D0049467

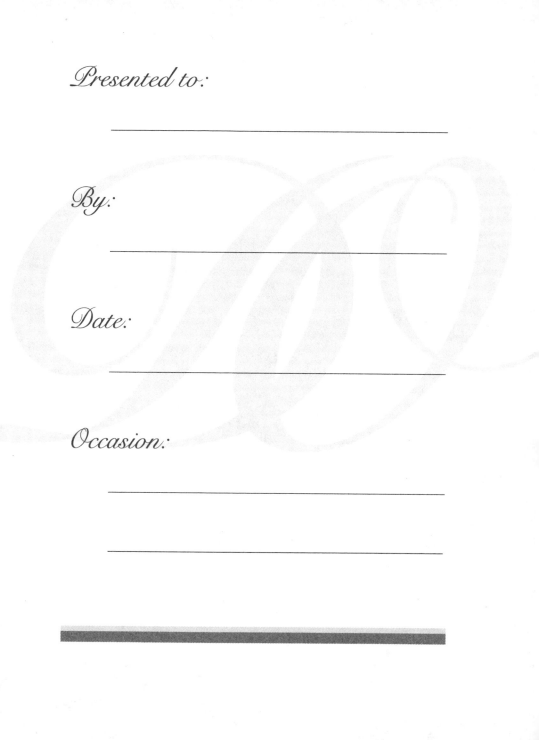

Presented to:

_____

By:

_____

Date:

_____

Occasion:

_____

_____

Choosing Life

One Day at a Time

A Daily Devotional for Men and Women

DODIE OSTEEN

WITH A FOREWORD BY JOEL OSTEEN

HOWARD BOOKS
AN IMPRINT OF SIMON AND SCHUSTER
New York   Nashville   London   Toronto   Sydney   New Delhi

HOWARD BOOKS
An Imprint of Simon & Schuster, Inc.
1230 Avenue of the Americas
New York, NY 10020

Copyright © 2001 by Dodie Osteen
Foreword copyright © 2006 by Joel Osteen

All rights reserved, including the right of reproduction in whole
or in part in any form.

This Howard Books hardcover edition 2015

HOWARD and colophon are trademarks of Simon & Schuster, Inc.

For information about special discounts for bulk purchases,
please contact Simon & Schuster Special Sales at
1-800-456-6798or business@simonandschuster.com.

The Simon & Schuster Speakers Bureau can bring authors to your live event. For more
information or to book an event contact the Simon & Schuster Speakers Bureau
at 1-866-248-3049 or visit our website at www.simonspeakers.com.

Manufactured in the United States of America

10   9   8   7   6   5   4   3   2

ISBN 978-1-4165-4302-2
ISBN 978-1-4165-4764-8 (ebook)

Unless otherwise indicated, all Scripture quotations are taken from
The Living Bible © 1971, by Tyndale House Publishers.

Dedication

✣

I dedicate this book in grateful tribute to my beloved late husband of 44 years and pastor, John Osteen, who was my partner in life and faith. He gave me five beautiful children and served as my spiritual teacher, encourager, prayer warrior, and inspiration – as he was to thousands around the world. Together we saw a daughter healed from a birth injury and rejoiced over my healing of metastatic cancer of the liver in 1981.

This book is also dedicated to my awesome children, Paul, Lisa, Tamara, Joel, and April, who have stood with me through thick and thin and are all involved in full-time ministry.

Special thanks to Renee Branson, who not only has been a personal secretary for us, but also has been a loving and devoted friend. Thank you for the countless hours you spent editing and proofreading this book.

Foreword

❦

I was privileged to grow up in a home full of love, support, and encouragement. I can't remember a day that went by when I didn't see my parents, John and Dodie Osteen, sitting in our family room, drinking coffee, and reading the Bibles and praying. They knew that the Word of God was their source of strength and wisdom.

My mother often spoke words of life and hope to everyone around her. Proverbs 18:21 declares, *"Life and death are in the power of the tongue."* Everyday, as we left for school, she would remind us that *"with God all things are possible"* or *"you can do all things through Christ who strengthens you"* or *"you are more than a conqueror."* As I reflect back on her words I realize that she was speaking truth, life, and hope into each of our lives. She did not see us as a nuisance, irritating, or trouble . . . she saw us exactly the way God sees us, full of purpose and with a divine destiny.

The example of my parents in both their actions and words played a significant role in my life and the lives of my brother and three sisters, who are now serving the Lord Jesus in fulltime ministry.

Now, Victoria and I are passing on the legacy of John and Dodie Osteen to our children. We are setting the example of godliness for their lives, and we are speaking the same words of life over our children each and every day.

The Scripture encourages us in Isaiah 55:11 when it says, *"My word that goes forth out of My mouth: it shall not return to Me void [without producing any effect, useless], but it shall accomplish that which I please and purpose, and it shall prosper in the thing for which I sent it."* The words in this devotional will be a source of encouragement and strength in your life. When you apply the scriptures, insights, and prayers in these pages, you will begin to see relationships restored, finances recovered, addictions overcome, and sicknesses healed. Don't wait another day. Begin living the life of victory that the Lord has in store for you.

Remember—life and death are in the power of your tongue. Today, Choose Life!

Joel Osteen

Introduction

❦

*M*any of you know that in 1981 I was miraculously healed of metastatic cancer of the liver. In my book, *Healed of Cancer,* I share the struggles and battles I had to fight, how God's Word helped me to overcome, and how God completely healed me. I believe that as terrible as that experience was, it has given me a special understanding of how God wants to heal us in every part of our lives today.

I thank God that I had His Word to depend on in that dark hour, as well as the good teaching of my late husband John Osteen, and other great men and women of God. If it hadn't been for the Word of God, I would have died. As John used to say, "If you will put the Word of God in your heart when you don't need it, God will bring it out when you do need it." I hold fast to God's Word daily. My life depends on it, and yours does too. God exhorts us as His children: *...give attention to my words; incline your ear to my sayings. Do not let them depart from your eyes; keep them in the midst of your heart; for they are life to those who find them, and health to all their flesh. Keep your heart with all diligence, for out of it spring the issues of life* (Proverbs 4:20-23 NKJV).

I encourage you to read your Bible daily. If you don't have a Bible reading plan of your own, I have included the one I have used for years in the back of this book. Your spirit needs spiritual food just like your body needs physical food. It is the Word of God that has given me life and hope. I trust that as you read these daily devotions and your own Bible every day, that you will be a doer of the Word and not a hearer only. A doer is someone who sows the seed of the Word of God into his or her heart and obeys it. One way to sow the Word of God into your heart is to "confess" or "say the same thing"

God says in His Word. As you daily say what God says, you'll get the same results God does.

Whether you need healing in your body, family members to be saved, a marriage restored, to grow in your Christian walk, or to be made whole from a fragmented life, this book will help you. I encourage you to be assured that it is always God's will to save, heal, deliver, and prosper you as you continue to choose life…one day at a time.

May the Lord richly bless you,

Dodie Osteen

Choosing Life

Choose Life!

"I call heaven and earth to witness against you that today I have set before you life or death, blessing or curse. Oh, that you would choose life; that you and your children might live!"

—Deuteronomy 30:19

*T*his scripture says we have a choice to live or die...to be blessed or cursed... to serve God or not to serve Him. God wants us to enjoy the good life He made possible for us, but we are the ones who must make the choice. Deciding not to serve Him can cause us a lot of trouble. But if we do choose to serve Him, we receive wonderful benefits. Verse 20 says, *"Choose to love the Lord your God and to obey him and to cling to him, for he is your life and the length of your days."* So if you want to live a long life, make a quality decision—choose to serve God, obey Him, and cling to Him. You'll be glad you did!

❦

Oh, God, I thank You that You came to give me life, and I choose this day to serve You, love You, obey You, and cling to You. I know that You are my life and the length of my days—and I choose to enjoy the abundant life You provided for me.

Stop and Think about Eternity

*"All of us must die eventually; our lives are like water that is
poured out on the ground—it can't be gathered up again."*

—2 Samuel 14:14

*I*f you know and love the Lord Jesus, then you won't be concerned about
this scripture. But if you're not serving God, perhaps you ought to stop and think
about it. Someday you're going to die. Eventually all of us will die. Those of us
who are Christians will go up to meet Jesus. But if you're not a Christian, it will
be as if your life had been poured out on the ground with no way to gather it up
again. Some people say you'll come back as somebody or something else after
death. But that's not true. The Bible says in Hebrews 9:27 (KJV), *...it is appointed
unto men once to die....* So if you're not right with God, ask Him to come into
your heart today. Then when you die, you'll go to heaven and spend eternity
with Jesus.

*Jesus, I know that one day I will die, but I don't want to die lost for all eternity.
So I ask You to come into my heart and be my Lord and Savior. I want my life to
count for You here and in heaven.*

You Must be Born Again

Jesus replied, "With all the earnestness I possess I tell you this: Unless you are born again, you can never get into the Kingdom of God." "Born again!" exclaimed Nicodemus. "What do you mean? How can an old man go back into his mother's womb and be born again?" Jesus replied, "What I am telling you so earnestly is this: Unless one is born of water and the Spirit, he cannot enter the Kingdom of God. Men can only reproduce human life, but the Holy Spirit gives new life from heaven; so don't be surprised at my statement that you must be born again!"

—John 3:3-7

Thank God, when we receive Jesus, we are born again. We experience the new birth when the seed of God's Word is planted in our spirit. Nothing productive can take place in our lives until we have God's Word planted inside us. The incorruptible, imperishable Word of God lives forever!

Have you and your family received Jesus as Lord? What about your neighbors and co-workers? John 1:12,13 says, *But to all who received him, he gave the right to become children of God. All they needed to do was to trust him to save them. All those who believe this are reborn!....*

When you're born again, God puts a light on the inside of you. You become the light of the world (see Matthew 5:14). Your light attracts others to you because God, who is Light, dwells in you, and your light will never go out!

Lord, I thank You that I am born again. I am a new creature. By the power of Your Holy Spirit, I will boldly testify of Your saving grace to my family, friends, and neighbors that they too may experience Your wonderful peace.

A New Life in Christ

For you have a new life....
—1 Peter 1:23

If you have been born again, you have a new life. It was not passed on to you from your parents, for the life they gave you will fade away. This new one will last forever, for it comes from Christ, God's ever-living message to men.

God never changes, but people do. Have you ever said, "I wouldn't be so quick to make that mistake if I had it to do over again"? Well, Jesus has taken care of that for you by going to Calvary to pay the price for all the sins of mankind— even yours. It's not too late for you to start over. A "new life" can be yours beginning right now.

Romans 10:9 says, *For if you tell others with your own mouth that Jesus Christ is your Lord, and believe in your own heart that God has raised him from the dead, you will be saved. For it is by believing in his heart that a man becomes right with God; and with his mouth he tells others of his faith, confirming his salvation.*

Welcome to your new life. Live, love, and enjoy the benefits spelled out in God's Word—His letters written to you with all His love.

❧

Father, thank You for my new life. I turn away from the past and press forward to the good plan that You have had for me from the beginning. Help me to live my new life in such a way that I may draw others into Your kingdom. ❧

Don't Wait to Share Salvation

First, I want to remind you that in the last days there will come scoffers who will do every wrong they can think of, and laugh at the truth.

—2 Peter 3:3

For years people have predicted that Jesus was coming back soon, and likewise, the scoffers have spent years saying, "Things are just the same as they've always been. People have been saying that Jesus was coming back ever since the day He left the earth, and He hasn't come back yet. If He's coming back, there's no reason to get excited. It can't be that soon."

Well, 2 Peter 3:9 says that God isn't being slow about His promised return, even though it may sometimes seem that way to us. Instead, He is providing more time for sinners to repent because He is not willing that any should perish.

We should rejoice that God is giving us more time to get His message of salvation out to others. Time is short, and we need to take advantage of every opportunity we have to share the good news of Jesus Christ. Why not share your friend, Jesus, with someone you know today?

❧

Father, thank You for allowing me more time to tell others about Jesus. I will tell them that Jesus is coming soon even if they laugh at me, so they will have an opportunity to be saved.

God's Word is Nourishment

And now just as you trusted Christ to save you, trust him, too,
for each day's problems; live in vital union with him. Let your roots
grow down into him and draw up nourishment from him....

—Colossians 2:6,7

*O*nce you decide to give your heart to Jesus, you need to trust Him every day in every way. Acknowledge Him in all your ways, and you will find out that little things will just begin to happen—and when they do, don't act as though they didn't. Give Jesus praise and glory for every little blessing—from finding a good parking space to receiving an unexpected financial gift. Let your roots grow down into Him.

And how do your roots get nourishment? By studying the Word of God and listening to His Word being preached. Faith comes by hearing...and hearing...and hearing. Even if you think you've heard it all before, you'll still learn something new that will strengthen your walk with the Lord.

❦

Dear heavenly Father, I praise You today for Your faithfulness to me. I appreciate all the little kindnesses You send my way. Every good and perfect thing comes from You, Lord, and I give You thanks for loving and blessing me.

Read God's Instruction Book

Every young man who listens to me and obeys my instructions will be given wisdom and good sense.

—Proverbs 2:1

*W*hen you purchase something new—a dishwasher, a stove, a TV, a vacuum cleaner, or even a new car—you receive an instruction book that tells you how to operate it. You don't have to read the instructions that come with a product, but when you do, you'll have a better understanding about all the features. And you'll know what to do when something goes wrong.

The Bible is an instruction book, and it is one book that we can't afford not to read. The instructions in God's Word told me how to be saved, filled with the Holy Spirit, and healed...and knowing that information kept me from dying in 1981. The Word continues to instruct me on how to have joy and live a happy life.

Once you've read the directions that come with your new car, you rarely have to read them again. But that's not true with God's Word. You need to read God's instruction book every day, because you will find something new that you hadn't noticed before. You'll learn to apply it to all the situations you face in life and gain victory over circumstances that completely baffle those who don't have a close relationship with God.

❦

My Father, I love Your Word. It is filled with wisdom and instruction for my life, and I need Your guidance every day. I commit to You now to set aside time each day to read and meditate on Your Word.

January 8

God's Word Always Proves Right

...Though everyone else in the world is a liar, God is not.... God's words will always prove true and right, no matter who questions them.

—Romans 3:4

*D*o you want to please the Lord Jesus Christ? I do, and that's for sure. You probably do too. The Apostle Paul in his letter to the Romans wrote that although everyone around you may be lying, God will not lie. His words will always prove true and right no matter who questions them.

Whenever anybody says something that disputes the Word of God—whether they are the world's greatest theologian or the world's greatest scientist—they are wrong. God's Word is always right, so hide it in your heart and keep it. Store it up for a time when you will need it, and you'll be happy that you did. When you store the Word of God in your heart when you don't need it, God will bring it out when you do need it!

❧

Father, I ask You to help me stay in Your Word this year. Your Word is always true and right. Thank You that You are faithful to guide and direct me through Your Word every day.

Your Guide and Instructor

I will instruct you (says the Lord) and guide you along the best pathway for your life; I will advise you and watch your progress.
—Psalm 32:8

The Word of God is so strong and powerful. When it is planted down deep in your heart, it will help you in times of discouragement and minister joy to your heart. Psalm 32:8 is like that for me. Personally, I like the idea that God has promised to watch out for the pathway of life that is best suited for me. And I love the instructions of the Bible—God's instruction book.

Now, I don't usually like to read instructions that come with a new appliance. I just want to plug it in and hope it works. But I like God's instructions. Why? Because they promise to guide and direct my paths toward the very best that He has for me. That's what I want, especially in these times.

Further, God promises to observe my progress. That means if I take a wrong turn, I'll feel a little nudge in my heart, and He'll tell me to go in a different direction. You and I can trust God. He has always given me good advice, and He'll do the same for you.

❦

Father, I love Your guidance and instruction. Keep me on the path that You would have me follow, and don't let me veer off in a direction where I should not go. Thank You for advising and watching me daily.

The Truth You Know Will Set You Free

And you will know the truth, and the truth will set you free.
—John 8:32

I can't stress how important it is to read the Word of God. It contains all the truth we will ever need to conquer all of the problems we will ever encounter. We just have to open up the Word and find the place where it is written. The Word says that our bodies can be healed, our families can be saved, our finances can be abundant, our fears can be conquered, our relationships can be healthy and whole, our churches can make a difference in the world, and on and on it goes.

I read and stand on the truth of about 50 Scripture passages every day because I know that it was the truth in God's Word that kept me alive when I was going to die of metastatic cancer of the liver in 1981. I exhort you to find out what the Bible says about your need, apply it to your life, and let the truth of God's Word set you free!

❧

Lord, I ask You today to help me find the truths in Your Word that will set me free. Your Word is life and health and peace in the midst of every problem. I choose to apply the truth of Your Word to my life and walk in Your freedom.

Believe the Truth You Have Been Taught

But you must keep on believing the things you have been taught. You know they are true for you know that you can trust those of us who have taught you.

—2 Timothy 3:14

I often think about the great truths that are taught at our church. They are so good—so simple and yet so profound—that they literally save lives. People come to the church not only because the Word of God is taught there but also to witness actual signs, wonders, and miracles! People know they can trust us because we teach them only what the Bible says—and that's all.

In fact, I tell people, "If we ever teach anything that can't be backed up by the Word of God, don't you believe it." I mean that. I appreciate the fact that people come and sit under our teaching because they know they can trust us to teach them things they need to know—things that will help them throughout their lives.

God is so good to give us His Word. The more we hear it, the better off we will be in every way—socially, emotionally, financially, and physically.

Lord, I am being taught Your Word, and I believe that I receive everything You have to offer me in it. I choose to keep on believing what I have been taught because it lines up with Your Word, and Your Word is truth.

The Word of God Changes You

I don't mean to say I am perfect. I haven't learned all I should even yet, but I keep working toward that day when I will finally be all that Christ saved me for and wants me to be.

—Philippians 3:12

*W*e received a letter from a lady in our area who doesn't attend our church, but she watched our television program. She said, "Your sermons have helped me to change. I've always thought I was a Christian, but since I've been listening to you, I've realized that I was a passive sort of person and not an active, working Christian.

"I'm still not where I need to be," she went on to write, "but I've started by being a witness to my own family. I have been a sinner, but with your guidance, I have asked for forgiveness, and I know that God has answered my prayers. I have been forgiven."

This little message was and is encouraging to us. And I want you to be encouraged today. None of us are "there"—we have certainly not reached perfection. But when you know that you've been forgiven, you can be a positive witness in the lives of your family, friends, and co-workers. Tell someone today about Jesus Christ. Your testimony to His goodness in your life could be exactly what someone needs to hear.

Father, I want to be a bold witness to Your goodness in my life. Your Word promises me that I can ask You for anything in line with Your will, and Your will is for all people everywhere to hear about eternal life in Jesus. So I ask You for boldness and courage to share my testimony of Jesus with others so they too can be saved.

Do You Need a Miracle?

The Lord is good, a stronghold in the day of trouble; and He knows those who trust in Him.

—Nahum 1:7 NKJV

I didn't know in October 1981 that I was going to need a miracle just to live. I had many plans for the future when symptoms began to appear in my body that led to the diagnosis of liver cancer. Given only a few weeks to live, I was certainly a candidate for a miracle, and after many months, tests confirmed that God had indeed performed a miracle in my body. Tests revealed that the cancer was gone! Glory to God!

Maybe you need a miracle today—in your body, in your finances, or in your family. Be encouraged! Our God delights in your faith in His ability to turn your negative situations into positive testimonies to His grace and mercy. Trust, lean, and depend on Jesus to heal you in the area of your need, and you too can receive a miracle from God.

❧

Father, I take refuge and trust in You. You are my strength and stronghold in times of trouble. Thank You for Your miracle-working power that is operating in every area of my life.

God Still Works Miracles

Now when the sun was setting, all they that had any sick with divers diseases brought them unto him; and he laid his hands on every one of them, and healed them.

—Luke 4:40 KJV

*E*ach service we have a special time of ministry at Lakewood Church when we have believers pray individually for those who have needs. We lay hands on the sick as Jesus commanded in Mark 16:17,18—*"And these signs shall follow them that believe; In my name shall they cast out devils; they shall speak with new tongues; they shall take up serpents; and if they drink any deadly thing, it shall not hurt them; they shall lay hands on the sick, and they shall recover* (KJV)."

When God dramatically healed me of cancer in 1981, I learned how important a touch from God really is. And God's touch is not just for physical healing. We also believe God for miracles in families, financial situations, jobs, and any other important needs that people have. We have found, through prayer, that God still works miracles in the lives of His people.

❧

Jesus, I thank You that You never change and that You still want to touch me, answer my prayers, and bring the miracles I need in my life. I'm glad that You're still working miracles today.

Jesus Is the Miracle Worker

*Jesus traveled all through Galilee teaching in the Jewish
synagogues.... And he healed every kind of sickness and disease.
The report of his miracles spread far beyond the borders of Galilee
so that sick folk were soon coming to be healed from as far away as
Syria. And whatever their illness and pain, or if they were possessed
by demons, or were insane, or paralyzed—he healed them all.*
                                                —Matthew 4:23,24

*A*t some time everybody in the world is going to need a miracle from
God. No matter what kind of disease in your body, your mind, your family, your
finances, on your job, etc., that you have, it's not too difficult for God. Jesus went
around Galilee more than two thousand years ago performing all the miracles
described in Matthew's gospel and He can still do those same things now. He
hasn't changed! He is still the Miracle Worker, and the fame of His name has
continued to spread throughout the world.

We see signs and wonders and miracles when we pray for people, because
Jesus has given us His authority, according to Matthew 10:1. So if you're sick,
be encouraged. There is hope for you!

*Father, in the name of Jesus and on the authority of Your Word, I believe in
the miracle-working power of God to heal my body (family, relationships, job
situation, etc.). I believe I receive everything You have for me. I am healed. I am
whole. Thank You, Jesus, for the power of Your Word, Your name, and Your blood
that was shed for me at Calvary and causes sickness and disease to flee from me!*

God's Miracles Demonstrate His Majesty

You have given him fame and honor. You have clothed him with splendor and majesty.

—Psalm 21:5

God's miracles demonstrate His honor, His majesty, and His eternal goodness. I want to publicly thank God for His miracle of healing me of cancer. The best of doctors could give me no hope to live, but God stepped in and altered the devil's plan for me.

He intervened on my behalf, setting my feet on firmer ground. He made a way for me where there was no way. *But God*—two wonderful words that changed my life, as well as the lives of my family, my church, and my world—demonstrated His honor toward me as well as His majesty and eternal goodness.

God is no respecter of persons. If you need a miracle, He'll do it for you. He will demonstrate His honor and majesty toward you.

❦

God, You are a miracle-working God, and Your Word promises to make a way for me where there appears to be no way. I'm counting on You to demonstrate Your honor and majesty toward me, and I'll be sure to give You all of the praise.

Let Miracles Become Commonplace

He sighed deeply when he heard this and he said, "Certainly not. How many more miracles do you people need?"

—Mark 8:12

*R*eading Mark 8 and 9 every now and then will bless you because it describes some of Jesus' miracles. In verse 12 of chapter 8, He had miraculously fed 4,000 people, yet they still asked Jesus to make something happen in the sky, saying then they would believe in Him (see verse 11).

It's hard to imagine people being so difficult after having just seen Jesus perform a great miracle of feeding thousands of people. Finally, the Bible says, Jesus sighed deeply and asked how much more proof they needed to believe in Him.

Our church has become a place where miracles are commonplace. We love miracles. Every time I step up to the platform, our congregation sees a miracle because I was supposed to die around the end of 1981.

How many more miracles do you need in order to believe? If you aren't aware that Jesus still does miracles, you might do well to recall the fact that just your being alive today is a miracle. The fact that you're on your way to heaven because Jesus has saved your life from the pit of hell is a miracle. It is a miracle that the sun came up in the east this morning and will set in the west! You see miracles every day! How many more do you need?

Just look around you at the large and small miracles of your own life. Miracles are more common than you may realize. All you have to do is open your eyes! Look at the miracles all over the world, and you won't need any more proof. Jesus is the Miracle Worker!

Lord Jesus, I don't need any more proof of who You are. But I want You to know how thankful I am for miracles—both large and small. Thank You, for the miracle of my own life.

The Key to Miracles

Jesus Christ is the same yesterday, today, and forever.
—Hebrews 13:8

*W*hen the truth of that statement sinks into your spirit, it will eliminate your fears and doubts about healing. This scripture tells us about Jesus. It declares something about what He was in the past, what He is today, and what He will always be in the future.

What kind of a person was Jesus? You have to agree that He was a Healer of the sick. You couldn't read His Word and doubt this. Matthew 9:35 says, *Jesus traveled around through all the cities and villages of that area, teaching in the Jewish synagogues and announcing the Good News about the Kingdom. And wherever he went he healed people of every sort of illness.* The King James Version says He went about *...healing every sickness and every disease among the people.*

If He is the same today as He was then, there is hope for you and every sick person! God is no respecter of persons. He does not love others more than He loves you! Matthew 6:7,8 says, *"Don't recite the same prayer over and over as the heathen do, who think prayers are answered only by repeating them again and again. Remember, your Father knows exactly what you need even before you ask him!"*

God will hear you. You are as important to Him as anyone else. Jesus is the key to your miracle. Trust in Him!

I thank You, Jesus, that You are the same yesterday, today, and forever. I thank You that just as You healed in Bible days, You still heal people today. You are the mighty Miracle Worker, and I ask You to heal me today from the top of my head to the soles of my feet. Thank You for my miracle. Amen!

Rise Up and Walk!

The Lord, the Maker of heaven and earth—Jehovah is his name—says this: Ask me and I will tell you some remarkable secrets about what is going to happen here.

—Jeremiah 33:2,3

*W*e are sons and daughters of God. He has given us power through His name to command demons, trouble, and disease to leave, and our words will come to pass!

John's sister Mary is a great example. She was desperately ill some years ago—she could not walk or feed herself, and seemingly she had lost her power to reason. She was in agony.

We wanted God to heal her! John said when he saw Mary, he got mad at the devil and all the power of evil that had caused her condition. So he took a deep breath and commanded the devil and demons to depart and the sickness to go—and they did!

Immediately Mary jumped out of bed and ran through the house praising God! Later she went to the table and fed herself! Her reasoning returned, and the sickness vanished, never to return!

Later he asked Mary, "Why did you leap out of bed so suddenly?" She said, "John, I heard the voice of the Ancient of Days—the Eternal God—say from His throne, 'Rise up and walk.'"

John said, "No, Mary, I said that to you." She said, "No, it was not you that I heard, but the voice of God spoke this command to me, 'Rise up and walk.'"

When we step out on God's promises and exercise commanding power, our voices blend with the voice of God and the impossible happens! (You can read John's sister's full testimony in his book, *You Can Change Your Destiny.*)

❧

Oh my Father, thank You for giving us Your power to cast out demons and heal sickness and disease. I want to hear Your voice tell me remarkable secrets about how I can pray for others today. I long to know Your secrets and Your ways of healing and delivering people. I'm glad Your voice joins with mine when I boldly speak Your Word in faith, and I expect to see miraculous results.

God Cares About You

"...take care of my sheep," Jesus said.
—John 21:16

A man wrote a letter thanking us for caring for people. He said, "Because of your television program, I asked God to come into my heart and be my Lord and Savior every day. May God bless all the people at Lakewood Church because you really care for people."

It is thrilling for us to know that people who watch our TV program can see that we really care for them. When Jesus left the earth and ascended into heaven, He sent the precious Holy Spirit to help us spread the good news of Jesus' saving grace.

The Holy Spirit also reflects Jesus' wonderful way of caring for and about all people everywhere. We are so grateful to have the privilege of spreading the word that Jesus cares about people.

Jesus cares about you. Whatever you're going through today, know this: Jesus cares about it. He is concerned about what concerns you. Take a moment right now and welcome Him into your day. Ask Him to guide you through it as if He were going everywhere you go, talking with everyone you talk with, running all of your errands with you, and completing that work assignment that has an "impossible" deadline.

He knows what's on your mind anyway, so why not let Him help you carry the load?

Jesus, thank You for caring for me. I have so much to do today, but I know I'll be able to accomplish it with You at my side. I appreciate You wanting to be involved in my day. Come on and let's do it together!

Open Your Heart's Door

"Look! I have been standing at the door and I am constantly knocking. If anyone hears me calling him and opens the door, I will come in and fellowship with him and he with me."

—Revelation 3:20

Too many people today are depriving themselves of life's most wonderful experience...simply because they won't open the door. God respects our right to choose, and He will never push His way in, but He continually stands at our heart's door and knocks, hoping we'll allow Him to come in and fellowship with us.

If you haven't yet responded to His knocking on your heart's door, won't you consider doing it now? He is patiently waiting for you...longing to fellowship with you as His child. If you'll open the door and respond to His love, you'll experience the most wonderful relationship of your life. What a wonderful opportunity to fellowship with your heavenly Father. Don't miss out on it!

Heavenly Father, thank You for loving me and patiently knocking on my heart's door. I open wide the door of my heart and ask You to fellowship with me today. I look forward to developing a close relationship with You so I will hear You when You call.

January 22

Tell God, "I'm Yours!"

I would have despaired and perished unless your laws had been
my deepest delight.

—Psalm 119:92

After I was diagnosed with liver cancer, this scripture really helped me. And verse 94 says, "I am yours!"

That's the way I feel about God. I owe my life to Him. I am His. And I know that whether or not God has done anything special for you, your life needs to be His.

I owe a lot to Jesus. He saved my life. He kept me from dying of cancer. It was His Word that I depended on and the healing virtue of the Lord Jesus that kept me alive.

Those words are like medicine to me. Why don't you start today to tell God that you know you are His child too? I like knowing that I belong to Him. He saved me from the pit of hell when He went to Calvary in my place. Later He saved my life from the debilitating cancer that tried to take hold of my body and shut down its God-created functions. *everythg, everyone, anythg*

I'm thankful today that I belong to Jesus and He belongs to me. How about you?

❈

I thank You, Lord, that I am Yours. I would have despaired of life if You had not reached out to me. I would have perished and been lost without Jesus as my Lord and Savior and Healer. I owe my life to You, and I will serve You all the days of my life.

Acquaint Yourself with God

Acquaint now thyself with him, and be at peace: thereby good shall come unto thee.

—Job 22:21 KJV

*D*o you realize that in this day and age, the only way you can have peace is to be acquainted with God? People who are acquainted with almighty God don't react to trouble the same way as those who have never had a relationship with Him.

Those of us who are acquainted with our heavenly Father know the secret to letting go of things we cannot change. We have learned to let God in and give Him charge of our lives, our situations, our challenges, and our circumstances.

Take a moment today to get quiet and listen. If you and God have grown apart, I believe your effort to become reacquainted with Him will result in God speaking to you in the midst of your deepest troubles.

Stay acquainted with Him, and the next time trouble knocks at your door, you can open it with confidence in God.

❧

Father, I desire to begin a deeper walk with You today. I know that when I draw near to You, You draw near to me. When I feel that You are far away, I know that all I have to do is step toward You and You will meet me. I long to know You as my personal friend and to have Your peace and goodness in my life.

God Will Never Forsake You

..."I will never, never fail you nor forsake you."
—Hebrews 13:5

*W*e sometimes leave God and forsake Him, but do you realize that He will never leave nor forsake you? It's true. He is a merciful Savior who will never forsake you. I encourage you today to trust in God. He is a God of mercy and of love. Right now an open pair of hands is waiting for you to take hold, and those hands are attached to arms that are reaching out to bring you hope, comfort, and love.

If you find yourself far from God today, reach out toward those hands, clasp them in your own, and know the security that comes from walking hand-in-hand with Jesus. It will change your life forever.

I stretch forth my hand toward Your outstretched hand today, Lord, and take comfort in the mercy and love that You are extending to me. I know You will never fail me nor forsake me. Thank You for showering me with Your amazing grace and peace.

Strength for Each Day

...And your strength shall be renewed day by day like morning dew.

—Psalm 110:3

This scripture became so real one Sunday morning when we came to church early and dew covered the grass.

It reminded me that when you are in a battle and you don't feel strong enough to fight, it is good to get up early in the morning and look at the grass. Almost every day of the world there will be dew, which should remind us that there is enough strength for that day—strength to keep on going.

Isaiah 27:5 (KJV) says, *...let him take hold of my strength, that he may make peace with me....* Just reach up and take hold of God's strength when you notice the dew on the grass, and make peace with God in your heart concerning the things that face you today. He will be your strength in the midst of every situation.

Father, I thank You for Your Word that says my strength will be renewed daily. As I consider the morning dew, I know I'll have the strength that I need for today— and You'll also take care of tomorrow as You did yesterday. Thank You for providing the strength I need for every day of my life.

Cast All of Your Care on God

Let him have all your worries and cares, for he is always thinking about you and watching everything that concerns you.

—1 Peter 5:7

First Peter 5:7 in the King James Version reads like this: *Casting all your care upon Him....* But *The Living Bible* says to just let God have your worries and cares. The truth is that at this time in history, there are just too many cares and worries for any of us to handle. Most of the things that upset us so much are things we really have little or no control over and can do little or nothing about anyway.

Why not turn your cares and concerns over to Jesus? You're always on His mind anyway, so let Him take care of whatever is worrying you. Whatever it is, He can handle it...and He does it because He wants to!

I don't know anybody who wakes up in the morning and thinks, "What can I worry about today?" But wouldn't it be great to wake up and think, *Jesus, whatever comes along today, I'm asking You to handle it. I can't do it as well as You would anyway, and I know You love me so much that You don't want me to waste any time worrying.*

❧

Lord, You know how easy it is for me to worry, even though I realize that my worrying won't change the situation at all. So I cast today's cares and worries over on You because I know You are watching over everything that concerns me.

God Is a God of Mercy

Come and have mercy on me as is your way with those who love you.

—Psalm 119:132

*W*e need mercy many times in our lives, don't we? I do, and I imagine that you do too. When I think about it, we don't go through a day that we don't require mercy. We are so capable of disappointing people, breaking our promises, or failing to follow through on some task.

God's Word has many references to His patience and mercy with us. Psalm 103:8-11 explains how God deals with that. It says, *He is merciful and tender toward those who don't deserve it; he is slow to get angry and full of kindness and love. He never bears a grudge, nor remains angry forever. He has not punished us as we deserve for all our sins, for his mercy toward those who fear and honor him is as great as the height of the heavens above the earth.*

What an example God is in dealing with the injustices of life! May we learn to show mercy today to others as God has shown His mercy to us.

❧

Lord, I am so grateful that You have not punished me for my sins as I deserve. There is truly none like You. As You have extended Your mercy toward me, I will show mercy to others. It is comforting to know that Your mercies are as great as the heavens are high!

Confess and Forsake Sin to Have God's Mercy

He that covereth his sins shall not prosper: but whoso confesseth and forsaketh them shall have mercy.

—Proverbs 28:13 KJV

People can confess their sins over and over and over, and feel good about receiving forgiveness from God, but then keep on doing whatever sin they were confessing. That's not what the Bible says to do. It says you have to *confess* your sins and *forsake* them. *Forsake* means "to go away from; leave; abandon forever."

If you forsake sin, that means you don't repeat it. Then you don't have to continually ask Jesus to forgive you for it. The result of forsaking sin is something we all need daily—mercy!

You will not prosper if you keep doing what you know is not pleasing to God. So if you want to have the mercy of God (and who doesn't?), confess and forsake sin. You'll enjoy the rewards of God's infinite mercy and have a wonderful life.

❀

God, I come to You today to forsake the sins of my past—especially the ones I seem to commit over and over. I turn my back on those habits and activities that I know are not Your will for my life. Give me strength, I pray in Jesus' name, to overcome the sins that have held me captive, and set me free!

Do What God Tells You to Do

Loving God means doing what he tells us to do, and really, that isn't hard at all; for every child of God can obey him, defeating sin and evil pleasure by trusting Christ to help him.

—1 John 5:3,4

We can see by this scripture that the way to defeat sin and evil pleasure is by trusting Jesus Christ. Getting to know Him by reading His Word will help you develop that trust. If you don't know what's in the Bible, then you don't know Him and how He feels about sin and many other important things.

Remember that God has a place in mind for you and a plan for getting you there. It may not always be clear, and you might get sidetracked for a time, but if you trust Him and obey His Word, nothing can really hinder His will for your life. I exhort you today to work at defeating any sin in which you take pleasure. Leave it at the feet of Jesus and let Him help you conquer it once and for all.

❧❧

Father, I know that You have a good plan for my life—help me to find it. When I get sidetracked, bring me back to Your path. My faith and trust are in You. Help me to defeat every desire to sin and to become the strong Christian You want me to be.

God Wants to Forgive Our Sins

If we confess our sins, he is faithful and just to forgive us our sins, and to cleanse us from all unrighteousness.

—1 John 1:9 KJV

Are you one of the many people who feels condemned by past sins? If so, this scripture in 1 John 1:9 is for you.

Isn't it wonderful to know that all we have to do is to confess our sins to God with a truly repentant heart, and He will not only forgive us, but He will also cleanse us from all unrighteousness!

It's because He loves us so much. He wants to do it because His Son Jesus died for us. He doesn't want you to feel guilty and condemned! Let the past go, and don't live in it any longer. Just go on with your life. Start afresh and anew.

Get things between you and God straightened out and be free!

Father, I confess my sins to You. Thank You for being faithful and just to forgive and cleanse me of all sin. Take my past—and even the memory of it—and toss it into Your sea of forgetfulness, to be remembered no more. I forgive myself and put the past behind me too.

God Does Forgive and Forget Your Sins

Lord, if you keep in mind our sins then who can ever get an answer to his prayers? But you forgive! What an awesome thing this is!
—Psalm 130:3,4

Are you still haunted by the sins of your past? Have you done something that you're ashamed of, and you think God hasn't forgiven you? Here is some good news for you: When you ask God to forgive your sins, He does, and then He forgets they ever happened! What an awesome thing this is.

If God can forget your sins, you need to let them go too. Live your life as if you've been forgiven. After all, you have! Accept as fact that Jesus paid for your sins at Calvary, and be quick to forgive yourself after you've accepted God's forgiveness. Then forget about the past, and move forward into the good life Jesus paid a very high price for you to have.

Father, thank You that You always forgive me when I sin. I accept as fact that Jesus paid for my sins at Calvary, and I am forgiven! I forgive myself, too, and when I pray, I know You always answer me. You are truly an awesome God!

God Clears Your Record

What happiness for those whose guilt has been forgiven! What joys when sins are covered over! What a relief for those who have confessed their sins and God has cleared their record.

—Psalm 32:1,2

Four or five men who had just been released from prison visited our church, and we were so glad to have them. When I met them, I thought of this scripture from Psalm 32 because I thought it really applied to them. But then I started thinking, *This applies to us all—for all have sinned and fallen short of the glory of God. What happiness there is for all whose guilt has been forgiven!*

What a joy when our sins are covered over! What a relief when we have confessed our sins before God and our record is cleared! Glory, hallelujah!

No matter what you have done, if you come to Jesus with a repentant heart and ask His forgiveness, He will clear your record and erase any and all traces of your sins—never to remember them again! Now, that is good news!

God's mercy works. Why not receive it today?

❧

Father, what a relief and joy it is to know that when I confessed my sins that You covered them over with the precious blood of Jesus, never to remember them again. I praise You for clearing my record and making me clean and happy in You.

Go Back to the Fork in the Road

When a person falls, he jumps up again; when he is on the
wrong road and discovers his mistake, he goes back to the fork
where he made the wrong turn....

—Jeremiah 8:4,5

*G*od had told Jeremiah to go tell the people some important things. He said to tell them that He wasn't pleased with them because they were refusing to listen to Him. They needed to go back to the fork in the road where they had taken the wrong turn, but they would not.

We're like that sometimes. We head off in a direction that is going to lead to destruction, and God tries to tell us where we got off course, but we refuse to listen. Then we're disappointed with the results and wonder how we got into such a mess.

If you've ever made a mistake in judgment, just go back to the place where you started to make the wrong turn, get headed in the right direction through obedience to the Lord, and you will be very happy with the results!

❧✿❧

So many times, Father, I have taken a wrong turn on the road to Your perfect
will for my life. Yet You have always restored me, shown me where I missed it, and
pointed me in the direction that You would have me go. I am so grateful. Please
continue to direct my steps toward the goals You have set for me. I truly desire to
follow You.

God Is our Refuge in Times of Trouble

All who are oppressed may come to him. He is a refuge for them in their times of trouble. All those who know your mercy, Lord, will count on you for help. For you have never yet forsaken those who trust in you.

—Psalm 9:9,10

*H*ave you ever been oppressed? *Oppress* means "to crush or overwhelm, to weigh heavily upon." Have you ever had anything come against you with such force that you just couldn't seem to shake it off?

All of us have had trouble at one time or another, but if we go to God, He will help us. He'll be there in our time of trouble and be a refuge in our storm.

If you know that God is merciful and that He loves you with a compassion that never ends, then you can count on Him for help because you know He always wants to help you. He will never, ever ignore your cries for His help.

In times of trouble, run to Jesus—He will be your refuge.

I place my trust in You, Lord, because I know Your tender mercies are directed toward me and that You always hear my cry for help. I thank You because You are my refuge and You will never forsake me.

February 4

Armed with Strength for the Battle

For You have armed me with strength for the battle....
—Psalm 18:39 NKJV

David said in Psalm 18:6, *In my distress I screamed to the Lord for his help...* Have you ever done that? I screamed to the Lord when I was dying with cancer. I wanted to live, and I screamed for help.

Then David said in the latter part of verse 6, *...And he heard me from heaven; my cry reached his ears.* And then he said in verse 32 of the same Psalm, *He fills me with strength and protects me wherever I go.* This is such good news!

We went through so much years ago when my husband faced emergency bypass surgery. He prayed over the globe of the world before he went to the hospital for the heart catheterization procedure that morning. My husband wanted to live to keep evangelizing the world. During the heart catheterization procedure, emergency surgery was required, and the surgeons started immediately to save his life. It was such a stressful day.

I picked up my Bible and read that He has armed me with strength for the battle. Yes! I had quoted Ephesians 6:11-18 that morning, and I had on the whole armor of God, including my feet shod with the preparation of the gospel of peace. But it was great to be reminded that He had also armed me with strength. Another scripture says, *He covers my head in the day of battle.* So our heads are covered too.

John recovered from surgery and continued to preach the Gospel all over the world for many years until he went to heaven in 1999.

If God is our God and Jesus, His Son, is the Lord of our lives, then we're covered from top to bottom...head to toe! And He arms us with strength!

I thank You, Lord, that my cries always reach Your ears. I praise You that I am dressed for battle and You have armed me with the strength I need to press through to victory!

February 5

Be a Good Soldier in God's Army

And as Christ's soldier do not let yourself become tied up in worldly affairs, for then you cannot satisfy the one who has enlisted you in his army.

—2 Timothy 2:4

Are you aware that you are a soldier in the army of the Lord? You weren't drafted—you enlisted in the army of God when you made a decision to accept Jesus Christ as your Lord and Savior. As a young recruit, you must train spiritually for spiritual warfare. Why? So you'll be prepared for battle—because battles come to all of us!

Spiritual training includes reading and studying the Word of God, attending a good Bible-teaching church, participating in Bible studies, prayer groups, and outreaches that touch your community.

Good training will help you when you need it most—in times when you have to go to battle for your health, your finances, your family, or your friends. These battles are sometimes long and difficult to deal with, but ultimately, you will win your war against the enemy if you've taken your training seriously and followed the One who enlisted you.

You are very important to the Captain of the Host—God Almighty! Make your best effort to obey Him and not be tied up in worldly affairs, and He will be satisfied to call you a member of His troops.

❧

I praise You, Lord, for teaching me in Your Word how to win the battles I face in this life. I am serious about becoming fit for battle. I refuse to become tied up in worldly affairs. I want to be a good soldier in Your army. Thank You for enlisting me and giving me the desire to follow You as my Commander-in-Chief.

Jesus Will Calm Your Storm

And there arose a great storm of wind, and the waves beat into the ship, so that it was now full. And he was in the hinder part of the ship, asleep on a pillow: and they awake him, and say unto him, Master, carest thou not that we perish? And he arose, and rebuked the wind, and said unto the sea, "Peace, be still." And the wind ceased, and there was a great calm.

—Mark 4:37-39 KJV

When Jesus spoke to the sea and rebuked the wind, the raging waters settled down. All of a sudden, it was calm all around the area. Matthew 8:27 says the disciples marveled, asking themselves what manner of man this was that even the winds and sea obeyed Him. This is the man that we spend our lives talking about—the Lord Jesus Christ.

He wasn't just in their boat on that one stormy night—He is still available today. Most of us encounter storms in our lives at one time or another, and how comforting it is to know that the Master doesn't want us to perish...that He's there to calm our storms. My family and I have been through many storms, but Jesus has always been there to speak peace, no matter what the circumstances were.

I exhort you to call on Jesus when you're facing storms in your life. He will be there to speak peace to your situation. Nothing that you're going through is too difficult for Him, and He will calm your storm. The winds will cease, and you too will say, "What kind of man is this that caused my storm to cease?"

❀❀

Thank You, Father, for sending Jesus into the storms in my life. I am so grateful that I can call on Him, knowing that He will speak peace to the winds and the waves and give me His peace.

God Himself Will Give You Peace

*May the Lord of peace himself give you his peace no matter
what happens. The Lord be with you all.*

—2 Thessalonians 3:16

*O*nly God can give you peace. In John 14:27, He calls peace a gift from Him to you. And He says His peace isn't fragile like the peace the world gives. He says His kind of peace will keep you from being troubled or afraid.

Isn't this the kind of peace you need in your life? Don't you want to experience the peace described in Philippians 4:7—that peace that is far more wonderful than the human mind can understand? I do. I need God's peace every single day of my life.

I experienced the most wonderful peace when my husband went home to be with the Lord. As Joel says, "God knew when Daddy was going, and He knew when we would be able to bear it and go on with the church, and with our own lives."

I want you to experience this glorious peace no matter what happens. You can—because the gift is for you! Open God's gift of peace. It will give you all the strength you need to continue doing great things for God.

❧

Lord, thank You for Your peace. It is certainly a gift that I need. So much that goes on in this world tries to steal my peace, but You are my peace and You are always with me. Today I choose to let Your peace rule and reign in my heart.

Regard the Word of God

"Quick! Bring in your cattle from the fields, for every man and animal left out in the fields will die beneath the hail!" Some of the Egyptians, terrified by this threat, brought their cattle and slaves in from the fields; but those who had no regard for the word of Jehovah left them out in the storm.

—Exodus 9:19-21

When Egypt's Pharaoh kept denying Moses the right to take the Israelites out of bondage and let them journey to the Promised Land, one of the plagues God sent to demonstrate His power was severe hailstorms.

God warned the Egyptians and the Israelites of the coming plague, and the people who were terrified by this threat gathered their animals in from the fields, but those who had no regard for God's Word left them out in the storm.

We live in times when our world is threatened by many disastrous things—from terrorism to weather—but many people still do not regard what God tells them to do.

I exhort you to listen to what God says in His Word. Don't be like Pharaoh and harden your heart. God can change your heart no matter how bad you think you are. Don't be one who disregards the Word of God.

You can protect yourself and your family from the storms that come against you by arming yourself with the Word! Start today!

❧

Father, I will be prompt in obeying Your voice. Thank You for helping me do what You say when You say to do it. I will obey Your commandments, Lord, and I know You will protect me as I hold Your Word in highest regard.

God's Strength and Protection

He fills me with strength and protects me wherever I go.
—Psalm 18:32

*I*f there was ever a time when we needed strength and protection wherever we go, it is now. In a day when sin and its dangerous effects are everywhere, it is so comforting to find in God's Word that He provides strength and protection *wherever* we go!

When you're out running errands or accomplishing certain goals today, keep in mind that God will fill you with all the strength you need to accomplish whatever it is He's called you to do today, and He'll give you protection wherever you go if your trust is in Him.

Just knowing this can cause today to be a wonderful day for you! Be blessed!

❦

God, I thank You that I have Your protection wherever I go and Your strength for whatever I need to do today. How blessed I am to have You walking beside me!

Don't Wait for Sorrow to Turn to God

For God sometimes uses sorrow in our lives to help us turn away from sin and seek eternal life....

—2 Corinthians 7:10

When I found this scripture, I was reminded of all of the funerals we've conducted at Lakewood Church over the years. Naturally, there is a great deal of sadness involved in the passing of a loved one. Many people are just heartbroken and almost inconsolable with grief. But God can use times of grief to quiet the spirits of the surviving family, friends, and acquaintances, and help them get their hearts right with Him.

My husband had a message entitled "Earthquakes That Bring You to God." I think the death of a loved one can be an "earthquake"—something that causes time to stop. It is one of life's great "interruptions" that causes us to pause and take note of what's really going on around us, and evaluate our own lives.

You don't have to wait until you have an "earthquake" to turn your attention to God. Stay close to His side when things are going well for you—then when sorrow comes, you'll be better prepared to handle it.

Lord, I pause to evaluate my life today, and I turn my attention to You. Draw me ever closer to You in times of peace and prosperity so that I will be prepared in spirit, soul, and body for the "earthquakes" life may bring.

Is Your Heart toward God?

And when he was departed thence, he lighted on Jehonadab the son of Rechab coming to meet him: and he saluted him, and said to him, Is thine heart right, as my heart is with thy heart?....
—2 Kings 10:15 KJV

The essence of this verse speaks of King Jehu's declaration of loyalty to Jehonadab—of his heart being right. We are to be an example to people, especially if we are parents. Is your heart right? Is your heart turned toward God, or is it turned toward someone else? Your children are looking at you and saying, "Where is your heart, Mother and Daddy? How is it turned? I'm looking to you, and my heart's turned like your heart is turned."

Be a good Christian example by loving God. If you are not saved, today is the day to make the decision to turn your heart toward God and get right with Him.

Then when people look at you, their heart will be turned right because your heart is turned toward God.

❧

Help me to always keep my heart right with You, O God. I want to live my life before my children and others with a heart turned toward You so they may follow my example as I follow You.

Water Your Spirit Every Day

*Those who forget God have no hope. They are like rushes
without any mire to grow in; or grass without water to keep it alive.
Suddenly it begins to wither, even before it is cut.*

—Job 8:11-13

*T*have lots of plants in my home. In fact, I almost have too many. When
the little leaves begin to droop, then I know they need water. And if I don't water
them, I know they will die.

That's the way it is with God. If you forget Him, you're going to get just like
my plants. You are going to wither and die—not physically perhaps, but you will
die spiritually. Spiritual death is separation from God.

Don't forget God. Invite Him into your day right now. Water your spirit
every day with the washing of the water of the Word, renewing your mind and
heart, and you'll never wither and die on the vine.

❦

*I thank You, God, that You are my hope. Because I remember You and water
my life with Your Word, I don't have to worry about withering away or dying on
the vine. I will never forget You, and I will continue applying the water of Your
Word to my life daily.*

Obey the Voice of the Lord

> *Then they said to Jeremiah, "Let the Lord be a true and faithful witness between us, if we do not do according to everything which the Lord your God sends us by you. Whether it is pleasing or displeasing, we will obey the voice of the Lord our God to whom we send you, that it may be well with us when we obey the voice of the Lord our God."*
>
> —Jeremiah 42:5,6 NKJV

*I*n this passage, the captains came to the great prophet, Jeremiah, asking him to pray and ask God what He would have them to do. They said they would do whatever God said, whether it was pleasing or displeasing.

A lot of things we do in life are not pleasing to us. In fact, they're very displeasing. I thought of a friend of ours, Dr. Reginald Cherry, who, for years, got up at 4:30 every morning to take care of his patients. Having to get up so early was probably not pleasing to him, but he did it because God had put it in his heart to care for people and to help them.

Perhaps you have to get up at a very early hour each day and find it most displeasing. But you do it in order to fulfill the requirements of the job you have agreed to do.

Lots of things in life are not pleasing to us, but we do them because we want to please God. Today, do whatever God asks you to do, even if it seems displeasing to you. Learn to be obedient, and then you'll be happy and it will be well with you.

❧

O Lord, I want to be obedient to Your directions whether they are pleasing to my flesh or not. Give me the grace to obey Your voice that it may be well with me!

Friendship with God

Friendship with God is reserved for those who reverence him.
With them alone he shares the secrets of his promises.

—Psalm 25:14

I love to think about Christians being called God's friends. I think of myself in those terms. How about you? What does friendship mean to you? The dictionary defines *friendship* as "persons who know, like, and trust each other; acquaintances; persons with whom one is allied in a cause; supporters; sympathizers."

Proverbs 17:17 KJV says, *A friend loveth at all times....* God loves you all the time—even when you're not very lovely to be around. He considers himself your friend whether or not you think of Him that way.

If you have a close friend, you know how nice it feels to be in such a relationship. The Bible says that Jesus is a friend who sticks closer than a brother. Begin to think of yourself as a friend of God. Share your most intimate thoughts and secrets with Him. He knows them anyway, of course, but it's good for you to put words to them in conversation, which is what prayer is.

If you have made Jesus your Lord and Savior, He is your friend and you are His. Listen as He shares the secrets of His promises with you. The more intimate you become, the more assured you will be of His friendship and His wonderful plans for your life—plans for your welfare and peace to give you hope for the future!

❀

Thank You, Jesus, that You are a friend who sticks closer than a brother. I'm glad I can have an intimate relationship with You. I reverence You and delight in sharing my intimate thoughts, hopes, and dreams with You. Thank You for revealing Your secrets to me too. I love You and appreciate our friendship deeply. I bless You today with my whole heart.

Father God, We Need You So

O Lord...Return and help us, for we who belong to you need you so.

—Isaiah 63:17

*N*ow, isn't that scripture true of these times in which we live? In these last days, we need to cry out to the Lord daily, reminding Him that we're here and how much we are depending on Him to help us.

If you don't know God as well as you'd like to know Him, now is the time to devote quality time to developing a more intimate relationship with Him. Set aside a specific time daily to talk to God and let Him talk to you through His Word.

If you do know Him, remind Him in prayer that you always need Him. That will thrill Him. Everyone needs to be needed—even God.

❧

I belong to You, Lord, and I do need You in these times in which we're living. These are perilous times, and many things happen where I need Your help. You are always a very present help in times of trouble, and I am thankful, Father, to be Your child.

Go Forward, Not Backward

*But what I told them was: Obey me and I will be your God
and you shall be my people; only do as I say and all shall be well!
But they wouldn't listen; they kept on doing whatever they wanted
to, following their own stubborn, evil thoughts. They went backward
instead of forward.*

—Jeremiah 7:23,24

If you want to keep going backward instead of going forward, then according to this Scripture, all you have to do is to be stubborn, follow your own way, and not listen to God.

If you want to go forward, however, and do something lasting for Jesus, then all you have to do is obey His commands. It seems simple, doesn't it? It is simple. The only way to live and be happy, moving forward and succeeding in life—both naturally and spiritually—is to simply be obedient to God.

He will never ask you to do the impossible. Following His guidance will always lead to happiness.

Don't go down the road that takes you two steps forward and one step back because of disobedience. Leave what's behind you and press forward to God's very best for your life. Why not begin today?

❧

*Lord, I choose to be obedient to Your will and keep moving forward with You.
I want my pathway to be ordered according to Your will, and not my own. Help
me to continue to obey You that all may be well in my life.*

Household Salvation

*He brought them out and begged them, "Sirs, what must I do
to be saved?" They replied, "Believe on the Lord Jesus and you will
be saved, and your entire household."*

—Acts 16:30,31

*D*id you know that if you are saved, salvation is also available to your
household? That's what the Bible says. We can believe that God will touch our
relatives and bring them into His kingdom. We cannot sit by and let our relatives
in distant cities and other states and around the world be untouched by our love
and concern for them.

You may be the only person who is praying for them. If so, you are the key to
their salvation. You have a responsibility to them, and God will use you if you are
willing to die to yourself and pour out your life for them. One day you will rejoice
because they'll come into God's kingdom.

Reach out in love—write a letter, make a phone call, and begin to pray for
your unsaved family members. John and I did that every day for our unsaved
relatives. We believed that any influence Satan had on them had to leave because
God's power in the name of Jesus drives the devil's power away.

Our relatives got saved, and yours will too. Don't leave your family members
in darkness! God will see them through to victory!

*Lord Jesus, I believe Your promise that says You will save both me and my
family. I realize that I'm the one who has to reach out in love and show them the
way. I am concerned about their eternal destiny. Father, I ask You to prepare their
hearts to receive Your goodness and mercy. I will keep loving them until they
respond to You as You call them out of the darkness of the devil's kingdom into Your
marvelous light.*

Today Is the Day of Salvation

(For he saith, I have heard thee in a time accepted, and in the day of salvation have I succoured thee: behold, now is the accepted time; behold, now is the day of salvation.)

—2 Corinthians 6:2 KJV

*O*ne of the ladies in our church recently told us a wonderful story. She said that she had been praying for her brother, who had been watching our program. At the end of one of the broadcasts, he dropped to his knees and accepted Jesus as his Savior. Big tears ran down his cheeks. That was an answer to her prayer. She said her brother wanted us to know that he found Jesus while watching our program.

Now, that's our desire for everybody. If you or someone you love doesn't know Jesus, remember that today is the day of salvation. Make this the day that you invite the Lord Jesus into your heart. If He already lives there, share Him with a loved one who may not realize that today is the accepted time to give his or her heart to Jesus.

❧

Father, I pray today for my loved ones to find You as a result of hearing a Christian radio or TV program. By the power of Your Holy Spirit, may they be touched and changed forever as they learn that today is their day of salvation!

God Has Summoned You

The mighty God, the Lord, has summoned all mankind from east to west!

—Psalm 50:1

*I*f a law enforcement officer comes to your house and serves you with a summons, then you are obligated by law to appear in court. Well, you and your family have a summons from the Lord Jesus Christ to appear with Him in heaven for all eternity! Hallelujah! And if you don't heed His summons—if those of you who labor and are heavy laden don't come to Him and allow Him to give you rest and be your peace—you are going to miss out on a lot of blessings.

Don't miss out on worshipping God and spending unending time with Jesus for all eternity. God has summoned you and your family to come to Him.

God, I don't want to miss spending eternity with You. I give my heart to You, Jesus, and ask that You cleanse me of all unrighteousness. Thank You for saving my family too, and giving us rest, peace, and blessings throughout all eternity. I rejoice that we will spend eternity with You.

Doing What God Says Can Save Your Family

Respect [handwritten]

By faith Noah, being warned of God of things not seen as yet, moved with fear, prepared an ark to the saving of his house; by the which he condemned the world, and became heir of the righteousness which is by faith.

—Hebrews 11:7 KJV

Do it! [handwritten]

There are some interesting things about the eleventh chapter of the book of Hebrews, known as "The Heroes of Faith Chapter." Do you know what Noah did when God told him to go and build that boat? The Living Bible says, *...When he heard God's warning about the future, Noah believed him even though there was then no sign of a flood, and wasting no time, he built the ark and saved his family....* When God tells you to do something, even though it doesn't look like it can be done, you need to go ahead and do it. Whether it involves salvation or your health, just believe God and follow His instructions. Even if the situation looks like it will never change or the symptoms just keep attacking your body, you still need to do what God tells you to do. And don't waste any time about it. It may save your life...or your family!

another's [handwritten]

I don't put off what God tells me 2 do. Job 36 esp in & w offering little things [handwritten]

Father, I thank You that You warn me to stay prepared to obey You so my whole family can be saved and healed. Teach me how to live my life to obey You, so I don't miss an opportunity to be a witness to my loved ones. I believe Your Word, and I am determined to be quick to obey in spite of what the circumstances around me may look like. By faith, I claim the inheritance of my family's salvation.

Acts 16:31 [handwritten]

my, mine's health, wealth, wholeness, prosperity, obedience, gratefulness, youthfulness, strength, favor, grace w/ You & everyone in every situation, circumstance [handwritten]

Household Salvation

Shine as a Beacon Light

...Shine out among them like beacon lights, holding out to them the Word of Life....

—Philippians 2:15,16

The huge Williams Tower stands tall in Houston's Galleria area, and at night, the tower has a light that beams around certain sections of the city. As I observed that light one night it made me think of the precious Christians in our church and around the world.

They get filled with the Word of God in their church services, Bible studies, and personal times alone with God. Then they go out into their own neighborhoods in the towns and cities where they live and shine as beacon lights, holding out the Word of Life to the people in darkness around them.

Even a tiny, little light forces darkness to back away. Don't ever allow yourself to believe that you can't make a difference in the lives of others. Keep on shining, because this world needs you as a light in the darkness.

❧

Lord, I want my life to make a difference. I choose to let my life shine like a beacon light to those in darkness as I hold out to them the Word of life.

Use the Word as a Witness

While they were living in Nazareth, John the Baptist began preaching out in the Judean wilderness. His constant theme was, "Turn from your sins...turn to God...for the Kingdom of Heaven is coming soon."

—Matthew 3:1,2

My family and I have always loved God's Word. We've used it countless times in innumerable ways to minister to the needs of others. You can face anything and anyone that Satan brings against you with the Word and come out a victor through Jesus.

But everybody needs to know that. Friends, loved ones, and co-workers are facing terrible challenges these days. It is heartbreaking to see the suffering brought into an entire family when a child is declared terminally ill or a breadwinner's career suddenly comes to an end.

Sadly, it often takes some terrible tragedy to motivate people to give God a try. In John the Baptist's day, he warned people of the seriousness of those times and paved the way for Jesus by announcing His coming. Some listened, but others did not, though John was a powerful witness.

You can share the good things God has done for you since you came to know Jesus in a personal way and change the lives of those closest to you.

You can use God's Word as a witness to others. "It is written" are three of the most powerful words in the Bible! Put them to work for you and those you love!

❧

Lord Jesus, I want to tell others about You. It is not hard to say: "Jesus loves you. He died for you. He took your sins so you could have eternal life in heaven. All you need to do is confess with your mouth that Jesus is your Lord and believe in your heart that God raised Him from the dead and you can be saved too!" (See John 3:16; Romans 6:23; Romans 10:9).

Thank You, Jesus, for Your Word that teaches me how to share Your truth with others.

Jesus Is the Living Light

... "I am the Light of the world. So if you follow me, you won't be stumbling through the darkness, for living light will flood your path."
—John 8:12

I like knowing that because I have made Jesus my Savior and the Lord of my life, He is flooding His living light on every path I take in this journey of life.

It assures me that I have nothing to fear. I have nothing to worry about. If I slip up and make a wrong turn, darkness will flood my path to let me know that I need to get back on the road where God's living light beams me home to safety.

Jesus is the Light of the world, and if you will ask Him, He will be your Savior. He will be the living light that will flood your path, showing you which way to go.

Allow Jesus to be the living light in your world.

❧

Jesus, You are the Light of the world. I follow You as You shed Your living light on my path so I won't stumble through the darkness and take the wrong road. I praise You and thank You, Lord!

Be Free from Anxiety and Fear

...May God bless you richly and grant you increasing freedom from all anxiety and fear.

—1 Peter 1:2

*D*o you have trouble? Does your heart ache? Are things coming against you that you just don't know how you can stand? I'll tell you how you are going to make it. God is going to bless you and help you today.

God said He would bless us and give us increasing freedom from anxiety and fear. Do you know how that happens? By reading and hearing the Word, by attending church, and by watching Christian teachers on television.

Being involved in a good, Bible-believing church and hearing the Word of God will increasingly free you of anxiety and fear because the peace of God has a way of overtaking fear and anxiety. As the Word of God gets down deep in your heart, you begin to realize that fear has no place in your life. You are a child of almighty God, and He did not give you a spirit of fear (see 2 Timothy 1:7). *Princess*

Yes, there is plenty going on in the world today to keep you anxious. But if you'll just listen to God, you will be free from anxiety and fear. Give Him praise for delivering you from fear. *His Word*

❧

Thank You, Lord, for setting me free from anxiety and fear, and for giving me peace. I am richly blessed in You.

Whom Shall I Fear?

*The Lord is my light and my salvation; whom shall I fear? The
Lord is the strength of my life; of whom shall I be afraid?*
—Psalm 27:1 KJV

*F*irst John 4:18 tells us that fear is a tormenting spirit. Fear and torment are attacking multitudes of people in our world today—and it is a sign that we are living in the last days. Jesus said that in the last days, men's hearts would fail them for fear (see Luke 21:26).

But Psalm 27:1 says, ...*Whom shall I fear?* There are so many things in the world today that people are afraid of, but fear can be overcome when we believe and know that the Lord is our light and our salvation.

God is our Father, and He loves us. We can always depend on Him. By the power of His Word, we can be lifted out of the darkness of intense, overpowering fear and oppression. We can make a habit of confessing the Word of God that specifically addresses the subject of fear—and there are many.

Begin to praise God that you have victory over fear. Thank Him for protecting you from torment and anxiety. Remember that you are strong in the Lord and in the power of His might. You are more than a conqueror through Christ Jesus!

❧

*Lord, I thank You that You are my light and my salvation. You are the
strength of my life, and I will not be afraid. You are the God of this universe, and
You are my very own Father! I will not fear or fret! I will not be anxious about
anything. You are my peace.*

We Don't Have a Spirit of Fear

For God hath not given us the spirit of fear; but of power, and of love, and of a sound mind.

—2 Timothy 1:7 KJV

*W*hat makes you fearful? I realize these are days when all of us could be afraid about many things that are happening in the world. But why are you fearful?

Have you ever thought about this scripture confirming that fear does not come from God? Don't you yet have confidence in Jesus? He is your only hope.

When the devil comes to you with all his suggestions that you should be fearful, replace his suggestions with scriptures on fear. Place your trust in God and let the Holy Spirit give you peace. *Lu 10:19 mark 5:34, 36 ***

Thank You, Lord, that I do not have a spirit of fear, but You have given me a spirit of power, and of love, and of a sound mind. I will not fear!

Your Heart Shall Know No Fear

Yes, though a mighty army marches against me, my heart shall know no fear! I am confident that God will save me.

—Psalm 27:3

$\mathcal{I}$ read the book of Psalms every month, and I've read this verse many, many times. But as I read it again, the little phrase, "...my heart shall know no fear" stands out to me, and perhaps it will help you.

You know how it is when things come against us in this life—sickness, issues with children, relatives, friends, your job, and things like that. Sometimes it just seems like you're overwhelmed with fear.

We can either refuse to allow fear in our heart or we can be fearful. But this scripture says, "...my heart shall know no fear," meaning we don't have to have fear.

Now, we may feel like we're going to faint in our mind, but the Word of God says, "...my heart shall know no fear," and I believe it. If you have the Word of God in your heart, it will be protected and you can live your life without fear.

❧

Thank You, Lord, for giving me the assurance in Your Word that my heart will know no fear no matter what comes against me. Through You, I will live a "fear-free" life!

Don't Be Afraid—Let Jesus In

That evening his disciples went down to the shore to wait for him. But as darkness fell and Jesus still hadn't come back, they got into the boat and headed out across the lake toward Capernaum. But soon a gale swept down upon them as they rowed, and the sea grew very rough. They were three or four miles out when suddenly they saw Jesus walking toward the boat! They were terrified, but he called out to them and told them not to be afraid.

—John 6:16-20

*J*esus' disciples were consumed with fear at seeing Him walking toward them on the water, but He quietly assured them that they needn't be afraid. When they finally let Him into the boat, they immediately noticed that they had arrived at their destination.

Do you realize that there are frightened people floating around in a storm who haven't been willing to let Jesus into their boat? Are you one of those people? Now is the time to let Jesus in. Don't be afraid any more.

When you allow Jesus to get into your boat, you'll be amazed at the peace that will overtake your stormy sea of problems. And suddenly you'll be right where He wants you to be.

Jesus, I don't want to be floating around in the rough seas of life without You in my boat. I want to be where You want me to be, doing what You want me to do. If I'm headed off-course today, please steer me back to the right place. I want to arrive at the destination that You have planned for me.

Wrapped in Jesus' Arms

He that dwelleth in the secret place of the most High shall abide under the shadow of the Almighty. I will say of the LORD, He is my refuge and my fortress: my God; in him will I trust. Surely he shall deliver thee from the snare of the fowler, and from the noisome pestilence. He shall cover thee with his feathers, and under his wings shalt thou trust: his truth shall be thy shield and buckler.

—Psalm 91:1-4 KJV

People often write to tell us how much they love our church. One woman's letter made me stop and think about being wrapped up in the arms of Jesus—or sheltered under His wings, as the scripture says in several translations.

She said, "Sometimes I bundle up and just go outdoors because I want to be close to Jesus. I put on my coat, hat, and gloves, get a couple of blankets, and go outside. I feel close to the stars and know that Jesus is above the stars, so I'm closer to Him.

"I used to feel kind of foolish when I looked in the mirror and saw myself all bundled up like that. But then I heard that Pastor John would wrap up in a blanket and go sit out under a tree to pray. That really made me feel good."

Do whatever it takes for you to feel closer to Jesus. It's the fellowship with Him that counts.

Jesus, I wrap myself up in Your arms today. I choose to dwell in the secret place of the most High and abide under Your shadow. Almighty God, You alone are my refuge, my place of safety. You are my God, and I trust You. I thank You for sheltering me under Your wings.

Lie Down in Peace and Sleep

I will lie down in peace and sleep, for though I am alone,
O Lord, you will keep me safe.

—Psalm 4:8

A lot of people have trouble sleeping. People are fearful of putting their head down on a pillow at night because of all the things that are going on in the world. There are lots of things happening in families and individual lives. But Psalm 4:8 says, we can *...lie down in peace and sleep....* Notice that it says "in peace"—not "in pieces." *I will lie down in peace and sleep, for though I am alone, O Lord, you will keep me safe.* What a wonderful promise!

Sometimes it seems like we're so alone. It's so dark at the midnight hour and the early morning, but we're never alone because the Lord, who never leaves us, will keep us safe.

If you're having trouble sleeping, remember that you're never alone. Just put your head on the pillow and sleep in peace because God is right there with you, even as close as the very breath that you breathe.

❧❧

Thank You for Your Word, O Lord. I boldly confess that I will lie down in peace and safety because You are my keeper! I am never alone because You are always with me.

Where Does Faith Come From?

...faith cometh by hearing, and hearing by the word of God.
—Romans 10:17 KJV

*H*ow do we get faith? Where does it come from? The Living Bible's translation of Romans 10:17 says, *Yet faith comes from listening to this Good News— the Good News about Christ.*

If you don't have faith, you can get faith to come to you and live in your heart. If your needy family and friends don't have faith, you can get faith to come into their lives also. What makes faith arise from the throne of God and walk, run, or fly into our lives and produce His mighty works?

Faith comes by hearing and listening to the Word of God!

You cannot see God work without faith. Hebrews 11:6 says, *You can never please God without faith, without depending on him. Anyone who wants to come to God must believe that there is a God and that he rewards those who sincerely look for him.* You cannot have Bible faith without the Word of God.

The secret is to give people the Word of God. Apart from Bible faith there can be no salvation, no healing, no miracles—these only come from hearing, receiving, and acting on the promises in God's Word.

Release your faith. When you get faith into your heart and into the hearts of those who need help, then God will work in a miraculous way.

Father, I know that faith comes by hearing and listening intently to Your Word. As I hear the Word, by faith, I can "see" You working in every area of my life. There is no question that You will do what You promise. I place my trust in You, and I will share Your Word with my family and friends so they can have faith that works too.

We are Not Without Faith!

...God hath dealt to every man the measure of faith.
—Romans 12:3 KJV

*W*e know we cannot please God without faith—it's impossible. But there's no need to worry about not having faith because the Bible says that God has given faith to each of us. And faith will grow as we hear the Word of God.

When we take the time to hear and study the Word, it will produce in us a steady growth of faith. Our faith in the name of Jesus will result in beginning to see ourselves as redeemed, healthy, whole, happy, blessed, and prosperous.

With our measure of faith, we can speak out of the abundance of our hearts. Jesus said that a man will bring forth good things out of the good treasure of his heart (see Matthew 12:34,35).

Just a fraction of a measure of faith can help us refuse to deliberately sin. If we refuse to participate when the devil tempts us to sin, we won't always have to be going to the Father in shame and repentance.

Use the measure of faith that God has given you to fight the devil! You have everything you'll ever need to be victorious!

❋

God, You are so good and fair and impartial to give every person the same measure of faith so we can please You. I want my faith to please You, so I will get Your Word in my heart and let my faith grow. Then when I speak Your promises boldly, I will walk in victory over every circumstance.

Faith—Live Your Life by It

By faith Abraham, when he was called to go out into a place which he should after receive for an inheritance, obeyed; and he went out, not knowing whither he went. By faith he sojourned in the land of promise, as in a strange country, dwelling in tabernacles with Isaac and Jacob, the heirs with him of the same promise: for he looked for a city which hath foundations, whose builder and maker is God. Through faith also Sarah herself received strength to conceive seed, and was delivered of a child when she was past age, because she judged him faithful who had promised.

—Hebrews 11:8-11 KJV

Here's a paraphrase of these scriptures I love. By faith, John Osteen obeyed when he was called to go into the ministry, and he went out not knowing where he would be going. By faith, he sojourned in the land of promise and started Lakewood Church in an obscure place and began to teach God's Word to the heirs of His promise.

He reached out to tell the untold and to reach the unreached so the Bridegroom would come for His bride, the church, whose builder and maker is God.

By faith also Dodie herself received strength to fight cancer when she was sent home to die, and showed that there is victory in Jesus and the Word of God. She defeated cancer and death because she judged Him faithful who had promised.

I still judge God faithful. Insert your name and your situations in these scriptures as I did and see them come alive for you.

❧❧

Father, by faith I freely choose to follow You daily...just one step at a time. By faith I receive Your promises because You are faithful to fulfill Your Word in my life. I trust You to lead and guide me—just as You did Abraham and Sarah and the Osteens—to my inheritance so I can fulfill Your plan for my life.

Choosing Life—One Day At A Time

March 6

Hope—a Vital Link to Workable Faith

What is faith? It is the confident assurance that something we want is going to happen. It is the certainty that what we hope for is waiting for us, even though we cannot see it up ahead. Men of God in days of old were famous for their faith.

—Hebrews 11:1,2

In his book, *ABCs of Faith*, John spoke about hope being the climate in which faith works. I learned so much about so many things during our more than forty years of marriage, but one of the main things I learned is that without hope, faith alone doesn't produce results.

Hope is important. You have lost a lot if you've lost hope. Hope is a vital link to workable faith. My husband and I always mixed lots of faith with lots of hope.

Sometimes he'd get discouraged about something, and that's when I'd help him practice what he preached. Perhaps you feel this way. It's easy to know what you ought to do—that you can't allow yourself to lose hope, for example...yet go ahead and lose hope. You can say one thing and do another, but it won't work.

Look up all the scriptures about hope and write them down. When your list is complete, start confessing those verses every day. Hope will return, accompanied by faith and agreement with God and His Word.

You can create a climate for workable faith. Why not start today?

Father, my hope is in You today, and because You always do what You say, my faith in Your Word is unwavering. I have confident assurance that what I am now hoping for is waiting for me, even though I can't see it yet. I will keep my hope and faith in You, and You will surely bring it to pass!

The Power of Agreement

"Again I say to you that if two of you agree on earth concerning anything that they ask, it will be done for them by My Father in heaven. For where two or three are gathered together in My name, I am there in the midst of them."

—Matthew 18:19,20 NKJV

God always promises to answer any prayers that line up with His will (see 1 John 5:14,15) whether we are praying alone or with someone else. But verses 19 and 20 in Matthew 18 are a direct quotation of Jesus. He actually said that He gets involved—He is present, in other words—and there is power in times of united prayers between two or more believers.

Is the prayer of agreement a guarantee that God will answer in the way we want Him to? God would never grant a foolish or selfish request, but there is no question in my mind that prayers of agreement are special to God.

When John and I agreed in prayer for my healing way back in 1981, our prayer was strong and powerful to God, and to each of us. That prayer sustained me in the long months when my flesh sometimes wanted to give up my fight for life and health.

Find someone to pray with you—a prayer partner. Put together your list of requests for things about which you need God's wisdom. Prayer is simply communicating with God. Sometimes you talk while He listens, and other times He'll talk (you'll have impressions in your spirit) and you'll listen.

God is good all the time. Don't underestimate the power of agreement!

❧

Lord Jesus, I thank You for Your Word and the power of agreement. I thank You for being in our midst when I gather with other believers in prayer. Lord, I have confidence in You. I know our heavenly Father is pleased when we pray in unity and in Your Name. That's the kind of prayer He will answer.

How Big Is Your "Want To?"

> *As Jesus and the disciples were going to the rabbi's home, a woman who had been sick for twelve years with internal bleeding came up behind him and touched a tassel of his robe, for she thought, "If I only touch him, I will be healed." Jesus turned around and spoke to her. "Daughter," he said, "all is well! Your faith has healed you." And the woman was well from that moment.*
> —Matthew 9:19-22

*T*his passage speaks of healing strength that came as a result of this afflicted woman's determination. And it works for anyone who is willing.

A young lady who was within days of graduating from the police academy had a serious problem—to qualify for graduation, she needed to be able to run two miles in a certain number of minutes. She was very troubled because she had tried and tried, but so far, she had failed.

She tuned into our TV program and watched as John preached a message entitled "How Big Is Your 'Want To'?" After hearing the message, she decided that her "want to" was big enough to overcome this problem, and she ran that two-mile test in record time! She graduated with the rest of her class.

From where did this new level of strength come? Like the little lady with the issue of blood, her strength stemmed from a desire that exceeded all other things for that moment in time. It worked for her—will it work for you? It all depends on the strength of your "want to."

❦

Jesus, I am determined to run my race to do all You have called me to do in this life. Strengthen me as I reach out to touch You with my faith, because I really want to do my best for You in everything I do.

No Limits with God

Do not let this happy trust in the Lord die away, no matter what happens. Remember your reward!

—Hebrews 10:35

God gave us an example in the Old Testament of His ability to overcome natural circumstances by His miracle-working power. He led two million people through the wilderness for forty years—though they complained loud and often about their plight. There were no drug stores, no doctors, lawyers, housing units, or grocery stores, yet God took care of the Israelites and rewarded them.

He provided clothes and shoes that never wore out. When they needed water, it poured out of a rock. When they needed food, it rained down from heaven. There are simply no limits with God!

God has repeatedly demonstrated His power to help us rise above the natural into the supernatural.

Are you or someone you love involved in a crisis right now? Is there a problem in your home, with your children, or your spouse? Are there troubles on your job? I encourage you to look to Jesus today. He is your answer.

There are no limits with God. He constantly demonstrates His power to work at the end of man's limitations. In other words, when you are at the end of your rope—Jesus is right there, waiting to pour out His miracle-working power in your behalf. After you've done all that you can do in the natural, Jesus will do what you can't do.

Trust in Him no matter what happens and begin to enjoy what He has already done for you! He rewards you by causing everything to turn out all right!

Father, thank You for Your miracle-working power. I cast all my cares on You today because I know You are the answer for every need in my life. I may feel limited, but You have no limits. I gladly keep my trust in You.

God Pleads with You to Walk the Good Road

Yet the Lord pleads with you still: Ask where the good road is, the godly paths you used to walk in, in the days of long ago. Travel there, and you will find rest for your souls....

—Jeremiah 6:16

*H*as God been pleading with you to return to those roads that you used to walk before your thoughts were consumed with the cares of the world or with making money? Do you long to return to the roads that you walked when you were a child and knew that your mother was praying for you?

If you've been traveling a road that has led to nowhere, turn around today. You can go back. Just ask God where the good road is—He will help you find the godly path you used to walk. Travel the familiar roads you walked when you first met Jesus, and you will find rest for your weary soul.

❧

My Father, I need rest for my soul. I want to return to the good road less traveled—where my walk with You began. I thank You now for leading me there so I can walk in Your godly paths and find Your rest.

How Stupid Can You Be?

Woe to those who try to hide their plans from God, who try to keep him in the dark concerning what they do! "God can't see us," they say to themselves. "He doesn't know what is going on!" How stupid can they be!...

—Isaiah 29:15,16

*T*hese scriptures are so interesting. It probably doesn't apply to you, but that doesn't keep it from being true. How could anybody try to hide his or her plans from God? Don't they know that God is omnipotent, omnipresent, and omniscient? He's all powerful. He sees everything. And He knows everything that's going on with every one of us.

In case you forget that God sees and knows all, I'm reminding you today. It doesn't make any sense to think you can hide anything from Him. He's God!

Today, remember that you are always on God's mind—He even has your name tattooed on the palm of His hand (see Isaiah 49:16)!

Father, I've done plenty of things I wish You had not seen, and I repent. I am perfectly aware that You see and know everything about me. How great it is to know that I am on Your mind and my name is engraved in Your hand.

Let's Not Be a Stumbling Block

*O Lord God of the armies of heaven, don't let me be a
stumbling block to those who trust in you....*

—Psalm 69:6

What if I told you that people are observing you? They are, you know.
One preacher says, "Many folks are not reading their Bibles—they're reading you!"
Now, this is serious because they could get confused when they see someone who's
supposed to be a Christian doing things that aren't very Christ-like.

When that happens, you become a stumbling block for their salvation. That's
a serious responsibility for which God will hold you accountable.

Today and every day, be careful about the way you live. Put God first in your
life, and cause Him to be proud of you. One thing I definitely don't want Him
to say to me is, "So and so didn't make it to heaven after observing you in this
situation." How ashamed I would be to hinder anyone's Christian walk or
entrance into eternal life by my lack of Christ-like behavior. How about you?

*Lord, don't let me be a stumbling block to someone's trust in You. May I never
be a negative influence on anyone else's life. Instead, I want my life and the way I
live my life to draw others to You.*

It Is Our Duty to Obey God

Here is my final conclusion: fear God and obey his commandments,
for this is the entire duty of man.

—Ecclesiastes 12:13

Solomon, the author of Ecclesiastes, was a very wise man. And in this verse, he says it is our *duty* to praise and fear God, and to obey His commandments. Our *duty*. It's not a choice...it's a duty!

Webster defines *duty* as "an act or a course of action required of one by position, custom, law, or religion; a moral obligation; a service, action, or task assigned to one...."

Nearly everybody has to work at a job in order to live. From the first date of employment, we are expected to perform certain duties in exchange for a salary. A job well done is usually compensated with some type of recognition—verbally, financially, or both.

I believe God compensates us accordingly when we fear or reverence Him and obey His commandments. Our actions will result in our being blessed or cursed. Fearing and obeying God is not optional for Christians who want to be blessed! I am a Christian who enjoys God's blessing! How about you?

I exhort you to make it a priority to walk in obedience to the Lord. Demonstrate your respect for God by obeying Him and you will experience having His blessings overtake you every day.

❧❧

I accept my duty to fear and reverence You, God, and to obey Your commandments. Strengthen me in my weaknesses and give me the determination to be all that I can be for You.

God Is Grieved When We are Unhappy

Then they destroyed their foreign gods and worshiped only the Lord; and he was grieved by their misery.

—Judges 10:16

I recently read this story in Judges 10. The people of Israel had turned away from God and were worshipping idols. They had sinned against God and forsaken Him. As a result, He had grown angry and weary of dealing with them.

In verse 14, God says, *"Go and cry to the new gods you have chosen! Let them save you in your hour of distress!"* But the people begged and pleaded with God to save them, and even though they had strayed from Him, verse 16 says that their misery grieved or hurt God.

It is good to know that we serve such a compassionate God. Perhaps you have grieved the Father's heart. Maybe you have backslidden, and you are miserable. God doesn't want you to be unhappy—that makes Him unhappy!

Always remember that God only wants the very best for You. He will always take you back because He is a God of compassion. When you are not serving God, His heart is grieved. But if you'll just turn your life toward Him, He'll welcome you back with open arms.

Lord, I never thought of You being unhappy when I'm unhappy. Forgive me when I'm outside of Your will, and help me to live my life in such a way that You won't be grieved. I'm glad You always extend Your love to me. Thank You for being so kind and compassionate.

Let's Please the Lord in All We Do

> *But just when Rehoboam was at the height of his popularity*
> *and power he abandoned the Lord, and the people followed him in*
> *this sin... But he was an evil king, for he never did decide really to*
> *please the Lord.*
>
> —2 Chronicles 12:1,14

*T*think it is interesting to read about the kings in the Old Testament. King Rehoboam was serving the Lord when his reign began. And for three years, everything went extremely well because of his obedience to God.

Then he openly abandoned the Lord because he had never truly committed himself to please God, resulting in all of his people following his lead. Needless to say, everything went bad for everyone. Verse 15 concludes by saying there were continual wars. Rehoboam's choice brought death, destruction, and fear into the whole kingdom.

Just like King Rehoboam, you have a choice to make today. You can choose to go another way, or you can make up your mind to really please the Lord in all that you do. Choosing to please God will have the opposite result of Rehoboam's choice. Instead of evil, you'll enjoy life!

I encourage you to make the right choice today, and choose to please the Lord in all that you do!

❧❧

Lord, I ask You to help me make right choices today, and keep me from all evil. I choose to please You in all that I do.

Love God and Fit in with His Plans

*And we know that all that happens to us is working for our
good if we love God and are fitting into his plans.*

—Romans 8:28

For years I've heard people say, "All things work together for good." But there's a stipulation that goes along with that in the book of Romans. If you don't love God and are not fitting into His plans, then you don't have the promise that everything is going to work out for your good.

First of all, it's important that you accept Jesus as your Savior. Then let Jesus become Lord of your life, and allow Him to direct your paths. When you are led by God, you will discover how easy it is to fit into His plans.

When He tells you to go to church on Sundays, get yourself and your family up on Sunday morning and go to church together. Be there when the doors open. Don't forsake assembling with other believers to worship Him.

When God says to bring the tithes into the storehouse, do it. When He says to love your neighbor, love your neighbor.

When you are obedient, you can expect God to work for your good.

Lord, I am willing to give up all my plans and follow Your plan for my life. I know that as I line up with Your will, You will make everything work for my good.

God Is Good to Those Who Wait for Him

The Lord is wonderfully good to those who wait for him, to those who seek for him. It is good both to hope and wait quietly for the salvation of the Lord.

—Lamentations 3:25,26

There is more to salvation than accepting Jesus Christ as your Lord and Savior, believing He died and rose again to give you eternal life. Salvation includes healing of the mind and body, and deliverance from all that holds you captive and hinders your walk with the Lord. I'm talking about things like fear, rejection, the past, lack, a negative attitude, etc.

Learning all of the benefits of salvation enables you to quietly wait for God and believe He will act on your behalf. You can pray, "God, I need this or I need that. It's included in salvation, and I need it."

Then wait quietly for your answer and have hope in Him. He is a wonderful God who always fulfills His promises because all of His promises are "yes" and "amen" when we wait for Him and seek Him.

❦

Just knowing that You are wonderfully good and that You are there, Lord, encourages me to wait for You and seek You. How grateful I am for my salvation. Help me to receive all the benefits of salvation You have for me, as I wait for and hope in You.

We're Always in God's Thoughts

*O Lord my God, many and many a time you have done great
miracles for us, and we are ever in your thoughts. Who else can do
such glorious things? No one else can be compared with you. There
isn't time to tell of all your wonderful deeds.*

—Psalm 40:5

Although it may be hard to believe, you are always on God's mind. There
is never a time when His thoughts are not directed toward you. And He can do
things for you that nobody else can.

You can sit and look at an idol and pray to it all day long, but it's not thinking
about you. It can't do anything for you. It's made of china, porcelain, wood, or
clay. Why would anyone think an idol could perform miracles?

But we serve a God who can and does specialize in miracles. Think about what
you really need today. Are you single and looking for a mate? Are you married
and having some challenges in your relationship? Are you the parent of a teen who
has decided that following your rules is out of style? Perhaps you are living in a
retirement center or a nursing home, feeling as though life has passed you by.

Do you believe God is thinking about you? Do you think He can take care of
your situation for you? Do you believe He will?

Be assured that God can and will handle any circumstance you're facing. He
freely gives His love to all. Why not accept His love right now?

❧

*Father, I do believe that I am always in Your thoughts. I know that You are
well able to do great and glorious things for me. You still perform miracles for
me when I need them. There is no one like You. Your deeds are wonderful!*

God Will Instruct and Guide You

*I will instruct you (says the Lord) and guide you along the best
pathway for your life; I will advise you and watch your progress.*
—Psalm 32:8

*G*od will guide you—not on the path that's not good for you, but the one
that's best for your life.

See what God tells us: He says He will instruct us, guide us, advise us, and
watch what we do. That's all the heavenly help we could ever need! As we listen to
His instructions and obey Him, He will lead us to the best pathways for our lives.

What a joy and comfort to know that God is watching our progress, and that
He's always ready to point us in the right direction. My desire is to be obedient to
His voice so He will be pleased with my life and continually guide and instruct me.

❧

*Father, I thank You that You are continually watching my progress and giving
me direction when I need it. I love You, Lord, and I trust You. I want Your
instruction, guidance, and advice in all that I do. Help me to stay in the best
pathway for my life.*

God Never Sleeps

Shall I look to the mountain gods for help? No! My help is from Jehovah who made the mountains! And the heavens too! He will never let me stumble, slip, or fall. For he is always watching, never sleeping. Jehovah himself is caring for you! He is your defender. He protects you day and night. He keeps you from all evil and preserves your life. He keeps his eye upon you as you come and go, and always guards you.

—Psalm 121:1-8

Jehovah God will never let you stumble, slip, or fall—He is always watching. He never sleeps, so there's no need for both of you to be awake. If He's going to be awake, you can sleep well knowing that He'll take good care of you. You are God's child, and He is caring for you now.

When our children were little, I watched over them very carefully. John watched over them even when they were grown, married, and had their own families. He was a good earthly father.

Your heavenly Father is even better than that. He is your defender and protector day and night. He keeps you from all evil and preserves your life. He keeps His eye upon you as you come and go. He always guards you.

Aren't you thankful for a God like that!

❧

O God, I am grateful that You are watching over me—protecting me right this minute so I won't stumble, slip, or fall. It is so good to know that I am constantly in Your care. You defend me, guard me, and keep me from all evil. Thank You, Lord.

His Wounds Have Healed Ours

*He personally carried the load of our sins in his own body when
he died on the cross, so that we can be finished with sin and live a
good life from now on. For his wounds have healed ours!*

—1 Peter 2:24

*B*ecause we serve the Lord Jesus Christ, we are blessed! Not only has Jesus carried away our sins, but He has also taken sickness and disease out of our midst. We can boldly confess long life because Jesus' wounds have healed all of ours. We are the healed of the Lord!

God is for us. He has always been on our side. When Jesus came, His name was called Emmanuel, which means "God with us." He was with us, and now He is *in us!*

Share the Good News of Jesus' saving and healing power with those around you. Let them in on the good report. God answers you when you call on Him in times of trouble. His wounds have healed you and me, whether or not we experience symptoms that make us feel otherwise. Share this Good News today— everybody needs to know!

Lord Jesus, You Yourself bore my sins on the cross so I could be finished with sin and live a good life. You were wounded for me so I could be healed. Bring someone across my path today so I can share Your healing power with them too. Thank You, for not only saving me but also making me whole.

That Same Spirit Dwells in You

*But if the Spirit of Him who raised Jesus from the dead dwells
in you, He who raised Christ from the dead will also give life to
your mortal bodies through His Spirit who dwells in you.*
—Romans 8:11 NKJV

This powerful scripture came to mind several years ago when my daughter, Lisa, was opening the mail in her office at our church and a box exploded in her lap. She could have been badly injured by a powerful pipe bomb that riddled her office with debris, nails, shrapnel, barbed wire, and set her office on fire.

Miraculously, Lisa's life was spared and not one piece of metal penetrated her body. Surgery was needed to close the wounds created by the explosion. One emergency official at the scene said, "Someone had to be standing between your daughter and that bomb." Thank God, *...the Angel of the Lord guards and rescues all who reverence him* (Psalm 34:7).

The same Spirit that raised Christ from the dead was dwelling in Lisa in her hour of need. It quickened her mortal body, and she rose up and overcame the enemy's attack.

You too can be unharmed by the devil's attacks. Why? Because the Spirit of the living God dwells in you!

O God, my Father, I thank You that You have assigned angels to guard and rescue me. The same Spirit that raised Christ from the dead also brings Your life to my body. Thank You for healing me, delivering me, and protecting me from all the attacks of the devil. I am an overcomer through Your Spirit that dwells in me.

You Can Have God's Favor in a Wicked World

When the Lord God saw the extent of human wickedness, and that the trend and direction of men's lives were only towards evil, he was sorry he had made them. It broke his heart.

—Genesis 6:5,6

Throughout history, the wickedness of the world has broken God's heart. That's how it was in Noah's day. It was so bad that God was sorry He had even created mankind! And today it seems even worse. There are many more people doing many more wicked things now than in Noah's time.

But the Bible says that even in all that wickedness, God saw Noah. He saw that Noah was living right and raising his family in a godly manner—and because of Noah's goodness, he found favor in the sight of the Lord. The world may have been in a terrible mess, but God noticed that at least one man was righteous and true, and He spared Noah and his family.

Our world may be in a mess today, but still there are people who are righteous and true—people who find favor in God's sight.

Rejoice that you are a child of Almighty God. Conduct yourself in a manner that gains God's favor and do your part to make this world a better place!

❧

Father, I thank You that I am in right standing with You through the Lord Jesus Christ. Help me to live right in all I do in the midst of this evil and perverse world. Show me ways that I can be of service to my fellowman so the world will be a better place.

Jesus Is Our Hero

But they could think of nothing, for he was a hero to the people—they hung on every word he said.

—Luke 19:48

The book of Luke is the most complete life story of Jesus we have. In the scripture quoted above from chapter 19, Jesus had just finished His triumphal entry into Jerusalem. Riding on a lowly donkey, He was on a mission of peace, but the priests, religious leaders, and merchants of the city would have no part of it. They desperately tried to think of something bad to say about Jesus because He was doing all kinds of miracles and endearing himself to the common people. But, they couldn't convince the people to listen to their negative comments—Jesus was the people's hero.

According to Webster's Dictionary, a *hero* is "a man noted for courageous acts or nobility of purpose, especially one who has risked or sacrificed his life." Jesus definitely qualifies to be called a hero.

A few days later in Jerusalem, Jesus gave up His life on the cross as a sacrifice for our sins, and He is still our hero today. He is about the only One that you can really trust in this whole world. Only He can save you, give you peace and joy, and heal your body. He is the ultimate hero.

Commit yourself to Him. Spend time worshipping and praising Jesus and His wonderful grace and mercy. Make pleasing Him your number-one priority, and watch Him bless you in every area of your life.

❈

Jesus, I thank You for giving up Your life on the cross for me. You are my hero. I praise You, Jesus, for saving me, giving me peace and joy, and healing my body. I hang on to Your every word because Your words are life to me.

Jesus Wants to Do It All!

When Jesus saw how strongly they believed that he would help, Jesus said to the sick man, "Son, your sins are forgiven!" But some of the Jewish religious leaders said to themselves as they sat there, "What? This is blasphemy! Does he think he is God? For only God can forgive sins." Jesus could read their minds and said to them at once, "Why does this bother you? I, the Messiah, have the authority on earth to forgive sins. But talk is cheap—anybody could say that. So I'll prove it to you by healing this man." Then, turning to the paralyzed man, he commanded, "Pick up your stretcher and go on home, for you are healed!"

—Mark 2:5-11

There wasn't room for the paralyzed man to be brought into the house where Jesus was teaching, so his friends cut a hole in the roof and lowered him on a stretcher through the hole. When Jesus saw this, He forgave the man's sins.

The man's sins certainly needed to be forgiven, but at the moment, his physical healing was uppermost in his mind. Doesn't this scripture show you that Jesus not only can save you and cleanse you from your sins but also heal you?

Jesus has the power not only to forgive our sins but also to heal our diseases. Jesus wants to do it all for us, but some people don't know that. Everything that is included in the Bible is for YOU. Lay claim to your inheritance today!

❧

Thank You, Jesus, for providing both salvation and healing in my life. You are everything I need. I claim all of my inheritance today, and know that You not only have forgiven all my sins, but You have also provided healing for my body.

Jesus Bore Both Sins and Sicknesses

But He was wounded for our transgressions, He was bruised for our iniquities; the chastisement for our peace was upon Him, and by His stripes we are healed.

—Isaiah 53:5 NKJV

Do you really realize that Jesus not only took your sins on the cross but also your sicknesses? He bore in His body everything that causes you heartache—poverty, oppression, depression, pain, suffering. Jesus took it all so that you could live a victorious life and win every battle the future might bring.

Sadly, too many people are suffering. They are experiencing defeat in the area of their finances, in their mind, in their physical bodies, and in their relationships with family and friends. Why? They don't yet realize that Jesus conquered *all* the forces of darkness at Calvary.

Isaiah confirms that Jesus was wounded, beaten, and bruised for our sins (transgressions and iniquities) and with His stripes—the places where the whip cut into His flesh—He took care of all the sickness and disease we would ever have!

It is important for us to believe that whatever God said in His Word belongs to us. It is ours—yours and mine! Jesus took care of it all for us!

Jesus, I am so grateful to You for bearing my sins and sicknesses in Your body on the cross of Calvary. I am thankful that You have paid in full for my past mistakes and the curse of sickness that tries to attack my body. I praise You, Lord Jesus, for Your sacrifice for me. Thank You for paying the price so that I can walk in victory in every area of my life!

Look Intently at Jesus

The next day John saw Jesus coming toward him and said,
"Look! There is the Lamb of God who takes away the world's sin!
He is the one I was talking about when I said, 'Soon a man far
greater than I am is coming, who existed long before me!'"

—John 1:29,30

*J*ohn 1:33 says, '*...He is the one who baptizes with the Holy Spirit.'* And it goes on to say in John 1:35,36—*The following day as John was standing with two of his disciples, Jesus walked by. John looked at him intently and then declared, "See! There is the Lamb of God!"*

Did you know that Jesus likes for you to look at Him intently? He is the Lamb of God who takes away the sins of the world. But when we look at Jesus intently and focus in on Him, then He will move for us.

I encourage you to look at Jesus intently. He is the Lamb of God that takes away the sins of the world—even yours.

❧

Lord Jesus, I take time to get alone with You today so that I may quietly and intently focus on You, the wonderful Lamb of God. Thank You for being the world's sacrifice to take away all our sin and for baptizing me with Your own Holy Spirit.

72,000 Angels Could Have Rescued Jesus

"Don't you realize that I could ask my Father for thousands of angels to protect us, and he would send them instantly? But if I did, how would the Scriptures be fulfilled that describe what is happening now?"

—Matthew 26:53,54

Jesus spoke these words to His disciples when the soldiers came to Gethsemane to arrest Him. The King James Bible says Jesus mentioned "twelve legions of angels" who could come to help Him.

John researched these figures years ago in preparation for an Easter message, and I was intrigued to learn that a *legion* of Roman soldiers consisted of 6,000 men. Jesus said that His Father God would send *twelve* legions, or 72,000 angels, to rescue Him if He only asked. There was a lot of help available to Him! He didn't *have* to go through the horrible things that lay ahead for Him.

But it is important to realize that Jesus was not at the mercy of wicked men who thought they were in charge—it only looked that way to *them*. Jesus knew that He had come into the world to die.

We don't know what happened down in the dark regions of the doomed and the damned between the time Jesus left His body and rose from the grave. All we know is that on the morning of the third day, the glorious resurrection power of God burst that place open, and Jesus came out!

I'm glad 72,000 angels *didn't* come to rescue Him that day because, in dying, He rescued you and me for all eternity! Hallelujah!

❧

Thank You, Father, for the redeeming sacrifice of Jesus Christ. I praise You today for sending Him to the cross to pay for my sin. Thank You for His willingness to suffer the sentence of hell to bear the curse of sin, sickness, and death on my behalf, and for giving me His resurrection life!

Jesus Is Good News

"The Spirit of the Lord is upon me; he has appointed me to preach Good News to the poor; he has sent me to heal the broken-hearted and to announce that captives shall be released and the blind shall see, that the downtrodden shall be freed from their oppressors, and that God is ready to give blessings to all who come to him."

—Luke 4:18,19

*W*e're always preaching good news about Jesus. Why? Because Jesus is good news! He has never changed. If you need something from Him, all you have to do is ask Him, and He'll give it to you if you believe and have faith in your heart. Why? Because He is a good God, and He wants to do things that bless you.

Some people think Jesus is just out there somewhere—unable to relate to the issues that we face each day. That simply is not true.

Jesus can solve all our problems—whether large or small. Don't ever think that your problem is too hard for Him. If you have something wrong in your body, in your finances, or in your family and you think that no one can do anything for you, just remember that Jesus can.

Now, that's good news!

Thank You, Lord Jesus, that You never change. You are good and You do things that bless me. You can solve all my problems of lack, grief, personal needs, and oppression because nothing is too hard for You. And that is good news!

Women of the Word

Early on Sunday morning, as the new day was dawning, Mary Magdalene and the other Mary went out to the tomb... Then the angel spoke to the women. "Don't be frightened!...I know you are looking for Jesus, who was crucified, but he isn't here! For he has come back to life again, just as he said he would...."

—Matthew 28:1,5,6

Women are important. Throughout history, women have played a vital part in the success of a variety of endeavors. Take Mary Magdalene and "the other Mary," for instance. They were the first to see Jesus in His resurrected, glorified body! And He talked with them.

Jesus told them, "Go and tell the disciples that I'm alive! Go tell! Go tell! Go tell!" (see verses 8-10). And women are still telling it to this day. They're telling it on the mountain, in the city, and in the country!

He also appeared to men, and they began to tell it. He told them to "go into all the world and preach the gospel to every creature!" *Gospel* means "good news." And we are to tell the world the good news that there is life and hope after death!

I'm glad I have the hope of seeing my wonderful husband again. Glory to God! The Easter story gives us hope, and hope sustains us through even the darkest night.

The Bible says the sting of death is sin. Jesus took away our sin, so put your trust in Jesus, and you can know beyond the shadow of a doubt that death has no sting for you. Jesus said, "Because I live, you shall live also!"

Father, thank You for the faithful witness of women like Mary Magdalene that are found in Your Word. I will follow You today as Mary did, and share the Good News of Your redeeming love and resurrection power wherever I go. Give me opportunities today to tell this Good News.

The Empty Tomb

*Since we, God's children, are human beings—made of flesh
and blood—he became flesh and blood too by being born in human
form; for only as a human being could he die and in dying break
the power of the devil who had the power of death.*

—Hebrews 2:14

*W*e commemorate the resurrection of Christ around this time of year—
and we celebrate the empty tomb! Thank God, Jesus is not dead! He is alive!
Although He went to the cross—bearing our sins, sicknesses, and curses and paid
the price for our transgressions by tasting death, He arose to conquer all!

The world rejoiced that He was dead—they thought He was out of the
picture. But He became a human being so He could come out of the grave with
a glorified body that would never die again. He is immortal and eternal. And He
declared, "Because I live, you shall live also!"

Rejoice today and celebrate the empty tomb and resurrection life of the risen
Christ. And remember, He had you in mind when He willingly sacrificed His life.
Never let yourself forget that.

❧

*I rejoice today, Jesus, that You are risen from the dead! The grave couldn't hold
You, and You broke the devil's power of death and gave me Your resurrection life.
Because You live, I live also, and I will share Your resurrection life with others.*

Everything We Have Belongs to God

For the earth and every good thing in it belongs to the Lord and is yours to enjoy.

—1 Corinthians 10:26

People may wonder why we talk about the tithe in every service. Well, everything we have including our money—really belongs to God and not to us. He just asks us to be good stewards of what He gives us.

His Word says the earth is His and the fullness thereof. It says all the silver and gold belong to Him. It says He owns the cattle on a thousand hills. Everything on this earth is God's.

So pastors and church leaders aren't talking about *your* money when they talk about the tithe, which is the first tenth of your income. Leviticus 27:30 says the tithe is the *Lord's* and it is holy. When God says, "I want you to give the first dime out of every dollar to the kingdom of God," it is because He has a plan to bless you.

When you think of it in terms of one dime for every dollar you earn, it doesn't seem like such a sacrifice. John 3:16 says, *For God loved the world so much that he gave....* Why? Because it was His to give. Think about that the next time you think your pastor talks about your money too often. Remember whose money it really is, and honor God in your giving.

❧

Mighty God, everything I have comes from You. I want to be a good steward, so I make a fresh commitment to partner with You in Your work on earth, according to Your commandment to tithe and give offerings when You ask me to give over and above my tithe. Show me how I can be a good steward and manage my money wisely.

The Blessings of Giving

"...I will bless you and make your name famous, and you will be a blessing to many others."

—Genesis 12:2

*G*od told Abraham that He would bless him and make him a blessing. You cannot be a blessing until you're blessed. My husband always taught that we need to be a blessing to people, but in order to do that, we need to be blessed ourselves.

We believed then (and our family still does) that God blesses those who will do what is closest to His heart. What is closest to the heart of God? The closest thing to the heart of God is that every person on earth hears about His great love and the mercy He showed us in the death, burial, and resurrection of Jesus.

Our goal as a church has always been to spread the Gospel throughout the world—to give generously in order to bless the whole wide world with the truth of God's Word! We don't receive God's abundance to become rich and bless ourselves. No! We receive God's blessing to have more than enough to invest in sharing His Good News with everyone everywhere.

Our church annually gives millions of dollars through TV broadcasts and numerous other outreaches. Why? Because we expect millions of people to meet us in heaven as a result of our commitment to missions outreach. Those millions of people *are* the blessings we'll receive from our giving. Hallelujah!

Thank You, God, for including me in the blessing of Abraham as his seed through the Lord Jesus Christ (see Galatians 3:29). Your Word says Abraham was very rich in cattle, silver, and gold, but he used his wealth to bless others. I want to be blessed with wealth so I can give abundantly too. Thank You for blessing me so I can be a blessing to this generation.

Make Up Your Own Mind

Every one must make up his own mind as to how much he should give. Don't force anyone to give more than he really wants to, for cheerful givers are the ones God prizes.

—2 Corinthians 9:7

*P*eople often become uncomfortable when their pastor starts talking about money, but at Lakewood we always teach our people that God gives you the opportunity to make up your own mind about giving. He wants you to give cheerfully what He puts on your heart.

After all, God has done His part. He loves the world so much that He gave His only Son so that whoever believes in Him won't perish, but will have everlasting life (see John 3:16). Jesus did His part. He said His purpose in coming into the world was to die for sinners that He might bring us to God.

So what is our part? Our part is to carry this Gospel message throughout the entire world. God promises to bless us if we do that, but it takes money to spread the Gospel. We have the opportunity to use a portion of what God has blessed us with to bless others. The decision is entirely up to us.

Whatever you give to God's work, He will multiply back to you. As you continue to give, the financial seed you sow produces a harvest from which you can sow more seed. God is blessed, the lost and dying souls of the world hear the Good News and find Jesus, and your generous giving in obedience to God makes it possible. You're a blessing to the world!

Father, I choose to be a cheerful giver. Not only does my tithe belong to You, but everything I have is also Yours whenever You ask me to give it. I know You will bless what I give and will give me something even better as I put my trust in You. I have made up my mind to give liberally so others may be saved and blessed too.

Don't Let Money Control You

...the love of money is the root of all evil....
—1 Timothy 6:10 KJV

This scripture does not say that money is the root of all evil, but that the "love of money" is at the root of evil. Some people have lots of money and channel it in the right direction. They follow God's commands to give to the poor and to the church, and that's the right attitude to have about money.

But listen to what The Living Bible says, "For the love of money is the first step toward all kinds of sin. Some people have even turned away from God because of their love for it, and as a result have pierced themselves with many sorrows." Do you know that you can have money and be happy as long as you don't let money control you?

But there are many people who work and work and never know how much is "enough." Their families suffer because they are never at home. If you have money, be glad—but use it the right way and don't love it. You control it—don't let it control you.

❦

Oh, God, thank You for reminding me that money is not bad—but that it's good when it is used in the proper way. Help me to have enough money to tithe, pay my bills, and meet my needs, with enough left over to help others. I will not let the love of money just to gain wealth control me, but I will use money as a blessing.

God Has a Dream for You

For the Lord your God is bringing you into a good land of brooks, pools, gushing springs, valleys, and hills; it is a land of wheat and barley, of grape vines, fig trees, pomegranates, olives, and honey; it is a land where food is plentiful, and nothing is lacking....
—Deuteronomy 8:7-9

God has a dream for you. He wants you to be free of all debt so you can freely give. He wants you to shake off a spirit of poverty and get into His flow of blessings. God wants you to have enough money to meet your needs and to help evangelize the world.

Joel tells our congregation about God's dream for His children to be free from the strain of worry and anxiety about money—how to pay all the bills, have money for food and clothes, a house and transportation, unexpected needs, etc. You see, we can't be joyful givers like God wants us to be when we're saddled with lack ourselves.

God's dream for you includes financial freedom—to be all that you can be and do all that you can do to help those who struggle to get through each day, each month, and each year.

Develop a desire to live out God's dream for you in the area of giving. The blessing you'll know from giving is beyond anything you can imagine!

❧

Lord, thank You that Your dream for my life is to live without lacking anything and to have enough to help meet the needs of others. Your dream is that I would have plenty—more than enough—to have the freedom to give joyfully so others can receive Your abundant blessing too. Continue to bless me, Father, as I give.

God Gives You Much So You Can Help Others

Yes, God will give you much so that you can give away much, and when we take your gifts to those who need them they will break out into thanksgiving and praise to God for your help.

—2 Corinthians 9:11

*L*akewood Church is blessed, and we are thankful! We have a ministry of giving.

Why do we give and how are we able to minister to so many different needs? Because we have followed the principle outlined in 2 Corinthians 9:11. We realized from the beginning that God was blessing our ministry in order for us to be a blessing to others!

Verse 12 goes on to say that two good things happen as a result of giving—those in need are blessed, and their gladness overflows with thanks to God. People will know that your deeds are as good as your doctrine when you give. They will fervently pray for you because of the wonderful grace of God shown to them through you.

When you are obedient to God—doing what He says to do, giving to the poor, helping the world—then God will give you more and more and more! Obedience in giving is fun! Try it!

❦

Thank You, God, for giving me much so I can give away much. I desire to be blessed so I can be a blessing to others. Then they too can give You thanks and praise. Bless me so I can give generously to the poor as Your Word instructs me to do.

Love the Prisoner

"...I was...sick and in prison, and you visited me."
—Matthew 25:35,36

*I*t has always touched me deeply to receive letters from those who are in prison. One particular letter said, "We watch you on Sundays and any other time we can. It has made such a difference in my life. I thank God for leaders like you who take time for people who are locked away. It makes me feel special and wanted when your program comes on the air. You tell us that you know us, and welcome those of us who are watching from prison."

We love to minister to those who are in prison. We are glad that our program can go inside even prison walls to take the message of love to these precious friends of Jesus. How thrilling it is when prisoners who have watched our program are released and visit us at Lakewood Church, an Oasis of Love.

What a disappointment it would be to keep the truth of Jesus' love to ourselves and not be willing to share Him with everyone we possibly could.

Share Jesus with someone today. Many people you will meet today are in one sort of "prison" or another. They may only have the opportunity to meet Jesus through you. Don't let that window of opportunity pass you by.

Father, help me share Jesus with someone today. Everybody needs You, God, but sometimes they don't know it. Help me to love others with Your love and be Your hands extended.

God Hears the Cry of the Needy

For Jehovah hears the cries of his needy ones, and does not look the other way.

—Psalm 69:33

*O*nce I was handed a note from someone who attended one of our services. That note contained the heart cry of so many people in the world, and it broke my heart. It said, "I have a lot of turmoil and pain—I've had it for years. My mother and my father died, my son was murdered, and I've just been released from prison. Please lift me up in prayer."

So many people in the world have pain this severe. They've suffered agonizing disappointments and horrible tragedies—abandonment by divorce, a child running away from home, the death of a loved one—rejection of every kind. The diversity of awful things that happen to people is endless. But Psalm 69:33 says God hears the cries of everybody who is needy. He doesn't look the other way. Be encouraged today because Jesus loves you, and He will never forsake you.

❧

Thank You, Lord, for hearing the cries of the needy. What a blessing it is to know that You are always listening for our call...standing ready to meet our needs and heal our hurts. Thank You that Your eyes are upon me and Your ear is open to my cry when I am in need.

Desire a Clean Heart and Thoughts

Create in me a new, clean heart, O God, filled with clean thoughts and right desires.

—Psalm 51:10

*O*ur church has a wonderful street evangelism ministry, and one of our most effective volunteers in that ministry is someone who, as a young man, desired to become a gangster! He was absolutely fascinated by organized crime and made a decision at a very young age to become involved in it. He avoided giving his life to God because he knew it would stand in the way of realizing his dream!

After many years, he saw our television program one night and heard that anyone could be set free from their past—no matter what they had done. He gave his heart to Jesus that night, and then he came to our church. He does a wonderful job in the street evangelism ministry because he's been involved in some of the things some people on the streets believe they have to do to stay alive, like dealing in illegal drug activities, prostitution, and such things.

When this young man gave his heart to the Lord, his life changed dramatically, and he wanted a new, clean heart.

He's a living testimony to misguided people on the streets. His message of hope changes their lives, and many of the people he has witnessed to now have good, clean hearts too.

Nothing is too difficult for our God. He always turns our bad times around and makes something useful out of them when we let Him. Won't you ask Him to wash away your past and set you on a new course that will cleanse your thoughts and leave you with a desire to bring others into God's kingdom?

❧

Create in me a new, clean heart, O God. Fill me with clean thoughts and right desires. Help me to live right and do right and tell others that they can be free of their past and have a new, fresh start with Jesus too.

God's Plans Are for Good, Not for Evil

For I know the plans I have for you, says the Lord. They are
plans for good and not for evil, to give you a future and a hope.
—Jeremiah 29:11

I shared with our congregation a letter I received that said, "I had been shooting drugs for 26 years when I started watching your TV program, and I prayed the sinner's prayer with Pastor Osteen. I've stopped doing drugs. I also have my first job in 20 years. All praise to the Lord Jesus Christ."

This man now has a job after 26 years of drug addiction! God had plans for him—and His plans were for good and not evil. For 26 years, he probably went through hell on earth. But now that he has accepted the Lord Jesus, he has a future, and he has hope.

I thank God for this testimony. It demonstrates to all of us that God is still on the throne and in control of what's going on down here on earth. Wherever you are today in this journey called life, don't get discouraged. God has a good plan for your life, and one way or another, He'll see to it that you succeed.

❧

I know that You have a good plan for my life, God. Therefore, I will not worry
or be anxious about it, but I'll look to the future with hope in You.

Let God Take Control of Your Life

He was the one who prayed to the God of Israel, "Oh, that you would wonderfully bless me and help me in my work; please be with me in all that I do, and keep me from all evil and disaster!" And God granted him his request.

—1 Chronicles 4:10

*F*irst Chronicles tells of a man by the name of Jabez, whose mother so named him because she had difficulty delivering him. His name means distress or sorrow or pain. So Jabez had to go through life being constantly reminded that he had caused pain and sorrow.

Maybe you have a bad name, not from the name your mother gave you, but because of problems or troubles that have plagued you. Do you know what Jabez did? No matter what his name was or what it meant, he prayed to the God of Israel to wonderfully bless him and help him in his work and keep him from evil and disaster.

And do you know what God did? He granted his request. It doesn't matter how bad your name is. Your name may have "murderer" or "adulterer" behind it—it doesn't matter. When you turn to God and look to Him as your Savior, He will grant you peace.

Let go of your past if it is troubling you, and let God take control of your life.

Right now, Lord, I let go of everything that I don't like about myself and my past. Bless me and help me and keep me from all evil. Thank You for hearing and answering my prayers, and being with me in all that I do.

Let Jesus Conquer You

*Yet the Lord still waits for you to come to him, so he can show
you his love; he will conquer you to bless you, just as he said. For
the Lord is faithful to his promises. Blessed are all those who wait
for him to help them.*

—Isaiah 30:18

The Lord is waiting. He's been waiting...perhaps for a very long time. And
if you've been running away from Him, then you need to stop running—because
He's waiting...for you.

When you give your heart to Jesus, allow Him to conquer you. Don't live
partially in the world and partially in the spirit. Allow Jesus to conquer you and
bless you just as He said.

Have you ever thought of waiting for God to help you when you're making
decisions? Have you ever tried to run ahead of God? I have, and it's not much
fun. I'd rather wait for Him and let Him conquer me, bless me, and show me
how much He loves me. You can do that too.

❧

*Lord, I long to have my fleshly will conquered by Your Spirit. Strengthen
me as I surrender to Your will for my life. I say, not my will, but Yours, Lord,
be done. I stop running and allow You to conquer me and bless me. Thank You
for Your faithfulness.*

Seeking the Peace of God

May the Lord of peace himself give you his peace no matter what happens. The Lord be with you all.

—2 Thessalonians 3:16

*I*f you read the newspapers or watch TV, you know what a mess this world is in. There is turmoil everywhere. God is the only One who can give you peace in these perilous times.

Many things come against us in life. Psalm 34:19 says the righteous will suffer many afflictions, but God delivers us out of them all!

Even if you lived a wicked life before you met Jesus, you are now the righteousness of God in Christ Jesus, and you are entitled to His peace.

If your world is turned upside down and you aren't experiencing God's peace today—a peace that you can't get from any source in this world—then today can be your day. Seek the peace of God, and when you find it, remember to thank Jesus for it.

Lord Jesus, I thank You that I have Your peace today in every situation. Help me to remember that no matter what comes along, You are with me. I praise Your name!

Children Need to Be Saved

But Jesus said, "Let the little children come to me, and don't prevent them. For of such is the Kingdom of Heaven."
—Matthew 19:14

*W*e received the sweetest letter from a little ten-year-old girl who wrote: "I used to hate watching television. I didn't want to watch you or Kenneth Copeland or anybody else. But I gave my heart to the Lord, and now I love to watch your program. I'm having such a good time praying with you.

"God delivered me from listening to bad music and saying ugly words. All of the miracles God has done for our family since we've gotten saved are just wonderful!"

It is such a blessing for us to know that our simple and yet profound message of Jesus' love reaches the hearts of God's children of all ages. Are your children saved? They deserve to know Jesus as early in their lives as possible.

Don't hesitate to tell your children about Jesus—His love for them, His sacrifice for their eternal lives, and the opportunity they have to spend eternity in heaven. Knowing Jesus at an early age can help to prevent them from making many of the mistakes we parents have made.

❧

Father, I desire that my children be saved and have the opportunity to spend eternity with You in heaven. O Lord, I lift up my children to You today. I pray that You will give them understanding hearts as I explain their need for salvation. Help me to live a godly life before them. I entrust our home to You in Jesus' name.

God Listens to His Children's Prayers

For the Lord is watching His children, listening to their prayers; but the Lord's face is hard against those who do evil.
—1 Peter 3:12

When I was thirteen years old, I made the choice to accept Jesus Christ into my heart and to serve Him all of my days. And if I had that choice to make now that I'm older, I would do it all over again. Why? Because I am God's child, and I like knowing that He hears my prayers.

I never, ever want the Lord's face to be hard against me for any reason, least of all because I've done something evil in His sight. I always want Him to be happy when He sees me, thinks of me, and hears my prayers. Don't you?

If you're not serving the Lord today with all of your heart, it is a good time to start again. I know that you want Him to hear your prayers, and He will when you ask Him to be your Father and you are willing to be His child.

❧

Lord, I thank You for hearing my prayers. I know that You are always watching me and listening to me. I choose to serve You with my whole heart as your child and please You in all that I do.

God's Face Is Toward You

"For if you turn to the Lord again, your brothers and your children will be treated mercifully by their captors, and they will be able to return to this land. For the Lord your God is full of kindness and mercy and will not continue to turn away his face from you if you return to him."

—2 Chronicles 30:9

*W*hen our children were small, every night after they were tucked in bed, each child hollered from their respective bedrooms, "Good night, Momma and Daddy. I love you."

We didn't realize it at the time, but our oldest son Paul was frightened of being in his room alone. One night after the other children had said "good night," little Paul asked, "Daddy, are you there?"

John said, "Yes, son, we're here."

Then Paul asked, "Daddy, is your face toward me?"

It was so touching to me that this little boy would have been more frightened to think that our faces were turned away from him. Knowing that we were lying on our sides and facing his room made him feel secure.

That's the way God is. His face is always turned toward you. He will never ignore you. Let's be obedient to God so He will keep His faced turned toward us.

❧

Lord, I do want Your face to be toward me—Your eyes and ears to see and hear me. I desire to be obedient to You so that You will delight in me and never have cause to turn away Your face from me.

Trust in God As a Little Child

..."Let the little children come to me! Never send them away!
For the Kingdom of God belongs to men who have hearts as trusting
as these little children's...."

—Luke 18:16

Little children have trusting hearts. They trust their moms and dads because they don't know anybody else when they're first born. But if we, as adults, could have hearts like little children and just trust Jesus for our needs, I think we'd receive a lot more from Him.

Jesus wants us to come to Him as a little child—loving without conditions and trusting without requiring proof that He's trustworthy. He wants us to be carefree, happy, and confident because we know that all of our needs are being met.

If you've been concerned about praying—perhaps even concerned that you don't pray right—just begin to pray the simple prayer of a little child. Jesus will hear you and answer you.

❦

Lord, You are my Father. I thank You that I can crawl up into Your lap and that You'll give me whatever I ask from Your Word because You love me. You love me unconditionally, and I trust You to always hear and answer my prayers.

God Takes Joy in our Expectation of Him

But his joy is in those who reverence him, those who expect him to be loving and kind.

—Psalm 147:11

*H*ave you ever noticed how much joy grandparents get from their grandchildren…and how grandchildren seem to think grandmother and granddad are the most special, loving and kind people in the whole world? That is because of the special love between them.

It is the same way with God. He delights in us as His children. He is happy to answer our prayer requests, and He likes for us to expect Him to be loving, kind, and generous. God has been so loving and kind to me that nobody could ever convince me that He could be any other way. He deserves our love and respect, and I'm so happy to be serving Him.

❦

I want You to have joy today, Lord, because I do reverence You and I expect Your love and kindness in my life. I have confidence in You and Your loving kindness to me as Your child.

Receiving the Strength of God

*Reverence for God gives a man deep strength; his children have
a place of refuge and security.*

—Proverbs 14:26

*W*hether you're a male or a female believer, and whether you have the responsibility of being a single parent or are raising children with your spouse, you can have deep strength according to this verse in Proverbs. All you have to do to get this strength is to reverence God—love and fear Him (not in the wrong sense, but have great respect for Him). When your children sense that deep strength, they will feel safe and secure.

I encourage parents today to reverence and love God, and one way to do this is to get involved in a good, Bible-teaching church. Your failure to love God and belong to a good church may ruin not only your life but the lives of your children as well.

Be a man or woman of deep strength, and your children will have a refuge. They'll be able to come to you and say, "Dad, I need prayer," or "Mom, I need you to pray for me."

They will feel your strength and it will cause them to feel secure. In a day when there are so many insecure children, you can raise wonderfully secure children who are totally aware that they have peace and safety.

❦

My God, I bow before You with reverence for who You are. I thank You that as I honor and revere You, my children will recognize the deep strength I receive from You and have a powerful sense of security. You are our refuge and strength.

Guard Your Children Carefully

*Then Rizpah, the mother of two of the men, spread sackcloth
upon a rock and stayed there through the entire harvest season to
prevent the vultures from tearing at their bodies during the day and
the wild animals from eating them at night. When David learned
what she had done, he arranged for the men's bones to be buried in
the grave of Saul's father, Kish....*

—2 Samuel 21:10-12

This story really touches my heart. It's a sad story of a devoted mother
guarding the bodies of her dead sons. In those days, they didn't bury their dead
in the ground. Her sons were just laid out on a hill. From April until October,
Rizpah stayed on that mountain and guarded their bodies to keep the vultures
from eating their flesh. When David found out, he had their remains placed in
a grave where the vultures couldn't get to them.

We know that the spirits of Rizpah's sons were either in heaven or hell at that
time—it was too late then to protect them. But Rizpah was doing the best she
could with the knowledge she had.

But those of us who have living children today need to carefully guard them
in these days. We must watch over them continually to keep the "vultures" from
getting them. We need to protect them from gangs, drugs, and the evil one—and
the best way to do that is to place them in the divine care of our loving God.
Guard your children, cover them with your prayers, and faithfully give God your
praise for keeping them from harm.

*Lord, I want to keep my children from being led away by the snares of the
enemy and the "vultures" of the world. I ask You today to guard them and protect
my children from all evil. With You watching over them day and night, I know
they will be kept safe.*

Choosing Life—One Day At A Time

God Keeps Every Promise

But happy is the man...whose hope is in the Lord his God—the God who made both earth and heaven, the seas and everything in them. He is the God who keeps every promise.

—Psalm 146:5,6

$\int$tep outdoors today and take a close look at the beautiful trees and flowers, the earth and sky, and the birds that sing to you each morning. If God made all of these for your pleasure and enjoyment, will He not also keep all of the promises He's made to you in His Word? God loves to make and keep promises to you as His child because He loves you so dearly.

Whatever happens today, know that God can handle it. It won't be too hard for Him. His Word is packed with promises that everything is going to turn out for good for those who love Him.

Enjoy the beauty of God's wondrous creation today. Hope in the Lord and rejoice in the fact that His promises belong to you!

❧

Lord, I rejoice today in all of Your creation. Thank You for Your promise that I can be happy because my hope is in You. I am grateful that You keep all Your promises and they are all mine!

When Our Faith Is Weak, God Is Faithful

Even when we are too weak to have any faith left, he remains
faithful to us and will help us, for he cannot disown us who are
part of himself, and he will always carry out his promises to us.
—2 Timothy 2:13

I would have died in the early '80s had I not known that God still heals—
had I not believed that Jesus still heals today, and that He is the same as He's
always been. Sometimes people get so weak and sick, or they have so many things
come against them, that they don't feel as if they have any faith left.

But God always carries out His promises to us. All of His promises are yes
and amen! And when it seems like we are too weak, too sick, or too down to have
any faith left, still He remains faithful to us.

Sometimes we drift away from Him and are not faithful to Him, but He
remains faithful to us because He loves us. He will never disown us because we are
part of Him. He needs us in this world to help bring the good news of His gospel
to others.

That's good news! You and I are alive today because of God's promises to us.
In Psalm 107:20 (KJV), it says, *He sent his word, and healed them, and delivered*
them from their destructions. This promise says you have been delivered from
destruction. Hallelujah!

Father, even when my faith is weak, Your faithfulness is strong. You always
help me because I am your child. Thank You for always carrying out Your promises
to me.

A Doubting Mind Needs a Steadfast Heart

Let us hold fast the profession of our faith without wavering;
(for he is faithful that promised).

—Hebrews 10:23 KJV

I stood on this scripture for so long when I was fighting a battle to live back in 1981, after being diagnosed with cancer.

One day I was really disturbed because my heart knew that I was healed on December 11th, but my symptoms kept telling my head that I wasn't healed. I talked to my husband about it.

He said, "Your heart knows that God's Word is right, doesn't it?"

I said, "Yes, it does. My heart is sure that I received healing of cancer on December 11th."

He then asked, "Can't you see that it's your head doubting, and not your heart?"

He was right. If you're standing on a promise of God today, I encourage you to hold fast to your confession of faith without wavering. Even if your head wavers, your heart knows that God's Word is true, and that He will not fail you.

I hold fast the profession of my faith without wavering, Father God, for You are faithful who promised. Even if my mind has doubts, my heart steadfastly believes Your faithful promises.

God Does Exactly What He Says

...I have been telling you about Jesus Christ the Son of God. He isn't one to say "yes" when He means "no." He always does exactly what he says. He carries out and fulfills all of God's promises, no matter how many of them there are; and we have told everyone how faithful he is, giving glory to his name.

—2 Corinthians 1:19,20

God will never tell you one thing and do another. If you have asked Him for something, all you have to do is search His book. It's full of wonderful promises... and they are for you! If God says He'll do something for you, He will do it. You have His Word on it!

God is not a man that He would lie. And Jesus is more than happy to fulfill all of the promises of His Father. So ask God for what you need. You'll be glad when He does something special for you.

❧

O God, I give glory to Your name—the name that endures forever. Your faithfulness is known to every generation because You always do exactly what You say in Your Word. I thank You that Your promises are true and that You are faithful to fulfill them in my life.

Greatly Delight in God's Commandments

He does not fear bad news, nor live in dread of what may happen.
For he is settled in his mind that Jehovah will take care of him.
—Psalm 112:7

I love to read Psalm 112 from beginning to end. It is so encouraging in these days when dread could try to take over our thoughts. The news reports alone could trigger dread and fear in us, but we don't have to dread, worry, or be anxious about what may happen.

Verse 1 says that *...all who fear God and trust in him are blessed beyond expression. Yes, happy is the man who delights in doing his commands.*

Do you want to be happy? Of course you do. If you greatly delight in following God's instructions, you will be happy and according to verse 6, you won't be *...overthrown by evil....*

Verse 7 promises that you won't have to fear bad news when it is settled in your mind that God will take care of you.

It is settled in my mind that Jehovah God has taken care of me, is taking care of me, and will continue to take care of me. Why? Because I delight in His commands.

How about you?

Lord, I do trust You and delight in doing Your commands. You always take care of me, so I will not live in fear or dread. My mind and heart are settled and happy in Your promises.

God's Tender Mercy Is For You

He is merciful and tender toward those who don't deserve it....
—Psalm 103:8

*D*id you ever feel like you didn't deserve God's mercy or His tenderness? I have. But He's tender and merciful anyway. That is the very nature of God. He literally cannot be any other way—it just isn't in Him to be unmerciful and harsh toward His family.

You may think, I've never thought of myself as part of God's family. If you are born again, you are a very important member of the family of God. You are welcome at God's table. You are heir to a great inheritance of love, joy, peace, patience, kindness, goodness, gentleness, faithfulness, self-control, and more! These are the nine fruit of the Holy Spirit, and He has promised they belong to you!

Whether or not you feel deserving of God's glorious gifts and fruit, He has decided that you are. After all, He was wounded at Calvary and shed His blood to purchase your pardon. He rose from the grave to forever defeat death so you wouldn't have to struggle and fight to conquer it.

Isn't it time you just started to let yourself enjoy God's tender feelings toward you? Isn't it time to allow His mercies to cover you? See yourself as God sees you for a change. You will never be the same.

What a joy to be part of Your family, God! Your gift of salvation and eternal life is glorious, and You have given me the fruit of Your Spirit as a promised inheritance, though I have done nothing to deserve it. Jesus has demonstrated Your great tenderness and mercy toward me, and I thank You for Your goodness.

Don't Let Others Spoil Your Faith and Joy

Don't let others spoil your faith and joy with their philosophies,
their wrong and shallow answers built on men's thoughts and ideas,
instead of on what Christ has said.

—Colossians 2:8

It is important for you as a Christian to be careful of who and what you allow to influence you. Don't let the philosophies of others—their beliefs, views, and values—convince you that they are right and God is wrong.

God is not a man that He would lie. His Word—the Bible—is filled with His promises to you. His Word endures forever, so His promises are forever too.

Many would like to convince you that God no longer heals, that He wants to keep you humble by keeping you poor, or that His Word has no application for today.

But I encourage you to just stay in the Word of God, believe His promises, and trust and rely on Him. Then watch the blessings of God flow toward you! Take what you have learned and influence others with what Christ Jesus has said.

❦

Father, I will not allow other people to spoil my faith and joy in You. I will listen to what You have to say instead of the thoughts and ideas of men. I thank You that You are God and You cannot lie. You will do what You promise every time.

God Made You Special

I will praise thee; for I am fearfully and wonderfully made....
—Psalm 139:14 KJV

When John and I were first married, I was just a 21-year-old who had recently graduated from nurses school. I knew nothing about being a pastor's wife. I felt as though I had been ushered into an entirely new realm.

I had had a plan. My plan was to spend the rest of my life single—I was going to work as a nurse all of my life. I was never going to marry. Well, that changed a lot!

I remember saying, "Sweetheart, I can't play the piano. I can't sing. I can't teach a class. I can't do anything a pastor's wife is supposed to do."

He answered, "Dodie, I didn't marry you to play the piano or sing or teach a class. I married you because I love you, and I like you just the way you are."

That set me free and made me to know that I'm an original. I'm the only me in the world. Thank the Lord, I can just be myself. I don't have to be like someone else.

If you've ever felt less than perfect or as though you don't measure up to someone else's expectations, just relax in the knowledge that God made you, and He knows all about you. You can be yourself—that's exactly who God created you to be. Be an original.

❧

Thank You for making me the way I am, Lord. It is amazing to think that I don't have to be anyone else but me. I am grateful for the gifts and talents you have placed in me. I am unique—one of a kind. Help me to follow Your plan for my life. I praise You because I am fearfully and wonderfully made.

Understand Who You Are

"In solemn truth I tell you, anyone believing in me shall do the same miracles I have done, and even greater ones, because I am going to be with the Father. You can ask him for anything, using my name, and I will do it, for this will bring praise to the Father because of what I, the Son, will do for you. Yes, ask anything, using my name, and I will do it!"

—John 14:12-14

John always said—and I agree—that many of us fail to understand who we are through God's grace and mercy and what He has promised to do through us because of the death, burial, and resurrection of Jesus Christ, our Savior.

Who are we as Christians? We are blood-bought children of God who have accepted Christ as our Savior, believing that Jesus' blood was the price paid for the remission of our sins. We are new creatures in Christ Jesus, bone of His bone and flesh of His flesh! We have become partakers of His divine nature through the blood He spilled for us at Calvary.

Realizing who we are and what God has promised in His Word that we could do in the name of Jesus, we should rise up and exercise commanding power. We are sons and daughters of God. He said that He has given us power through the name of Jesus to command demons, sickness, trouble, and disease to leave, and it will come to pass! Praise the Lord!

Father, because I believe in Jesus, I know I can do the same miracles He did by asking You for them in His name. And You will grant them for me, just like You did for Jesus. I am Your child, and I believe I can do what You say I can do. I determine to act on Your Word like Jesus did, starting today. You are all powerful, and I thank You that You will do anything I ask in Jesus' name.

See Yourself As God Sees You

The Angel of the Lord appeared to him and said, "Mighty soldier, the Lord is with you!"

—Judges 6:12

This verse in Judges talks about a great soldier in the army of the Lord whose name was Gideon. The Amplified Bible says that God called Gideon a mighty man of fearless courage. But that is definitely not how Gideon saw himself. His perception of himself was very different from God's. He didn't think he was fearless or courageous at all.

In verse 15, Gideon tells the angel how poor his family in Manasseh is and that he is the least thought of in the entire clan! Gideon was a lot like most of us. He finds it hard to believe that God knows who he is and chooses to bless him with His favor anyway!

God doesn't call us to do things that we aren't equipped to handle. He sees us so differently than we see ourselves. Don't listen to the voice of discouragement that plays like a recording in your mind. Don't listen to the people around you. Don't look at your circumstances. If you do, you'll never be able to accomplish anything.

Just begin to see yourself as God sees you—fearless and courageous, mighty and bold! The choice is yours to make. It may look impossible to you, but trust in God—He can do the supernatural. It's time for you to step into the abundant life God has for you!

❦

Father, I want to see myself as You see me—strong and courageous in the power of Your might. I desire to accomplish what You ask me to do. I appreciate Your confidence in me. Help me to always hear and believe Your voice of encouragement.

God Honors Those Who Serve Jesus

"If any man serve me, let him follow me; and where I am, there shall also my servant be: if any man serve me, him will my Father honour."

—John 12:26 KJV

This scripture has blessed me through the years. It tells me that when we serve the Lord Jesus Christ, the Father will honor us. It is awesome to realize that God will honor us for serving His Son. There are many ways to serve Jesus.

Serve means "to be of service or use." People who are involved in church serve in the areas of praying, greeting, ushering, singing in the choir, teaching special classes, children's church, working with youth, volunteering in the office, answering the telephone, making calls to newcomers, visiting those in the hospitals and nursing homes, and many, many more.

Whenever you do or say something positive and productive to serve another of God's creations, God the Father in heaven loves you with an everlasting love and He will honor you.

Honor means "title conferred for achievement."

Serve the Lord with gladness and give Him the opportunity to honor you.

Lord Jesus, I desire to follow and serve You, not to bring honor to myself but to honor You. You served others when You lived on the earth, and I praise You for opportunities to be of service to You through the church, and in my relationships at home and at work. And I choose to serve You with gladness!

God Is Directing Your Steps

Since the Lord is directing our steps, why try to understand everything that happens along the way?

—Proverbs 20:24

*I*f you trust in God with all your heart, He will direct your steps. He purchased your salvation at Calvary, and as you allow Him to be in charge of your life, you will become the victorious Christian He intends for you to be.

When disasters come along that you don't understand—things like heart disease, cancer, runaway teenagers, the loss of a loved one or a job—it doesn't mean that God has stopped directing your steps. He will just cause you to be able to handle it in the power of His Spirit.

You can rule and reign in life as a king (see 2 Timothy 2:12). He will cause all things to work together for your good if you trust in Him (see Romans 8:28 KJV). Remember that regardless of your circumstances, He is directing your paths.

Don't reason and try to understand everything. Just let God give you strength, and you will be an overcomer. You'll be more than a conqueror because He's directing your steps!

❧

Thank You, Lord God, that You are always directing my steps even in the times I don't understand what is happening to me and around me. I put my trust in You because I know You will always cause all things to work together for my good.

He Will Perfect What Concerns Us

The Lord will work out his plans for my life—for your loving kindness, Lord, continues forever. Don't abandon me—for you made me.

—Psalm 138:8

*P*eople have many concerns these days—it seems as though there is always something to be concerned about. I think of this scripture when I begin to get concerned about anything. The King James Version says, *The Lord will perfect that which concerneth me: thy mercy, O Lord, endureth for ever: forsake not the works of thine own hands.*

This scripture tells me that whatever concerns you and me also concerns God. Whenever you seek Him and talk to Him out of your heart like a little child, He'll perfect that which concerns you.

Perfect means He'll make perfect whatever you need.

Be encouraged that Jesus knows all about your needs, and He is concerned. He will take whatever concerns you and turn it into something wonderful—something without a single flaw and lacking absolutely nothing!

Lord God, I believe You will work out Your plans for my life. Thank You for Your loving kindness that will continue toward me forever. I know You will never abandon me. I'm glad You are concerned about what concerns me. You made me, and You work all things together for my good.

Check Your "Victory File"

Remember ye not the former things, neither consider the things of old. Behold, I will do a new thing; now it shall spring forth; shall ye not know it? I will even make a way in the wilderness, and rivers in the desert.

—Isaiah 43:18,19 KJV

I was impressed with a message Joel taught our congregation about having a healthy, positive outlook on life. Joel had read that psychologists say there are two main files in every person's memory. One file is filled with all of your failures, defeats, painful memories, and hardships. File number two is your "victory file." It contains your accomplishments and all those things that you're most proud of.

The psychologists said that a person's disposition is usually dependent on which file you keep going back to.

To which file do you refer? Too many folks keep going back to their "failure" file—they feed their spirit on past disappointments, hurts, and pain. And their "victory" file never gets opened!

I encourage you to quit living in the past. Philippians 3:13 tells us to forget those things that are behind and reach for what is ahead. When you go back in your memory, go back to your "victory" file. Even if you have only one victory, go back to that one. And if you don't remember any victories, remember the time that God saved you—that was the greatest victory of all!

❧

Lord Jesus, I thank You that nothing in my past compares to all the good things that You have planned for my future. Therefore, I will forget those things that are behind me and reach for what is ahead. I will close my failure file and keep my victory file open!

Jesus Is Whatever You Need

But Moses asked, "If I go to the people of Israel and tell them that their fathers' God has sent me, they will ask, 'Which God are you talking about?' What shall I tell them? 'The Sovereign God,'" was the reply. "Just say, 'I AM has sent me!'"

—Exodus 3:13,14

*N*ot long ago I was praising God and talking to Jesus as I worked around my house. When I got to the refrigerator, I said, "Jesus, You are my Healer." I listed several other things that Jesus Is, and suddenly I thought, Well, I can't think of anything wonderful that Jesus is not. I've said everything about Him that I know.

That just showed me that Jesus is the great I AM—He is whatever we need. Whatever you need Him for, He is that. If you need help with your finances or for a child who is on drugs...or you need healing for your body—whatever it is—Jesus is that. Just tell Him what you need, and He will be that for you.

❧

Jesus, You truly are the great I AM. There is none other like You. Whatever I need, You have provided. Oh, how I praise You, Lord, for who You are. You are the Sovereign God, and I give You glory, honor, and thanksgiving. You are worthy of all praise!

He's Always God

How can we describe God? With what can we compare him?
—Isaiah 40:18

How can God be described? He is everything. There is nothing that you can compare Him to because He is it. He's all of it. He's always there.

He is the Great I Am. He is for us and never against us. Whatever we need, He is there to provide for us. He's merciful when we really don't deserve it. He loves us because that's what He wants to do.

God is so full of compassion for His children that He only wants us to have what's best for us. And He's forgiving. He forgives our sins. Isn't that wonderful? Nobody else can forgive our sins, and He not only forgives them, He *forgets* them! We usually remember them, but He doesn't ever bring them back to His remembrance.

God is also awesome—just because He's God. And I like Him just like He is. Whatever we need—He is it!

❦

God, You are so wonderful. There is no one else to compare with You. You are the only God. You are everything I need. You are ever-merciful and compassionate, and I love You. You are an awesome God!

God Is Not Weak, But Well Able!

*The people were soon complaining about all their misfortunes...
and they wept, "Oh, for a few bites of meat! Oh, that we had some
of the delicious fish we enjoyed so much in Egypt, and the wonderful
cucumbers and melons, leeks, onions, and garlic!"*

—Numbers 11:1,5

God provided so miraculously for His people all the time they were
wandering in the wilderness. Manna fell like dew during the night—they didn't
even have to fish or hunt for food! God himself delivered food to them every day,
yet they grumbled about what they were missing from their land of bondage!

Moses finally asked God why he had to be in charge of these grumbling
folks. Then the Lord said to Moses, *"When did I become weak?"*... (v. 23).

Then God miraculously brought quail in from the sea (v. 31)—more than
they could eat. Even though He was angry with them for complaining, He still
provided for them.

People complain today about all the things they want and don't have. Many
are never satisfied even when they have everything they really need.

Thank God for His infinite mercy to us. Despite our tendency to complain,
He often goes to any length necessary to provide for us when we belong to Him.
That's really good news!

*I praise You, Lord, for being merciful to me even when I complain. You have
been so good to me, and I really have no reason to grumble. I repent and ask You to
forgive me. You always provide for me and supply my every need. I just want to say
thank You today.*

Don't Be Faithless—Believe!

Then he [Jesus] said to Thomas, "Put your finger into my hands. Put your hand into my side. Don't be faithless any longer. Believe!"

—John 20:27

*F*rom time to time, we need to be reminded of the story of Jesus' crucifixion and resurrection. Mary Magdalene couldn't find Jesus when she visited His grave. Naturally, she was distraught, thinking Jesus' body might have been stolen—when, suddenly, Jesus was standing right there in front of her! He told her to go and tell His brothers that He was alive! So Mary went and found them and told them what she had seen and heard.

The same day Jesus appeared to ten of the disciples, but Thomas was not there. Eight days later, Jesus walked right through the walls of the building where the disciples and others had gathered. Thomas had said he wouldn't believe Jesus was alive until he felt the nail prints in His hands, so Jesus showed Thomas the wounds and charged him with these words, *"...Don't be faithless any longer. Believe!"*

Jesus went on to say in verse 29, *"You believe because you have seen me. But blessed are those who haven't seen me and believe anyway."*

Jesus hasn't changed. He's exactly the same as He has always been. Whatever you need today, don't be faithless about it any longer—believe!

❧❧

Father, I choose to be faithful in believing what Jesus has done for me. Even when I don't see the answer immediately, I know I am blessed because my faith is in You. You always meet my needs when I believe Your Word.

Trust God When Your Sun Goes Down

...Her sun is gone down while it is yet day....
—Jeremiah 15:9

Throughout our lives we encounter times when it seems as though the sun has gone down while it is yet day—or seeming disaster has occurred and nothing is the same as it was before. The sun went down while it was still day for me when I was diagnosed with terminal liver cancer. For my husband, the sun went down when he faced heart bypass surgery years ago. Other friends of ours have experienced the sun going down in their lives while it was yet day.

It looked as dark to us as it does at the midnight hour, yet we knew that God's Word is true and healing would come. All of us came out of the darkness with the help of the Lord Jesus. Our sun may have temporarily gone down, but it didn't stay down long. And praise God, when the sun came out again, it remained bright!

If the sun has gone down in your life, please know that Jesus is in control, and it will come out again, shining on your life like a beacon. The entrance of God's Word brings light!

My Father, thank You for being with me in the midnight hour. You always strengthen me when darkness tries to overtake me. I take hold of Your Word because You are my light and my life.

Look at Jesus

*Then he spat on the ground and made mud from the spittle and
smoothed the mud over the blind man's eyes, and told him, "Go and
wash in the Pool of Siloam" (the word "Siloam" means "Sent"). So
the man went where he was sent and washed and came back seeing!*
—John 9:6,7

I am always touched by the story of this man—blind from birth—whose
eyes Jesus covered with mud moistened with His own spittle. Nobody really
understood who it was that had healed him, including the man himself.

When Jesus heard this, He returned to the man and asked him, "Do you
believe in the Messiah?"

The man answered, "I want to, Sir, but who is He?"

Jesus said, "You have seen Him, and He is speaking to you." Isn't that exciting?

I have never physically seen Jesus, but I have seen Him in His Word...and in
the things He's done for people, including me. I clearly saw Jesus in my healing
from cancer. We know Jesus performed great miracles while He was here on earth,
but I want you to know He is still doing them! He'll give you the miracle you
need...and He'll make sure your miracle is right on time!

Look to Jesus, and be obedient—He'll never let you down. Whatever you
need, He is there for you.

*What a blessing to know, Lord, that You are still performing miracles! Thank
You for all the miracles You have done in our lives. Thank God we can look to
Jesus for any miracle we need, and He will do it!*

The Lord Delivers from All Afflictions

Many are the afflictions of the righteous: but the LORD delivereth him out of them all.
—Psalm 34:19 KJV

God will deliver us from *all* afflictions—not just a few but all of them! That little word, "A-L-L" means so much. The dictionary defines *all* as "every; any whatsoever; everything one has."

Every one of us has afflictions. The Bible says many are the afflictions, but the Lord delivers...out of them ALL. That little word ALL takes care of the afflictions, doesn't it?

You might say, "Well, God delivers me if it's not too hard for Him." Well, the Bible says nothing is too hard for God—nothing—zero.

You might say, "Many are my afflictions, but He will deliver me if He's not sleeping." According to Psalm 121:4, God never slumbers nor sleeps.

Remember those two words *many* and *all* today. It doesn't matter how many afflictions come today, God will deliver us out of them all. He will never break His covenant with us.

Jeremiah 33:20,21 (KJV) says, *Thus saith the LORD; If ye can break my covenant of the day, and my covenant of the night, and that there should not be day and night in their season; then may also my covenant be broken....* Nobody can stop the day or the night, so God won't break His covenant either!

❧

Thank You, Lord, for delivering me out of all my afflictions. No matter how serious the conditions may be, You never slumber nor sleep and You are a mighty Deliverer. Thank You for always keeping Your Word.

My Family and I Will Serve the Lord

"...But as for me and my family, we will serve the Lord."
—Joshua 24:15

We heard from a lady who was anxiously waiting for her 16-year-old daughter to return home from a mental institution. She had been in rehabilitation for six months. The mother had recently been saved, but the daughter had not yet accepted Jesus into her heart. The desire of this mother's heart was for her family and home to come together and to glorify the Lord as a unit.

A lot of people in the world are hurting. Their children are on drugs or some other bondage has control of their lives. It is very stressful and painful to every family member.

If you and your family are going through a stressful time, I exhort you to start believing God for deliverance and stand on the Word of God in faith believing for that deliverance. He will hear and answer.

Be diligent and patient—don't grow weary and give up when you don't see immediate results. Your answer is on the way!

❦

Mighty God, Your Word works, and I know it. I claim my family for Your kingdom—we will follow after You, and we will serve You. Deliver us from the works of the devil. Thank You for bringing peace to my home.

Do Your Best, and God Will Be Pleased

Let everyone be sure that he is doing his very best, for then he will have the personal satisfaction of work well done, and won't need to compare himself with someone else.

—Galatians 6:4

Are you doing the very best you can for the Lord Jesus? If you're not, you're going to be comparing yourself with somebody else. Somehow, most people fall short when they compare themselves to others. The result is a feeling of inadequacy, incompetence, even a lack of ability. Those feelings sometimes cause people to quit trying.

I've often seen little plaques and cards that say something like, "God isn't interested in your ability—He is interested in your availability." You should always strive to do your very best in your marriage, your relationship with your children, on your job, in your giving, etc. Your best is all that God requires. He only expects you to do what you can—not what someone else can do.

Do your very best for God, and He will be pleased with you.

❀

Father in heaven, I'm doing the best that I know how to do, and all I can do is my best. I don't try to compare myself with others. I just want to please You.

Let Miracles Affect You Permanently

"But watch out! Be very careful never to forget what you have seen God doing for you. May his miracles have a deep and permanent effect upon your lives! Tell your children and your grandchildren about the glorious miracles he did."

—Deuteronomy 4:9

*W*hat God told to Moses and the Israelites still applies to us today. Although we weren't there at that time to see those glorious miracles, we read about them in the Word and that should strengthen our faith to believe for miracles today. Once you've ever seen a miracle of God, you can't help being affected by it.

I know because I am a walking miracle—healed and whole because of Jesus' touch! And my children and grandchildren know what God did for me. My miracle has had a deep and permanent effect on our whole family and congregation.

We see miracles all the time, and you can too. Be careful to watch for them and be thankful for them. Don't disregard God's wonderful demonstrations of limitless love and grace in your life.

Thank You for miracles, Lord! Give me the spiritual eyes to recognize them when I see them...and to pass along to my children and grandchildren the knowledge of Your glorious miracles.

God Observes and Rewards Your Good Deeds

Day by day the Lord observes the good deeds done by godly men,
and gives them eternal rewards.

—Psalm 37:18

*E*ven though you do nice things for someone that nobody knows about, this scripture reminds us that God observes those things, and He keeps an account of your good works. Your account will be opened in heaven where you may redeem rewards that can never be taken away. Isn't that good news?

The Lord seeing what we do for others makes me think of mothers, who do so much for everyone—their husband, their children, and others. Be encouraged, mothers! God knows and writes it down when you fix nice meals that nobody thinks to thank you for. He makes a note of the loads of clean laundry the family enjoys but fails to comment about.

Whether anyone tells you or not how grateful they are for all the wonderful things you do for them, just remember that God observes it all. He keeps a record of your kindnesses toward others, and is planning a glorious reward just for you!

❦

Father, help me to serve others joyfully even if I am not thanked for my good deeds. Strengthen me when I'm tempted to feel "used" or "taken advantage of." Just as You bless me because You want to, I choose to bless others, knowing that my reward from You is eternal.

The Lord Is Searching for You!

For the eyes of the Lord search back and forth across the whole earth, looking for people whose hearts are perfect toward him, so that he can show his great power in helping them.

—2 Chronicles 16:9

God is always looking for people whose desire to serve Him is so great that they simply refuse to give up!

Jeremiah 29:13 says, *You will find me when you seek me, if you look for me in earnest.* Lots of people start out praying to be used of the Lord, and they keep at it for a couple of days—reminding God of their desires. They might even go a whole week, specifically praying each day. But if nothing happens by the end of a week, they just give up.

God wants people who are steadfast and strong. He's looking for people who will exercise their measure of faith. We have a harvest to gather in, and it will take multiplied thousands of us to accomplish the task.

We can be kind of fickle sometimes. We want a lot of things, but we don't want to sacrifice to get them. That's when we find out just how badly we really want what we've begged God for.

God says He will show himself strong in behalf of those whose hearts are perfect. In what condition is your heart? God needs you, and He has been looking for you. How great is your desire to serve Him? How persistent are you willing to be in your pursuit of Him? I pray that God will find a perfect heart in you, because He desires to bless you and demonstrate His great power for you.

❧

Lord God, I want to fulfill Your perfect will for my life with a heart that is fully turned toward You. Let Your eyes rest on me today and show Yourself strong in my behalf. I am willing to serve You without wavering in everything I do.

Don't Listen to False Teaching

Stop listening to teaching that contradicts what you know is right.

—Proverbs 19:27

If you're going to a church where healing isn't taught, or if they teach that Jesus has changed, then I suggest that you stop listening to that teaching.

Hebrews 13:8 confirms that Jesus is the same yesterday, today, and forever. What Jesus was yesterday, He is today, and He will be forever. He was a healer in the New Testament accounts, and He is a healer today!

I know Jesus heals today because He healed and delivered me from cancer. I'm a walking miracle. When my daughter, Lisa, was born, Jesus delivered her from symptoms of cerebral palsy. She is fine today—grown up and perfectly normal ever since the Lord Jesus made her whole.

Stop listening to false teaching and follow your heart! The Jesus of the Bible is the same today. He'll do for you what He's done for me and my family.

Don't be discouraged if your healing comes slowly. When you have discovered that Jesus hasn't changed—and understand the principles of healing presented in His Word—you will receive your healing.

Jesus, I know You have not changed, and You still heal today. I will not listen to false teaching that declares healing to be a thing of the past. I know it is for me and my family just like it is for Dodie and her family. I thank You for healing us and making us whole.

Watch What You Do and Think

*Keep a close watch on all you do and think. Stay true to what
is right and God will bless you and use you to help others.*

—1 Timothy 4:16

*I*f you get away from God and don't watch what you're doing and what
you're thinking, not only will you miss out on some of God's blessings but also
you won't be able to bless and help other people. God wants us to keep our minds
stayed on Him and on His Word, to think right and to do right. Sometimes this
is a big challenge—but the results are well worth the effort. When we obey God's
Word, He will pour out His blessings on us and help us to be a light to others.

❦

*Lord, just as You are a light in the darkness, so I desire to be a light in the
darkness of this world. Help me keep my actions and thoughts in line with Your
Word. Keep me true to what is right, and let my light shine before men and
women, boys and girls, in order that they may be drawn to You—the Light of
the world!*

The Power of the Holy Spirit

*"...I will pour out my Spirit upon all of you! Your sons and
daughters will prophesy; your old men will dream dreams, and your
young men see visions. And I will pour out my Spirit even on your
slaves, men and women alike, and put strange symbols in the earth
and sky—blood and fire and pillars of smoke."*

—Joel 2:28-30

This promise is being fulfilled today! Never in the history of the modern
church has there been such a stir as there has been in the last thirty-plus years.
God is pouring out His Spirit, and strange but biblical things are happening.

Ministers and members of all the historic denominations are receiving the
baptism in the Holy Spirit as on the Day of Pentecost (see Acts 2). They speak in
other tongues, prophesy, pray for the sick, cast out devils, and witness miracles.
The mighty gifts of the Spirit spoken of in 1 Corinthians 12 have been restored to
the body of Christ.

It's exciting to be alive at this time in history! Hurting people throughout the
world are stirring. Their hearts are open, and the harvest is ripe!

What a thrill for the blessed Spirit of God to move upon us, enabling us
to pray in other languages or give a message in tongues for the edification of
the church!

*Thank You, Jesus, for pouring out Your Spirit on everyone who is hungry and
thirsty for Your mighty power. I'm glad You are no respecter of persons. Your power
is available to men and women, sons and daughters, and people everywhere who
have a servant's heart. Thank You for pouring out Your power on me and my
household so that we may serve You with all our hearts.*

The Purpose of the Holy Spirit's Power

...Go ye into all the world, and preach the gospel to every creature.
...And these signs shall follow them that believe....

—Mark 16:15,17 KJV

John described the purpose of receiving the baptism in the Holy Ghost this way: "When I received the baptism of the Holy Ghost, I spoke in other tongues and continued to do so almost every day of my life. But the Lord did not baptize me in the Holy Ghost just so I could speak in tongues. This baptism was for the endowment of power to reach a lost world. He let me speak in tongues so I would know that I had received the baptism in the Holy Ghost, but the purpose of this experience was to give me power."

Ordinary methods of reaching people who are ready to believe and receive Jesus don't work. Many churches today have no appeal to these distraught captives. Jesus is baptizing people in the Holy Ghost and fire that they may—through signs, miracles, and wonders—convince the multitudes that Jesus is alive and will save those who come to God by Him.

If you are burdened for this lost world and desire every creature to hear the Good News, then signs and miracles will attend your life to help you effectively win them.

❦

Thank You, Jesus, for promising me the powerful signs of speaking in tongues, casting out devils, and healing the sick as a confirming witness of Your power when I preach the truth in Your Word. The fields of the world are white unto harvest, and as I minister Your Good News to everyone everywhere, signs and miracles will follow me.

Four Principles for Receiving God's Best

"You men who are fathers—if your boy asks for bread, do you give him a stone? If he asks for fish, do you give him a snake? If he asks for an egg, do you give him a scorpion? [Of course not!] And if even sinful persons like yourselves give children what they need, don't you realize that your heavenly Father will do at least as much, and give the Holy Spirit to those who ask for him?"

—Luke 11:11-13

*J*ohn always taught that there are four scriptural ways to receive the baptism in the Holy Ghost.

1. You must have *faith* to receive the Holy Spirit.
2. You must *believe* to receive the power.
3. You must *obey* God.
4. You must *ask* our heavenly Father.

Have faith, believe, obey, ask—these are the four words to remember when you want to have God's power. *To have faith* means you see it in the Word and know that God honors His promises. To *believe* means to act like God told you the truth. To *obey* means to remove any obstacle that stands between you and God's best. To *ask* is to come to the place where you can enter into His presence filled with faith and just ask Him for the very best He has for you!

❧

Father, I have faith in Your Word today. I believe what Luke 11:11-13 says—that if I ask You for this good gift, You will give me the Holy Spirit. So I obey Your Word and ask You to give me the Holy Spirit and fill me with Your presence today.

The Baptism in the Holy Spirit Is for You

And Peter replied, "Each one of you must turn from sin, return to God, and be baptized in the name of Jesus Christ for the forgiveness of your sins; then you also shall receive this gift, the Holy Spirit. For Christ promised him to each one of you who has been called by the Lord our God, and to your children and even to those in distant lands!"

—Acts 2:38,39

Through seeking the Lord, my husband and I received the baptism in the Holy Spirit in 1958 when he was a minister serving in our Baptist church. The experience revolutionized our lives and launched us into a worldwide ministry for Jesus.

We traveled throughout the world, taking the message of God's love, healing, and power to people of all nations. We started Lakewood Church as an oasis of love in a troubled world, a healing center, and a place where broken people are mended. My husband is now in heaven, but our church continues to grow by the thousands as our family continues to tell the world that God is not mad at them.

God gave the Holy Spirit so we could have His power in our lives to be bold witnesses of His goodness to us. Aren't you thankful that this wonderful gift is for everyone?

❧

Oh God, today I turn from sin, and I turn to You and ask You to forgive me for anything I have done in the past to displease You. I want the gift of the Holy Spirit that You have promised to pour out on all nations. I want power to be a bold witness for You.

Receive the Fullness of the Spirit

"Did you receive the Holy Spirit when you believed?" he [Paul]
asked them....

—Acts 19:2

$\mathcal{D}$oes the Bible say the baptism of the Holy Spirit is a separate experience
from the new birth? Yes, it does. Luke 1:35 and Matthew 3:16,17 show us that
Jesus was born of the Spirit but needed the fullness of the Spirit before entering
into His ministry.

The disciples were saved before Pentecost, but Jesus told them not to leave
Jerusalem until the Holy Spirit came upon them and gave them power.

Sinners who repent and accept Jesus as Savior are looking for salvation, and
they don't always ask for the Holy Spirit at that time. They are seeking forgiveness
and eternal life through the shed blood of Jesus. But once they have been cleansed
and made acceptable in the Beloved, they are to ask for the Holy Spirit—God's
gift to the saints.

Paul asked believers in Acts 19, "Have you received the Holy Spirit since you
believed?" They had not, so he laid his hands on them, and they were baptized in
the Holy Spirit and spoke in tongues and prophesied.

Paul wouldn't have asked this question if we automatically received the
Holy Spirit when we believed in Christ. The Bible teaches that the Holy Spirit
is received in His fullness *after* salvation. Receive the power—and all the
wonderful blessings God has stored up for you!

*Father, I know I have believed in Jesus and I am saved. But I did not receive
the fullness of the Holy Spirit when I believed on Jesus. Now I know I can have
Your power when I receive the Holy Spirit. So I ask for Your power through the
Holy Spirit, and I believe I receive that power now in Jesus' name.*

The Baptism in the Holy Spirit

More Than Speaking in Tongues

Then, what looked like flames or tongues of fire appeared and settled on their heads. And everyone present was filled with the Holy Spirit and began speaking in languages they didn't know, for the Holy Spirit gave them this ability.

—Acts 2:3,4

*J*esus has created a hunger for the power of the Holy Spirit within you. When you receive this experience, you will speak in other languages as they did in the Bible. You will have a beautiful prayer language to aid you every day of your life. And you will receive power to be a witness for Jesus. You will talk about Jesus wherever you go, and you will show love to all of God's people.

In Acts 2, the power of the Holy Spirit transformed the first-century Christians into fearless, flaming witnesses for Jesus. All the signs, wonders, and miracles recorded in the Bible are a direct result of what happened when they received the baptism in the Holy Spirit. Cities were shaken, nations were blessed by the good news about Jesus, and multiplied thousands found salvation through the blood of the Lamb—all because they had been clothed with God's power from on high.

It has been our privilege to help thousands of God's precious people from many religious backgrounds find this power.

Rejoice that you can receive God's gift today—the baptism in the Holy Spirit!

❦

Jesus, when the believers received the Baptism in the Holy Spirit on the Day of Pentecost, they received a supernatural language as a sign of Your baptism of power in their lives to be bold witnesses for You. I desire to have a prayer language too. I lift up my hands to You now to praise You from my inmost being in sounds of praise that may only sound like little syllables to me—sounds that You form into a language that will give You glory.

Now Receive the Holy Spirit

As the deer pants for water, so I long for you, O God. I thirst for God, the living God....

—Psalm 42:1,2

*D*oes your soul yearn for the Lord like that? If so, you are ready to receive the baptism in the Holy Spirit. Find a place to get alone with God. Lift your hands toward heaven and think about Him—focus on His Spirit dwelling within you. Quietly begin to rejoice in the Lord. Let worship and praise flow from your mouth.

As you worship God, you will sense the Holy Spirit rising up from your belly to your vocal cords. Now stop speaking in your own language, and let the sighs and yearnings from your innermost being tell God in little syllables of praise how much you love Him—more than you can tell Him with just your own language.

Speak out whatever sounds rise up from within you. As you submit to the Holy Spirit, more sounds will come. As you continue worshiping, your prayer language will begin flowing stronger. You won't understand your words because they are the language of the Holy Spirit speaking directly to God. You can speak in tongues every day now, so let this blessed experience revolutionize your life!

❦

Oh God, I don't have enough words to thank You for all You have done for me. I ask You to baptize me in the Holy Spirit right now, and I yield my tongue to You to form a new language of praise from my heart. I will speak in other tongues as I speak out the little syllables that are rising in my spirit now....

Trials Before a Victory

Dear friends, don't be bewildered or surprised when you go through the fiery trials ahead, for this is no strange, unusual thing that is going to happen to you. Instead, be really glad—because these trials will make you partners with Christ in his suffering, and afterwards you will have the wonderful joy of sharing his glory in that coming day when it will be displayed.

—1 Peter 4:12,13

*W*hen one of the young women in our church had triplets, she was unable to come to church for quite some time. During that time, being able to watch our program on television was a real blessing to her.

She said, "I had many fears and was plagued by anxiety—I was really under attack. I prayed that your message would uplift my spirit. I turned on the TV and the message was entitled 'Trials Before a Victory.' It was just what I needed."

She was strengthened in her spirit, and she did not faint in the day of adversity. And neither will you when you expose yourself to good teaching and the Word of God.

Life sometimes brings us trials, but in suffering the trials, we become partners with Christ.

❦

Lord, I'm so grateful that You are my partner when trials come my way. You understand suffering like no one else, and You provide just what I need to get me through. Thank You, Jesus, for the joy of sharing Your glory one day soon.

Living in
"The Nasty Now and Now"

"I have told you all this so that you will have peace of heart and mind. Here on earth you will have many trials and sorrows; but cheer up, for I have overcome the world."

—John 16:33

We like to talk about the slow pace of years gone by. Things seemed easier, better, calmer, slower, more comfortable, and less complicated in "the good old days." But my husband used to say that although it was pleasant to reminisce about the past, the truth is, "We're living in the nasty now and now."

We're living down here with problems and trials. The reality is that we all face challenges in life. And we need to know where to turn when peace of heart and mind are hard to find.

Let me encourage you to turn to Jesus. Allow Him to calm your fears and bless you with peace. Develop an unshakable confidence in God. Since the Bible says the Lord is directing your steps, why do you try to figure out everything that happens to you?

Just keep pushing through the trials of life to your personal land of promise. There is peace in the midst of the storm—not just after the storm has passed.

❦

Lord Jesus, I need your strength to live in the "nasty now and now." When everything seems to disrupt my peace of heart and mind, remind me to turn to You so I can avoid the pitfalls that bring sorrow and be cheerful in the midst of the storm. I know I will overcome because You have already overcome the world and given me Your victory.

Be Prepared for the Conflict

Go ahead and prepare for the conflict, but victory comes from God.

—Proverbs 21:31

How wonderful to know that our victories come from God—that He will keep us alive and well in times of conflict. But notice that He instructs us to go ahead and prepare for the rough times even before they come. Pray and draw closer to God daily. Get into the Word of God and find scriptures to hide in your heart.

Then in the day of trouble, when there's a battle raging in your spiritual life, your family, your finances, or your job, you'll be prepared for the conflict. God will give you the victory, but He wants you to be prepared—which requires studying His Word and developing an intimate relationship with Him. When you do this, you will have peace and assurance about facing any conflicts that life may bring your way.

I thank You, God, that You are my promise of victory. Without You, I would not be prepared to face times of stress and conflict. Help me to be prepared for any conflict that comes my way, as I diligently pray and study Your Word.

Prayer Turns the Tide of Battle

You have seen me tossing and turning through the night. You have collected all my tears and preserved them in your bottle! You have recorded every one in your book. The very day I call for help, the tide of battle turns. My enemies flee! This one thing I know: God is for me!

—Psalm 56:8,9

Have you ever tossed and turned through the night because you couldn't sleep? Have you cried to the Lord in the night, "God, where are You? Where are You? Come to me, Jesus." You know He's there—as close as the very breath you breathe. But sometimes it doesn't seem like it.

The Bible says God will wipe away all tears from our eyes (see Revelation 21:4). He has all of our tears on earth recorded in His book—all of the tears we've ever cried have been stored in a bottle!

You will see your battle turn when you call out to God for help. The enemy causing death, financial trouble, poor health, and wayward children will flee.

This one thing I know, God is for you. And if God is for you, who can be against you? The very moment you pray, the tide of your battle will turn! Glory to God!

❧

Lord God, in the battles of life I will remember to cry out to You to help me. You're always as close to me as the breath I breathe. The very moment I pray, I know You will turn the tide of battle in my favor. You will fight for me and my enemies have to flee!

The Marks of a Giant-Killer

As Goliath approached, David ran out to meet him and, reaching into his shepherd's bag, took out a stone, hurled it from his sling, and hit the Philistine in the forehead. The stone sank in, and the man fell on his face to the ground.

—1 Samuel 17:48,49

One Sunday John preached a message on what it takes to be a giant-killer. There are giants in our land today—principalities, powers, and the devil himself... and giants of sickness, trouble in the home, children having children, and more. Can you, like David, become a giant-killer? Here are some distinguishing factors.

1. *Consecration*—David was dedicated or consecrated to God.
2. *Confession*—David spoke the Word, believing, and God was with him.
3. *Courage*—David ran toward his enemy—he faced the giant in his life.
4. *Covenant*—David had a binding agreement between himself and God.

Jesus was the biggest giant-killer in the world. He defeated the devil and every demon—all for us. Because He did that, we have covenant rights with Him. Follow after Jesus and develop these four characteristics in your life, and you too will become a giant-killer!

❧

My Father, I consecrate my life anew to You today. I confess that You will help me defeat every giant I face with Your name and Your Word. I will not shrink back in fear, but I will boldly meet my enemy face to face because I am in covenant with You and You are my strength and my shield.

Protected by Angels

For he orders his angels to protect you wherever you go. They will steady you with their hands to keep you from stumbling against the rocks on the trail.

—Psalm 91:11,12

*W*hen you say, "God, I'm tired of sin, I'm tired of the world, I'm tired of burdens, and I don't want to go to hell," then God will save you. You will become a covenant person—totally committed to God (and He to you). You are forever bound by a covenant (contract or binding agreement), and God assigns angels to watch you and your family to see that no harm comes to you.

God charges the angels to see that no calamity or plague comes near your dwelling. He charges the angels to bear you up in their hands lest you dash your foot against a stone. When you enter into a covenant relationship with God, He puts everything He has at your disposal.

God is looking for committed covenant men and women who will respond to His instructions promptly and obediently. If He says, "Give $500 to My work," a covenant man or woman says, "To whom do you want the check made out, Lord?"

Years ago, God asked John to go across the nation, and John said, "I'll go." Then the Lord said, "Go to the Philippines," and John went. He spoke to us to pastor Lakewood Church, and we said, "We'll do it."

God will never disappoint you. You'll never go wrong by doing what God asks you to do. And He'll send angels to help you do whatever it is He asks of you!

❧

Thank You, Father, for the ministry of angels in my life and the lives of my loved ones. Because I am Your child, I believe and expect them to protect me and see that no harm comes to me today, in Jesus' name.

God Will Bring You Safely Through

Lord, with all my heart I thank you. I will sing your praises before the armies of angels in heaven. I face your Temple as I worship, giving thanks to you for all your loving kindness and your faithfulness, for your promises are backed by all the honor of your name.

—Psalm 138:1,2

*V*erse 7 goes on to say, *Though I am surrounded by troubles, you will bring me safely through them....* It doesn't say God will bring you partially through them and then you'll have to fight your way out. It says that God will bring you safely through them—all the way through!

Maybe you feel as if you're living in a tunnel now, with darkness all around you. That is very uncomfortable. I know...I've been there. In the natural, you can't see any way out—but if your trust is in the Lord Jesus, He will bring you safely through that tunnel of troubles, and you'll begin to see light. So start singing praises to God, thanking Him for His wonderful promises, and before you know it, victory *will* come! His promises are backed by the honor of His name.

❧

Father, thank You for Your loving kindness and faithfulness to me. When I am surrounded by trouble, I know that I can trust You to bring me safely through. I praise You for backing all Your promises to honor Your name.

Is Your House Happy or Crying?

Happy is that people...whose God is the LORD.
—Psalm 144:15 KJV

When our daughter and son-in-law, April and Gary Simons, moved to a home closer to the church, their son Garrison, who was two-and-a-half years old at the time, left the only home he'd known since his birth.

Walking out the front door, Garrison began to cry. He said, "I don't want to leave this home." His parents tried to assure him that it was all right. But Garrison said, "This house is crying 'cause we're not going to be here."

Of course, the house was not physically crying, but Garrison cried because the house was going to be empty without him, his parents, and his sisters.

Right away I thought what a good example this story is for parents. Maybe your house is crying—or perhaps your children think your house is crying—because Mother and Daddy don't love God.

Maybe it's crying because there is bickering, fussing, cursing, drugs, or alcohol in the house—or your children think the house is crying, when it's really the mother and daddy who are crying.

Let this be the day that you change. Let your children say, "My house is not crying anymore. My house is happy because we're going to church together as a family. My mother and daddy love Jesus. My daddy has quit drinking. My mother has quit doing drugs."

Don't let your house cry. Let your house be founded upon Jesus, the solid rock!

❧❧

Lord, I desire a happy home—filled with love for You. Help me to change whatever isn't like You, so with You as our God our family can be happy.

Don't Trust in a Spider's Web

A man without God is trusting in a spider's web. Everything he counts on will collapse. If he counts on his home for security, it won't last.

—Job 8:14,15

*T*hese scriptures speak to my heart relative to today's troubled families. Try to imagine walking on a spider's web. It's impossible to even imagine.

This is what it's like for two-parent families when the children's spiritual training is left to one parent or the other, but not both. The family structure is so fragile that, eventually, everything collapses. Raising successful children requires both parents to wholeheartedly serve God and take the children to church together. It will save the home from ruin.

Why? Because the father who doesn't assume his role as spiritual head of his household will soon see his wife taking this position. Then the family as a unit is undermined because this isn't God's will for families.

You don't have to watch your family fall apart. God has a plan for your family.

Husbands, don't depend on your spouse to be the spiritual leader in your home. Take your place as the spiritual head of your home. Wives, don't assume your husband's position as spiritual head of your home. Trust God, work together, and train up your children in the way they should go. Build your house on a rock-solid foundation—the Lord Jesus Christ. Your family will flourish and God will be pleased.

Father, I don't want my home and family to collapse because it's built on nothing more than a flimsy spider's web. I put my trust in You, God, to help us set our house in order and place You at the center of it. You are the firm foundation and security of our home.

Build Your Home on the Solid Rock

Know ye not that ye are the temple of God, and that the Spirit of God dwelleth in you?

—1 Corinthians 3:16 KJV

When God was leading the Israelites through the wilderness, they disobeyed Him, made idols, and committed all kinds of sin, but through it all He remained faithful to them because His Spirit dwelt with them.

If you have made Jesus your Savior, His Spirit lives inside your body. You are the temple of the Holy Ghost, and God will remain faithful to you. You, in turn, must choose to be faithful to Him.

What kind of home have you built? Is your home built on sand where the storms of life can wash it away? Or is it built upon the solid rock? Is it built upon crack cocaine? Is it built upon cursing, bitterness, and other things that aren't good for you?

Why don't you build your home firmly upon Jesus—the Solid Rock? He will gladly come to live in your home because He wants to live in your heart. That would make both you and Jesus very happy.

❧

God, You know that, at times, my house has not been built upon Jesus, the Solid Rock. But I love You, and I want the temple of my body to be a worthy dwelling place for You. I turn my back on all that would cause me to stand on shifting sand, and I make a firm decision to follow You daily.

Be Free from Civil War at Home

> ..."Any kingdom filled with civil war is doomed; so is a home filled with argument and strife."
>
> —Luke 11:17

Many homes today resemble battlefields. There is so much strife and tension living there that it seems as if you could cut through the air with a knife. If your home is like that, you can do something about it. If you'll read the Word of God and get God's precepts in your heart, you'll discover how to avoid the dangers of strife. Also, take your family to church. Soon you won't have civil war in your home, because strife cannot live where it isn't welcome. Your family doesn't have to be doomed when your home is founded on the Word of God, and Jesus, the sure foundation.

If you're having trouble in your home, I advise you to make sure Jesus is living in your heart, get involved in a good church, serve the Lord with all your heart, and take your children to church—then your home will be filled with peace instead of civil war.

❦

Lord, I dedicate my family to You. I declare that our home will stay founded on the Word of God with Jesus as our chief cornerstone. Thank You for blessing our home with Your peace.

A Miracle for Your Marriage

"...from the very first he [God] made man and woman to be joined together permanently in marriage...."

—Mark 10:6

*T*he devil is out to destroy happy homes. He wants to divide every husband and wife. He attacks families, leaving husbands, wives, and little children (grown children too) wounded and scarred.

If this kind of trouble is hitting your home or the home of someone you love, you need to know there's an answer. Thank God, Jesus Christ can heal broken marriages and families and bring joy and happiness back to homes!

God established the home first—even before He created the church—so your home is very important to His Kingdom. And the devil knows if he can destroy the family unit, he can destroy much more beyond that. But God is in the restoration business.

He can make a new man and woman out of two unhappy spouses and keep them out of divorce court. Yes, it requires a lot of work, continuing prayer, and surrounding yourselves with wise counsel, but happy marriages are worth it all.

Jesus will help in your own marriage, your neighbor's marriage, or your children's marriages, asking Him to intervene. Time and time again, Jesus has demonstrated His power to rise above natural circumstances to restore marriages and families—and He'll do it for you!

Thank You, Jesus, that You intended for us to have a happy home. It is the devil who works to divide and wound us, but Your plan is for us to be joined together permanently in marriage. You came to heal and mend broken hearts and homes. Thank You for restoring our home and strengthening our bonds of love so that we love each other as You have loved us.

Honor Christ by Loving Each Other

That is how husbands should treat their wives, loving them as parts of themselves. For since a man and his wife are now one, a man is really doing himself a favor and loving himself when he loves his wife!

—Ephesians 5:28

*E*phesians 5 talks about the role of the husband and father in the home. Throughout our marriage, my husband lived Paul's message to the church at Ephesus before our children, our church family, and me.

I remember one day, John got angry with me and decided he wouldn't talk to me for the rest of the day. So I hid behind a door and jumped on his back and held him around the neck, yelling, "I am not going to let you go until you give up!"

He got so tickled, he couldn't stay angry. He told that story many times and even included it in a book he wrote entitled *Love & Marriage.* My point in telling it again is this: when you honor your mate and show your affection, you'll have a happy home.

Thank Jesus for your mate! John and I always said we only fussed from the neck up, but we always made up. It never got to our hearts because we wouldn't let it.

Our children have never doubted that marriage is wonderful because we honored the Lord before them with love, joy, and happiness. Loving one another is the richest blessing you can give your children!

❦

Thank You, Father, for giving me my spouse as a treasured gift of Your everlasting love. I will honor You today by honoring my family in my conversation and actions—and will look for special opportunities to show them my love.

You Can Have Peace

"I am leaving you with a gift—peace of mind and heart! And the peace I give isn't fragile like the peace the world gives. So don't be troubled or afraid."

—John 14:27

*A*precious lady in our church wrote to say, "I love you so much, and I've learned a lot about the Word of God from Pastor's teaching. Years ago, I came here to church, and I was like a non-swimmer, tossed by the heavy waves of life." Just think about someone who can't swim being tossed by heavy waves and continually going backwards.

"I heard you telling me how I could have love, peace in my heart, joy, and happiness in Jesus. I cried throughout the service.

"I was staying in a bad marriage only because of my son. I had no hope. I wished with all of my heart that I could have peace like you said. But I thought it was impossible. However, my life changed that day. I found out that with God all things are possible.

"I gave my heart to Jesus, and I've done a complete about-face. All of you at Lakewood Church mean so much to me."

Despite the circumstances you find yourself in, you can have peace like this precious lady found. Jesus will be there for you like He has been there for her. Nothing is impossible with the Lord.

❧

Father, I need Your gift of peace of mind and heart today. The world is so filled with turmoil—even my little world gets confusing many times. But your peace isn't fragile like the peace the world gives. Thank You that when trouble or fear comes, You keep me in Your perfect peace.

Don't Wait for a More Convenient Time

A few days later Felix came with Drusilla, his legal wife, a Jewess. Sending for Paul, they listened as he told them about faith in Christ Jesus. And as he reasoned with them about righteousness and self-control and the judgment to come, Felix was terrified. "Go away for now," he replied, "and when I have a more convenient time, I'll call for you again."

—Acts 24:24,25

Paul had been arrested and ordered to appear in court before the unscrupulous governor, Felix, in order to file an appeal to Caesar. Governor Felix allowed the case to drag on for two years, so Paul used every opportunity to witness to Felix about Christ and his need to be saved. At one point, Felix began to tremble and sent Paul away until a "more convenient" time. The Bible doesn't indicate that a more convenient time ever came.

If you've been saying, "Go away, Lord Jesus, until a more convenient time," you need to realize that there may not be a more convenient time for you to get your heart right with God. You have no idea what will happen in your life today... or tomorrow.

Today is the day of salvation. I encourage you to take advantage of it by making sure Jesus is living in your heart forever.

❀

Today I fix my heart on You, Jesus, and I want to make sure You are in my heart to live forever as my Lord and Savior. I realize that today is the day of salvation—that there may never be a more convenient time to be sure my heart is right with You. I commit my whole heart and life to You, and I'll serve You all the days of my life.

Don't Just Pretend to Be a Christian

*Check up on yourselves. Are you really Christians? Do you pass
the test? Do you feel Christ's presence and power more and more
within you? Or are you just pretending to be Christians when
actually you aren't at all?*

—2 Corinthians 13:5

This scripture is profound. Almost everyone reading this book is probably
a Christian. If not, I believe that you will become a Christian as you study and
meditate on these little daily messages and experience new life in Christ Jesus.

There are those who just pretend to be Christians. You probably know some
of them. If you're not bearing fruit and don't feel Christ's presence more and more
in your life, then you ought to check up on yourself. Perhaps you aren't really
a Christian.

Once you're willing to put yourself to the test, if you find that you haven't
completely given your heart to the Lord and you haven't asked Him to come live
in your heart, then you're going to be glad you read this little message today—
because I believe you will give your heart to Jesus and be able to honestly call
heaven your eternal home.

I am glad to be a Christian, and I want everybody to be one. I'm the real
thing—not a pretender. How about you? Check yourself out!

*Father, I don't want to just pretend to be a Christian. More than anything, I
want to be the kind of Christian that You would have me to be. Fill my life today
with Your presence and power, and help me to serve You in sincerity and truth.*

Obey God's Word and Succeed

Despise God's Word and find yourself in trouble. Obey it and succeed.

—Proverbs 13:13

If you have known God in the past but you don't have as close a relationship with Him as you once had, you are miserable, aren't you? But when you go back and begin serving God again—living by His Word, being a doer and a hearer of His Word—you feel good inside. And your obedience brings success according to Proverbs 13:13.

I encourage you today to obey the Word of God. Don't waste another minute being separated from your Creator. He loves you, and He's always willing to forgive you and welcome you back.

His loving, outstretched arms are reaching out to you today. Stay on the road of obedience to God, and you'll always enjoy success.

❧

Father, I desire to be successful, and I know that obeying Your Word is one of the keys to success. I commit myself to be obedient to Your Word. Strengthen me daily as I walk this journey of faith with You at my side.

It's Perfectly Proper for God to Forgive You

But if we confess our sins to him, he can be depended on to forgive us and to cleanse us from every wrong. [And it is perfectly proper for God to do this for us because Christ died to wash away our sins.]

—1 John 1:9

*M*ost Christians have heard this scripture over and over, but I think it's important to remind you that you don't have to worry about anything you've ever done. It is perfectly proper for God to forgive you because of Christ Jesus, His Son, who took away the sins of the world.

If you just come to God and ask His forgiveness, He will forgive whatever is in your past that shames and embarrasses you. You don't have to feel condemned about it. Just be thankful that His Word assures you that it is perfectly proper for you to come to Him and be set free from sin's heavy burden!

❧

How grateful I am, Lord, that You find it perfectly proper to forgive my sins and cleanse me from all wrong. Thank You for dying to wash away my sins...and my heavy burden of guilt with it!

God Has Blotted Out Your Sins

I've blotted out your sins; they are gone like morning mist at noon! Oh, return to me, for I have paid the price to set you free.
—Isaiah 44:22

Are you concerned about the sins of your past? Have you done some things you're not proud of and let them temporarily separate you from God? Do you wonder if your sins are so terrible that God won't take you back?

Isaiah says that when you go outdoors early in the morning, you see a mist all over the yard. Everything is moist and damp. You go back inside, and when you go out again at noon, the mist and dew are all gone. They've just evaporated.

That's exactly what Isaiah is talking about in reference to your sins. So when you return to God, He'll take you back, and He'll be glad to blot out the memory of your sins. He loves you with an everlasting love. There's nothing you can ever do that is so wrong that God won't welcome you home when you repent, ask His forgiveness, and accept His pardon in Jesus' name.

❦

God, You are such a good and forgiving God. Thank You for paying the price to set me free by sending Your Son, Jesus, to shed His blood to blot out my sins forever. You even cause the memory of them to disappear like the morning mist.

God Helps Us to Forget the Past

*Joseph named his oldest son Manasseh (meaning "Made to
Forget"—what he meant was that God had made up to him for
all the anguish of his youth, and for the loss of his father's home).*
—Genesis 41:51

*M*ost people know the story of Joseph and how his brothers resented him
because he was his father's favorite son. Even though they sold him into slavery,
Joseph's exceptional gift for leadership caused him to be able to make the best of
the most unpleasant situations. Over the course of time, he went from being in
prison to being made a ruler in Egypt. Although he remembered the mistreatment
of his childhood, when his firstborn son came into the world, he named him
Manasseh, meaning "made to forget," as a tribute to God for all that He had done.

Perhaps you, or someone you know, should be named Manasseh because
you've endured much pain in your life. You may have a lot to forget, but God
will make it up to you for everything you've lost. Whenever you're tempted to
feel sorry for yourself because of bad memories, remember Joseph and his son,
Manasseh. Honor God with your determination to put the past in the past and
let Him compensate you for any losses you've sustained.

❦

*Father, I thank You because You have promised to restore to me what the devil
has stolen. I ask You now to help me forget the past and look forward to the good
things You have in store for me.*

Be a Citizen of God's Country

Now you are no longer strangers to God and foreigners to heaven, but you are members of God's very own family, citizens of God's country, and you belong in God's household with every other Christian.

—Ephesians 2:19

Citizens of God's country are people who are washed in the blood of the Lamb...people who have accepted Jesus as their Savior and are serving Him. As Christians, we are members of God's very own family and citizens of God's country.

Whether you live in Houston, New York City, London, or Nairobi, as a Christian, you are also a citizen of God's country, and you belong to God's household with every other Christian. Isn't that good news?

You're part of the big family of God. You're part of the household of faith. And someday you'll go to that big, beautiful place called heaven where we will all dwell together.

We who belong to the Lord Jesus Christ are all citizens of heaven. And I'm glad. Aren't you? Let's be good citizens!

❧

How I thank You, God, that I am no longer a stranger but a member of Your family and a citizen of heaven. What a privilege and honor it is to belong to Your household. I praise You for making it possible through the Lord Jesus Christ.

God's Yes Means Yes

*"Understand, therefore, that the Lord your God is the faithful
God who for a thousand generations keeps his promises and
constantly loves those who love him and who obey his commands."*
—Deuteronomy 7:9

*J*esus Christ, the Son of God, isn't One to say yes when He means no.
He always does exactly what He says He will do, and He carries out and
fulfills all of God's promises—no matter how many of them there are—for a
thousand generations!

The Bible is full of the promises of God. Jesus will always fulfill every promise
that He has ever made. So if you need something from God, find a promise in
His Book and be assured that Jesus will carry it out. He has not changed, and He
never will.

Psalm 149:4 says, *...Jehovah enjoys his people....* God enjoys being your Father.
He is delighted to keep all of His promises to you. Keep that in mind when you
feel lonely, distressed, anxious, or concerned that God doesn't know or care about
what you're going through. He cares so much that He stores your tears in a bottle
(see Psalm 56:8).

*Thank You, Lord, for Your faithfulness and love. I know I can count on
You to do exactly what You promise in every generation, even for my children
and grandchildren as we walk in obedience to Your commands. Truly there is
none like You.*

Rescued from Darkness

For he has rescued us out of the darkness and gloom of Satan's kingdom and brought us into the kingdom of his dear Son, who bought our freedom with his blood and forgave us all our sins.

—Colossians 1:13,14

If you have been born again, you have been rescued out of darkness. You never have to worry about the Satan-induced darkness of this world because you walk in the light of Jesus who is always with you.

He's always there for you, and He delights in answering the prayers of His righteous ones. You are righteous if you've been washed in the blood of Jesus.

If you're not sure you've been washed in the blood, then today is the day to take care of that. Ask Jesus to forgive your sins and invite Him to come and live in your heart. Make Him your Lord and Savior.

Now you are a member of the family of God! Jesus purchased your pardon at Calvary with His precious blood. Now let His light shine in you!

❧❧

Thank You, Lord, for rescuing me from the darkness of this world and bringing me into Your kingdom. I praise You for Your wonderful forgiveness and freedom. I will let Your light shine through my life to draw others to You too.

Admit Your Mistakes and Be Successful

A man who refuses to admit his mistakes can never be successful.
But if he confesses and forsakes them, he gets another chance.
—Proverbs 28:13

If you haven't been successful, maybe it's time to check up on yourself. Are you faithful in admitting your mistakes? Cleansing the conscience is good for you. If you continue to sin and say, "God forgives me," you won't be successful. You might as well stop and say, "I'm guilty, God," and openly name the sin as a confession of the heart. Then stop doing what you've been doing that is wrong.

If you confess your sins and forsake them, you'll get another chance. God is merciful. He wants you to be successful at everything you endeavor to do, but you must be honest and sincere with Him. Freely admit when you are wrong, and let Him reward your honesty.

❧❧

I want to be successful, Father, and if my success has been hindered by my neglecting to admit my faults, please forgive me. I confess my sins before You, God, and ask You to strengthen me to resist the temptation to return to them. In Jesus' name, I pray. Amen.

Don't Become Proud and Forget God

*I took care of you in the wilderness, in that dry and thirsty
land. But when you had eaten and were satisfied, then you became
proud and forgot me.*

—Hosea 13:5,6

*H*as God ever done anything for you? Has He ever seen you through a
hard time in your life? After it was all over, did you become proud and forget
about God? I hope that has never happened to you.

Don't we just love it when our children are sincerely grateful to us for
something we've done for them? Well, that's how God is. He doesn't expect you
to forget all about Him after He has given you what you needed. He certainly
wouldn't appreciate you becoming proud or haughty over having everything you
need or acting as though you won't need Him ever again.

When God does something for you, don't forget it. Let it be an inspiration
for you to serve Him even more because He brought you through. You may need
to call on Him again sometime.

❧

*Oh God, help me never to become proud and forget Your kindnesses. Help
me never to be arrogant because of the many blessings You have given me. Keep
me ever-mindful to thank You for everything and to always serve You with a
grateful heart.*

Listen Gladly to the Words of God

"Anyone whose Father is God listens gladly to the words of God...."

—John 8:47

*W*ho is your father? Do you listen to God or to the other voices that might be whispering in your ear? If you're not listening to God, you're going to make some mistakes that you'll be sorry for. Then you'll get caught up in guilt and condemnation. Don't do that. God sent Jesus into the world to convict—not to condemn.

Listen gladly to the words of God. He has wonderful things to say to you. He speaks through His Word, and He also speaks through your heart.

You are His child, and you want to please Him. When you listen and believe God's Word in your heart and confess it with your mouth over your life, God stands behind you to make good on His promises! Why not get started today?

❧

Father, I know Your Word is powerful, and that You speak to me through Your Word. I will listen gladly to Your instructions. You are my Father, and You know what is best for me.

Renew Your Mind

And so, dear brothers, I plead with you to give your bodies to God. Let them be a living sacrifice, holy—the kind he can accept. When you think of what he has done for you, is this too much to ask? Don't copy the behavior and customs of this world, but be a new and different person with a fresh newness in all you do and think. Then you will learn from your own experience how his ways will really satisfy you.

—Romans 12:1,2

Giving ourselves to God is a process that starts in the mind. We must keep a guard on our thoughts. We must watch what we read, what we look at, and what we let into our mind. Wrong thoughts cannot be allowed to linger there.

Romans 12:1,2 in the King James' translation says we are to be transformed. How? By the renewing of our minds. We have to *live* in the Word daily, learning from the lives of Abraham, Isaac, Jacob, Peter, Paul, and other great men and women of God. Take the hand of Jesus and walk with Him through Matthew, Mark, Luke, and John. I believe it will change your life.

My husband always taught that we should endeavor to *think* God's thoughts daily! Renew your mind. Learn to think like God thinks about salvation, forgiveness, mercy, sickness, healing, deliverance, love, goodness, and all the other wonderful things in His Word. The Word is filled with God's thoughts!

❀

Father God, I present myself as a living sacrifice unto You. I will not copy the behavior and customs of this world, but I will be transformed by the renewing of my mind. I will guard my thoughts and think Your thoughts today. I refuse to entertain wrong or negative thoughts. I take dominion over my thought life and will be satisfied by meditating on Your faith-filled promises instead.

Decide to Obey God

*Just tell me what to do and I will do it, Lord. As long as I live
I'll wholeheartedly obey. Make me walk along the right paths for I
know how delightful they really are.*

—Psalm 119:33-35

God would be so pleased if we would say, "God, I want to obey You. Just
let me know which way to go. Tell me where to turn, and I'll do it. I'll even do it
wholeheartedly, God, because I know how delighted You would be if I'd go in
Your way instead of my own."

Let's just say that to God right now, and let Him show us what to do today.
Follow that peace in your heart and keep on going. You'll be glad you did what
Jesus said to do.

❦

*Lord, just as the psalmist promised You that he would wholeheartedly obey
You, so I make that same commitment today. I will obey You. I'll go where You
want me to go. I'll do what You want me to do. Show me Your way today, and
I'll walk in Your delightful paths.*

Be Happy! Follow God's Laws

Happy are all who perfectly follow the laws of God.
—Psalm 119:1

*H*appy are all who perfectly follow.... Now, if you're not happy, maybe it's because you don't follow God's laws. Perhaps you have tried to do things your own way. Then when those things didn't work out, you were frustrated and disappointed. Maybe you even looked for someone other than yourself to blame. You may have even blamed God.

Many people do that—they blame God for things He had absolutely nothing to do with. Then they're unhappy and wonder why.

If you want to be happy, may I suggest that you make a quality decision to follow after God? His laws have been clearly set forth in the Bible—and there you'll find direction and guidance for your life, solutions to your problems, reconciliation for your broken relationships, and His unsurpassing love.

You'll be very happy when the peace of God takes over your life. Why not try God? No one else can do for you what He can.

❧

Father, I have not always followed Your laws, and I have been unhappy as a result during those times. Forgive me for wanting to do things my own way instead of obeying Your guidelines. Your Word shows me how I can happily serve You and have Your peace. Thank You for giving me wisdom and direction through Your Word.

Turn Around—Don't Grieve God

"I turned away from God, but I was sorry afterwards. I kicked myself for my stupidity. I was thoroughly ashamed of all I did in younger days."

—Jeremiah 31:19

Have you ever turned away from God? Were you so sorry? Did you feel grieved in your heart because you knew that you had grieved God? Have you ever wanted to kick yourself for your stupidity? I have. But God doesn't see us as stupid—He just sees us as learners. Although we make mistakes, He doesn't see us as failures, but as people who are seeking truth.

Sometimes we are thoroughly ashamed of all that we've done. Maybe you are ashamed of something you did recently. But remember—God forgives. If you are truly sorry about something you've done that you know is wrong, turn around. Take the right path. You'll feel good in your heart, and you won't have to be concerned about grieving God.

When you repent of your sins, you'll make the Lord proud of you.

❧

Lord, I have been ashamed of many things in my past. I have done stupid things that I am truly sorry for. Thank You that You see me not as a failure but as a learner. I know You have forgiven me, so help me to forget my sinful mistakes as You have...and move on to the right path You desire for my life.

Confess Sin Immediately and Receive Mercy

Let men cast off their wicked deeds; let them banish from their minds the very thought of doing wrong! Let them turn to the Lord that he may have mercy upon them, and to our God, for he will abundantly pardon!

—Isaiah 55:7

Some time ago, my little granddaughter, Christiana, was playing in my office. I had some little porcelain teacups there, and she knew she was not supposed to play with them, but her mother's back was turned, and Christiana picked one up. She was pretending to drink out of it, like little girls do.

All of a sudden, she put it down so hard that it rattled against the saucer and made a lot of noise. She looked up at her mother, and immediately said "I'm sorry, Mommy." She was really very sorry.

That's the right way to handle it! I thought. What a good lesson this incident was for all of us. If we'd be just like a little child and confess our sins immediately, we would immediately have God's mercy and forgiveness. Why? Because God can't resist our pleas for mercy when we're quick to repent!

❧❧

Father, I banish from my mind any thought of doing wrong. I ask You to have mercy on me and forgive me for disobeying You in any area of my life. Thank You for abundantly pardoning me!

Don't Wait until Tomorrow

Then the Lord said to Moses, "Instruct Aaron to point the rod toward all the rivers, streams, and pools of Egypt, so that there will be frogs in every corner of the land." Aaron did, and frogs covered the nation.

—Exodus 8:5,6

One of the plagues God sent to Egypt was frogs. It must have been awful! Frogs covered the entire land. Exodus 8:3,4 says that frogs filled the houses, the bedrooms—even the beds! When they opened the oven door, the oven was full of frogs. The Bible says the Egyptians were *...immersed in them!*

I've often thought about Moses asking Pharaoh, "When do you want the frogs to leave?" And Pharaoh said, "Tomorrow" (see verses 8-10).

Why would he want the frogs to leave tomorrow? Let them leave now! Who wants one more night with the frogs? He didn't consider his own discomfort—the palace had to be full of frogs—and he didn't consider the discomfort of his people!

People are like that today. They put off going to church, taking their children to church, and getting saved and filled with the Holy Spirit. They procrastinate about taking care of themselves—eating right, and not smoking, drinking, or doing drugs.

When are we going to stop living with the "frogs" in our lives? Today is the day to get things right with God. Start cleaning house right now. It's time to get rid of the frogs!

God, today I am cleaning house. I'm asking for Your help in getting the "frogs" out of my life. I have avoided dealing with certain things—thinking I would do that later. But I know You want to free me of those things. I'm ready to get rid of them today. With Your help, I'll start doing what is right in your sight.

When You Go Astray, Come Back to God

And if you leave God's paths and go astray, you will hear a
Voice behind you say, "No, this is the way; walk here."

—Isaiah 30:21

*I*n this scripture, God was talking to His rebellious children. The first verse in Isaiah 30 calls them "obstinate children" in some translations. Now I'm talking to those of you who have deliberately stepped off God's path and gone astray— you are today's "rebellious children." This may sound a little harsh, but does this describe you or someone you know and love?

God knows where you are. You can never stray so far from Him that He won't be able to woo you back into the comfort of His loving arms.

Somewhere, even along the path you may have chosen, you will hear His still small voice calling, "This is the way, walk in it," or, "Turn around, that's not the way you should be going. Come toward Me."

It takes a lot of energy to be obstinate and rebellious, so why not let go of those feelings and return to the One who loves you more than a brother? Come back to Jesus and let Him make His home in your heart again.

God, I ask You to forgive me for rebelling against You and Your plan for my life. I've put the distance between You and me, and I'm sorry. Help me to listen to You and obey Your still small voice.

God Is at Work in You

For God is at work within you, helping you want to obey him, and then helping you do what he wants. In everything you do, stay away from complaining and arguing, so that no one can speak a word of blame against you. You are to live clean, innocent lives as children of God in a dark world full of people who are crooked and stubborn....

—Philippians 2:13-15

*W*hether or not you realize it, God is working in you, helping you to want to obey Him. Isn't it good to know that even when we don't *feel* like being obedient, God loves us so much that He's willing to go the extra mile and help us to *want* to obey?

Our lives should imitate Jesus in every possible way. These verses encourage us to be humble like Jesus—refraining from arguing and complaining—so that no one can speak a word of blame against us.

When you imitate Jesus, no one will be able to find something wrong with you because you will be living a clean and moral life—above reproach. You will be an example to those who remain in darkness.

Lord, thank You for working Your will and Your way in me. I will not complain or argue or be crooked or stubborn, but I will live a clean and innocent life so others will see You in me. What a blessing to know that You will even help me to want to obey You.

It's Never Too Late to Come to God

Yet the Lord still waits for you to come to him, so he can show you his love....

—Isaiah 30:18

We often tell our congregation and the TV audience about a loving God who is always there for us. I ask you to ponder this scripture in Isaiah in your heart and mind.

Perhaps you have come close to giving your heart 100 percent to God, but because of the cares of the world—pleasures, your job, or some other reason—you haven't. You know about God, but you've never made a full, personal commitment to Him.

It's never too late. No matter how young or old we are, the Lord still waits for us to come to Him. This is an urgent message. God is still waiting. Take that step today. If you have a personal relationship with the Lord Jesus Christ, share Him with someone in your life who doesn't know Him.

Get down to business with God. You can settle once and for all where you will spend eternity.

❦

Lord, I appreciate Your patience with me. I realize from this scripture that You have been waiting on me to come to You. So today I give You my heart afresh and anew. I know You care for me and want to demonstrate Your great love for me.

God's Word Is Our Hope

Never forget your promises to me your servant, for they are my only hope.

—Psalm 119:49

This scripture really hit home with me when I was diagnosed with metastatic cancer of the liver and given only a few weeks to live. In the natural, I had no hope. The doctors knew of no effective treatment that would work because I had no primary tumor. I found Psalm 119:49 and started confessing, *May I never forget Your words, for they are my only hope.*

In the natural, I had no reason to hope. But in the spiritual realm, I took God's words on healing and applied them to my situation. Many people don't understand about healing, but I can testify that Jesus heals today! I took these words and devoured them. I read them every day of my life.

Now, decades later, I'm still healed and still reading these words every day because they are words that I cannot forget. They were—and continue to be—my only hope. Hallelujah!

❦

Your words are light and life to me, O God, my Healer and my Salvation. I will never forget them. How I praise You for restoring my hope, my health, and my life!

God's Word Brings Healing

And crowds came in from the...suburbs...and every one of them
was healed.

—Acts 5:16

*W*e received a letter from a former denominational preacher in our TV audience. He said he'd been in a serious automobile accident and sustained extremely severe injuries. Given no hope, he was just looking out the window of his hospital room when it came to mind that someone had given him a book by John. He thought, *Well, what have I got to lose? I can either sit here in a wheelchair or I can believe that God will heal me.*

He said he didn't really expect to be healed, but he did believe God's Word. When he began searching the Scriptures, faith came by hearing and by seeing God's promises. He was totally healed—but not instantly.

After his healing was complete, he took the time to write us a letter, telling us that John's book had really helped him. He encouraged us to keep doing all that we were doing for Jesus.

My point in telling you this story is to show the mercy of God toward those who diligently seek Him. This man even said he hadn't expected to be healed, but he knew that God's Word was true, and as he read it, his faith began to grow. When he searched the Word, he started believing something that his particular denomination doesn't teach—and he received his healing! Glory to God!

❧

Father, I thank You for Your Word and for the faith and healing that I find in its pages. When my faith is weak, I ask You to help me find and claim Your promises so I too can be healed.

God Is Abundantly Available to You!

God is our refuge and strength, a tested help in times of trouble.
—Psalm 46:1

*M*ost Christians are familiar with this verse, but in the footnotes of this verse in the New King James Bible, it says, "God is our refuge and strength, and He is abundantly available to help in the time of trouble."

I believe the key to insuring that God will be abundantly available to us is living a consecrated life. This involves dwelling in the secret place of the Most High as described in Psalm 91. I don't just visit God when I'm in trouble. I talk to God every day. I am His temple, His dwelling place in the earth. God lives in me.

I want to continually dwell in the secret place, and I want to be around people who dwell there. Why? Those who dwell in the secret place know that God is abundantly available to them at all times.

No matter what is trying to come against you, or someone you care about, there's one power that is greater than all: the most high God. He is no puny, little God. He is El Shaddai, the God who is more than enough. He is Jehovah-Rapha, your healer. He is Jehovah-Jireh, your provider.

And He is your Savior and your Lord—abundantly available to you at all times. He is your refuge and strength. You can call upon Him at any time, and He will give you peace in your heart that is beyond understanding.

❦

Thank You, God, that You are a very present help in time of trouble. You are my peace. I choose to dwell in the secret place today because You are the most high God who is abundantly available. You give me strength and protection 24 hours a day, and I thank You for it, in Jesus' name.

Live in Vital Union with Jesus

And now just as you trusted Christ to save you, trust him, too, for each day's problems; live in vital union with him. Let your roots grow down into him and draw up nourishment from him....

—Colossians 2:6,7

*I*s the dawn of every day accompanied by some kind of problem in your life? If that is how you see things, it is important for you to realize that although the devil is alive and causing as much mischief as he can, Jesus is more alive and is well able to overcome the devil's plans. Hallelujah!

When you live in vital union with the Lord Jesus, the everyday problems Satan uses to try and get you down won't work. Because your roots go deep in Christ when you hide God's Word in your heart and spend time in daily worship, you'll draw up nourishment from Him. He'll give you solutions to those problems, and pretty soon, you'll be able to face whatever comes along with confidence that with God on your side, you cannot fail!

Jesus is always right there with you. If you'll live in vital union with Him, He'll help you overcome all of your problems and live in victory.

Jesus, just as I trusted You to save me, I can trust You today with any and all problems I may encounter. As I walk in union with You and Your purpose for my life, I know You will nourish and sustain me in every situation and circumstance.

Victory over Life's Battles

He is my strength and song in the heat of battle, and now he has given me the victory.

—Psalm 118:14

I have good news for you if you're going through a battle—and so many of us are in these last days. God—the Great Commander of the armies of heaven—knows just how to lead us to victory. His marching orders can be found in His Word, the Bible.

Hide the Word of God in your heart, and when you have to do battle, God will be your strength and your song. He will see you through the heat of that battle, and then He'll give you the victory.

Father, I thank You for giving me Your strength to fight the battles of life. I even find my marching orders in Your Word. You always give me songs of victory in my heart. I praise You for You are my strength and song, and I come before Your throne today with thanksgiving for my victory!

God Gives Strength and Skill

Bless the Lord who is my immovable Rock. He gives me strength and skill in battle.

—Psalm 144:1

*H*ave you ever noticed how the tide of the battle turns when we pray and ask God to get involved? His Word promises that He'll be with us in the heat of our battles with health, prosperity, relationships, jobs, and anything else that presents us with a challenge.

But how do you obtain strength and skill to fight the battles of life? By knowing the Word of God, trusting in His wisdom, and believing that God hears, understands, and desires to help you.

Search out God's promises and let Him become your immovable rock. No matter what you're going through, He'll give you strength to face the battle and achieve the victory.

❦

My Father, You are my immovable Rock, my fortress, my high tower. When the enemy comes against me, he has to face the Rock of Ages who stands with me in battle. You give me strength and skill to battle my enemies, and You help me overcome them every time. Thank You, Lord!

Make the Lord Your Hope and Confidence

But blessed is the man who trusts in the Lord and has made the Lord his hope and confidence. He is like a tree planted along a riverbank, with its roots reaching deep into the water—a tree not bothered by the heat nor worried by long months of drought. Its leaves stay green, and it goes right on producing all its luscious fruit.

Jeremiah 17:7,8

*I*n the natural, drought conditions produce unrelenting heat that continues for days, weeks, and even months. No rain falls to cool things down and relieve the situation. It seems as though God is nowhere to be found!

It's sometimes like that when we're struggling with a serious problem. We pray and ask God for relief—but nothing appears to be happening. It's like a spiritual drought. We're tempted to worry, fret, and become fearful, but we don't give in to that temptation when our trust is rooted firmly in Jesus, the Author and Finisher of our faith.

Put your trust in Christ Jesus, and you can face troubles with confidence that your victory is coming. In due season, the rain will come and you will hear from heaven.

❧

My hope and confidence are in You, Jesus. I know that I can trust You to bring me through seasons of spiritual drought and send the refreshing rain of Your Holy Spirit to bring relief. I will not worry or fret or be fearful, for I am rooted and grounded in You.

Love God, and He Will Love You

Jesus replied, "Because I will only reveal myself to those who love me and obey me. The Father will love them too, and we will come to them and live with them. Anyone who doesn't obey me doesn't love me...."

—John 14:23,24

These scripture verses were written in reply to a question of Judas. He had asked Jesus, *"Sir, why are you going to reveal yourself only to us disciples and not to the world at large?"*

Jesus' answer gives us a little clue about why it is so important for us to have a relationship with God. What He's saying here is that if we don't know God, we're just out there in the world all alone. Then Jesus isn't going to come running to help us when we call on Him because He can't. If we don't have any interest in getting to know Him, His hands are tied! He's too much of a gentleman to force himself on us.

But if we obey and love God, He will love us and live with us. I don't know about you, but I need that. I want to feel the presence of His Holy Spirit with me all the time.

Ask God to reveal himself to you—to help you find answers to your questions and solutions for your problems. If you're in relationship with Him, Jesus will soon show up.

God, I love You and ask You to reveal yourself to me. I choose to obey You because I know You love me. Help me to find answers to my questions and solutions to my problems. I need Your wisdom and guidance.

Go to God

*"My advice to you is this: Go to God and confess your sins to
him. For he does wonderful miracles, marvels without number."*
—Job 5:8,9

*C*an you think of any better advice than going to God and confessing your
sins? I can't. Soul cleansing is necessary to living in intimate relationship with God.

Don't let sins of the past or present build up a wall between you and God. All
of us have stumbled, and many wonderful Christians have momentarily gone back
into their old lifestyles from time to time. But when you confess your sin, repent,
and ask for God's forgiveness, it's done immediately.

First John 1:9 (KJV) says, *If we confess our sins, he is faithful and just to forgive
us our sins, and to cleanse us from all unrighteousness.*

When you were saved, He put a light on the inside of you. According to
Matthew 5:14, you are the world's light...glowing in the night for all to see.

When you let your light shine before men, God can perform wonderful
miracles in your life. Waste no more time feeling guilty about sin—go to God
and make things right.

❦

*I want to have a clean conscience and walk in intimate fellowship with You,
Father God. I want no unconfessed sin to stand between You and me. Please
forgive me, Lord, for any wall I have built because of sin and cleanse me from
all unrighteousness. I thank You for Your faithfulness to me and marvel at Your
miracle-working power.*

Love God's Every Wish

Help me to love your every wish; then I will never have to be ashamed of myself.

—Psalm 119:80

*D*on't you love every wish that God has? Don't you want to try to please Him in everything you do?

If you'll love God's every wish and do what He asks you to do in obedience, then you will never grieve God and you won't have to be ashamed.

I am so ashamed of myself when I've been disobedient. I don't want anything that I do or say to disappoint God or bring shame to His name. I want God to be proud of me—I want Him to rejoice in how I react to unpleasant people and situations.

How about you? Obedience may not be easy, but it has such lasting rewards. Don't you think it's worth your time to obey God? Once you start, you'll never have to spend another day feeling sorry that you've disappointed Him. Isn't that a wonderful thought?

Father God, help me to love Your every wish. I want to do things that are pleasing to You—I want to do what You would do in the same situation. Thank You for placing Your desires in my heart so I will never bring shame to You, and I will never have to be ashamed of myself, either.

God Never Refuses to Be Kind and Loving

Blessed be God who didn't turn away when I was praying, and didn't refuse me his kindness and love.

—Psalm 66:20

In today's world, where most people are too busy to even notice others— let alone to be kind and loving—isn't it wonderful to know that we can depend on God? He's never too busy to hear our prayers, and He doesn't turn away from us. He delights in answering the prayers of His children, and He loves to show us His kindness and His love.

That's the kind of God we serve. Aren't you glad to be serving a God like that? I am.

❦

What a blessing to know, God, that I can always come to You with everything in prayer. Thank You for responding to me with love and kindness. You never turn away Your attention when I am talking to You, and I can count on Your tender mercies. Where would I be without You?

You Are God's Prize

The Lord will not forsake his people, for they are his prize.
—Psalm 94:14

Did you know that you're God's prize? When you love and serve Jesus and remain obedient to His Word, you are His child—His prize—and He will never forsake you. Doesn't that make you feel good? It certainly makes me feel good!

My children are my prizes—I'm proud of each one of them. And I think that's the way God feels about us. He's proud of us when we please Him, honor Him, and obey His directions.

Live your life in a manner that is pleasing to God, and when you get to heaven, He'll say, "I'm proud of you. You are My prize. Welcome home."

❧

Lord, I want to be a worthy prize. How wonderful You are to love me so much that You'll never forsake me. Help me to continually honor and obey You and to live my life in a manner that is pleasing in Your sight.

Yes, Lord, I'm Listening

...“I am the woman who stood here that time praying to the Lord! I asked him to give me this child, and he has given me my request; and now I am giving him to the Lord for as long as he lives.” So she left him there at the Tabernacle for the Lord to use...Little Samuel was helping the Lord by assisting Eli. ...One night after Eli had gone to bed...and Samuel was sleeping in the Temple near the Ark, the Lord called out, “Samuel! Samuel!”

1 Samuel 1:26-28; 3:1-5

I think one of the sweetest stories in the Bible is about Hannah taking her son Samuel to the tabernacle and giving him to God.

You know the story. Samuel didn't recognize the voice of God calling him and he ran to Eli, the priest, who realized that God was speaking to Samuel. Verse 10 says that Samuel finally understood that it really was God who was trying to communicate with him, and he said, “Yes, Lord, I'm listening.”

I think God liked Samuel's response, and He would like for us to recognize when He is speaking to us. We may not hear God talking to us audibly as Samuel did, but inside our hearts, we can hear and discern His voice.

When God calls your name and says, “I want you to do this,” or “I want you to do that,” hear Him in your heart and say, “Yes, Lord, I'm listening.”

Then do whatever He tells you to do, and you will be happy.

❧

God, let me hear and recognize Your voice. Speak to me, I pray, and I will listen. Guide my steps, and I will obey You.

You Are Blessed if You Doubt Not

Then give him this message, "Blessed are those who don't doubt me."

—Matthew 11:6

*W*hen Jesus told John's followers that those who don't doubt will be blessed, He was assuring them, as well as John, that He was truly the long-awaited Messiah.

The message to us is so simple—we must not doubt Jesus. We can doubt anybody in the world—professors, theologians, anybody—but we must never, ever doubt Jesus. Jesus can't bless you if you doubt Him, but I know you want to be blessed!

It really makes no difference who in the world you harbor doubts about— you just cannot doubt Jesus or His Word and still be blessed and have a good life.

So I urge you today to put your confidence in Jesus and His Word and enjoy the blessings He promises to give you!

❧

Lord, I ask You to forgive me for doubting You sometimes. I know You are always true to me and to Your Word, so I put my complete trust and confidence in You today and every day.

Run Your Race to Win

In a race, everyone runs but only one person gets first prize. So run your race to win. To win the contest you must deny yourselves many things that would keep you from doing your best.
—1 Corinthians 9:24,25

*H*ave you noticed how athletes train? They practice doing the same things over and over again. They never let a day go by without training. Runners often start their extensive training by attaching weights to their ankles. When they add lots of weight to their bodies, they can't run as fast, but they are training their bodies to endure the length of the race. They know, however, that they won't win a race with weights hanging on them.

I encourage you today to run the race of life to win. Just as an Olympic sprinter removes all the weights before competing on the track, set aside all those things that are hanging on you, weighing you down—the desires of the world, the flesh, and anything else that is holding you back.

Run your race with a heart and mind to win, and you will.

You'll feel good, and Jesus will be pleased.

Lord, I have decided to go for the gold and run my race to win. Cause me to see those things which keep me from doing my best. Thank You for bringing out the winner You see in me.

Do You Need to Have Your "I" Knocked Out?

Be kindly affectioned one to another with brotherly love; in honour preferring one another.

—Romans 12:10 KJV

*M*y husband often taught on maturing in our Christian walk. He said, "The spirit of the world exalts self. Gimmee, gimmee, gimmee, and get, get, get." This is a very unattractive attitude that, sadly, can be found even among Christians. It seems that some folks are determined to become famous and well-known regardless of who they have to knock over, step on, or drag down in the process.

It's a shame when people think only of themselves—the big "I"—and cease to care about others. That doesn't sound like Jesus, does it? John said, "They need to have their 'I' knocked out!"

We need to seek God until we have a spirit that honors others above ourselves. The Bible says we have not received the spirit of the world—we have the Spirit of God!

I encourage you to get your mind off yourself, and think about helping someone else. Visit someone who is sick, and count your blessings that you are healthy. Say "hello" to that lonely neighbor down the street, and thank God for your family and friends. Drop an extra check in the offering at church in support of someone on the mission field. Success isn't measured in what you accumulate for yourself—it's what you do for others that counts with God.

Father, forgive me for failing to consider the needs of others before my own. I will look for opportunities to serve and give of my time, talents, and money to show Your love and to honor my brothers and sisters in the body of Christ.

Do Everything God Asks You to Do

*They all responded in unison, "We will certainly do everything
he asks of us." Moses reported the words of the people to the Lord.*
—Exodus 19:8

When Moses returned from Mt. Sinai, he called Israel's leaders together to tell them what the Lord had said. God wanted Moses to remind the Israelites that He had delivered them from Egyptian bondage, and now He wanted them to be obedient to Him and keep their part of the bargain. God promised to bless them if they did. Verse 8 says they unanimously agreed to do anything He asked.

When God asks you to do something, do you do it immediately or do you postpone it until another time? What about your pastor? What happens when he asks for your help?

Do you and the people in your church do everything your pastor asks of you? Wouldn't God be pleased if you did? God has appointed and anointed pastors to lead His flock here on earth until He comes back to take us home to heaven.

When everyone does his part, churches thrive. See what you can do to help out at your church. You'll be blessed for being a blessing!

I know, Lord, that I need to obey You when You ask me to do something for You or my pastor or my church. Help me to know what You want me to do so I can serve You and be a blessing to others.

He Gives Power to the Tired

...Don't you know by now that the everlasting God, the Creator of the farthest parts of the earth, never grows faint or weary? No one can fathom the depths of his understanding. He gives power to the tired and worn out, and strength to the weak.

—Isaiah 40:28,29

*H*ave you ever been tired and worn out and needed strength? There have been times like that in my life. But just when I didn't think I could go on, I found scriptures like Isaiah 40:28,29. The Bible has just the right answer for whatever problem comes my way.

I've been sick—and tired of being sick—and His Word was there for me. I've experienced a doctor saying that my baby daughter would never be normal—but as my husband and I stood in faith and confessed God's Word, she was healed.

I could name countless other times when God has given me strength and power. Believe me, the One who never slumbers, sleeps, nor grows weary will give you power and strength when you're at your weakest point. Hallelujah! Doesn't that make you glad to serve Him?

I am glad to serve You, God. There is no other god like You. When I'm tired and weary, You are there to bolster me with Your strength. Great is Your faithfulness!

It's Time to Move On

The Lord is fair in everything he does, and full of kindness.
He is close to all who call on him sincerely. He fulfills the desires of
those who reverence and trust him; he hears their cries for help and
rescues them.

—Psalm 145:17-19

*I*f Jesus is your Savior and you have a heart that follows after God, you realize that He places desires, thoughts, and dreams inside of you. He gives you creative ideas and plans for things you want to see accomplished in your life.

Sadly, many times our dreams become blurred by the circumstances of life. Sometimes our dreams seem so unlikely that we begin to think we'll never accomplish them anyway, so we just give up.

My family and I could have grown discouraged and given up our dreams to accomplish great things for God after John went home to be with the Lord. But God had a different plan in mind and called Joel to pastor the church. He had never preached but one time and he stepped up as Pastor—and is tremendous.

Do you have some secret things you want to achieve for God? Don't let circumstances hinder you. Stir up the gifts God has placed in you. Rediscover your dreams, and feed, water, and cultivate them in the good soil of God's Word. Trust God and believe that your dreams will come to pass, and they will!

※

Lord God, You are fair and kind in everything You do. You draw close and rescue me when I cry out to You for help. Thank You for fulfilling the desires of my heart. My trust and faith are in You alone.

God Will Listen When You Call to Him

Mark this well: The Lord has set apart the redeemed for himself.
Therefore he will listen to me and answer when I call to him.

—Psalm 4:3

*T*he words "mark this well" mean we are to remember and pay attention to what is being said.

Just as you want your children to pay attention when you tell them something important—something that will protect them or provide a tidbit of wisdom that they can apply to many of the situations they'll face in life now and further down the road—God wants you to mark His Word. Take hold of it. Use it to tear down strongholds that keep you in bondage.

God intends for us to take our places as His children—we are the redeemed of the Lord. We are set apart for Him. He wants us to develop ourselves spiritually, and when we do that, then He's going to listen when we call to Him.

If you get into trouble, remember the authority you have been given to defeat the enemy of your soul. Start praising and thanking God for who He is in your life. Let rivers of living water flow through you. Call on Jesus. He'll listen to you, and He'll speak to you with His still, small voice.

Remember that you're one of God's sheep. You know His voice—so listen to what He says to you too.

Lord, I do pay attention to Your Word that says I am the redeemed of the Lord! I know I can call on You and You will hear and answer me. When You speak to me, I will know Your voice and listen to You too. You have set me apart for yourself, and as Your child I will overcome every situation through the authority of Your Word.

Seeing the Beauty in Everything

...Fix your thoughts on what is...lovely, and dwell on the fine, good things in others....

—Philippians 4:8

$\mathcal{I}$ had a beautiful experience while babysitting my grandson, Garrison, when he was very young. He asked if he could take off his shoes and socks, and I gave him permission. He had on little black tennis shoes and ordinary, little black socks. They were not pretty. They had been washed often and were faded.

When he took them off, he held them up and said, "Grandmama, isn't they pretty socks?" Now, his socks were not pretty—but that's the way he saw them. Out of the goodness of his heart, he saw beauty in those faded socks.

That made me think about how we as adults see things. Couldn't we do a much better job of living our daily lives by seeing the good in people and things? These were not expensive, designer socks—they were plain old little boy's socks. But he saw beauty in them.

How much better the world would be if we as Christians—with Jesus living in us—saw things that were good and fine in others, instead of focusing on the negative things.

I learned a lesson from Garrison that day. I'm proud of him, and I'm happy that we can see things through a child's innocent eyes of love as Jesus would like us to do.

Father, today I obey Your Word, and I choose to fix my thoughts on the lovely and good things in others. I will dwell on the fine things You have created in people, and see the good things in them through Your eyes of love.

Prayer Can Be Simple and Childlike

Jesus...said, "Unless you turn to God from your sins and become
as little children, you will never get into the Kingdom of Heaven.
Therefore anyone who humbles himself as this little child, is the
greatest in the Kingdom of Heaven."

—Matthew 18:2-4

As I was checking the messages on our answering machine one evening, I heard a pitifully weak voice saying, "Pastor, could you please come and see me?" We could tell this person was seriously ill, and we went to the hospital.

Although the caller had given his heart to Jesus as a child, then—at 30 years old—he was away from God when he was diagnosed with terminal heart and lung disease.

We asked him if he knew that Jesus heals. In his labored breathing, that barely audible voice said, "I don't know how to properly ask Him to heal me."

We said, "You don't have to pray a theological prayer. All you have to do is talk to Jesus out of your heart."

I think of that voice often and thank God that we have been so blessed to know the truth of His Word. All we need to say is, "Father, I don't know how to pray, but in the name of Your Son, Jesus, I want You to make me well."

If you need anything from God, all you have to do is know that His Word says you can be healed. Speak in faith as a little child, and Jesus will hear and answer your prayer.

Father, I need a touch from You, and I come to You now as Your child. I know
that You love me, and with childlike faith, I believe You will heal my body today.
Thank You for healing me.

Pour Out Your Longings to God

O my people, trust him all the time. Pour out your longings
before him, for he can help!

—Psalm 62:8

All of us have longings in our heart. And most people have longings that nobody can fulfill in this life except God. Some people long for their spouse, their children, or their parents to be saved. They long for the peace the Bible speaks of that passes our ability to understand it. Lonely people long for love, and sick people long for health. Our longings are varied and without end.

If you pour out your longings to God, He will bless you and help you, according to Psalm 62:8. This chapter concludes with these words, *He is loving and kind and rewards each one of us according to the work we do for Him* (verse 12).

I love knowing that God will bless and help me when I pour out the longings of my heart to Him, and that He'll do that just because He loves me. He loves to answer the prayers of His children. Why not have a "heart to heart" talk with God today and be blessed!

❀

Lord, You alone know my innermost longings. You alone can help and satisfy the deepest desires of my heart. I trust You, Lord, at all times and in all circumstances to fulfill Your promises in my life.

God Responds When We Cry Out

*"Oh, that we might know the Lord! Let us press on to know
him, and he will respond to us as surely as the coming of dawn or
the rain of early spring."*

—Hosea 6:3

I like to find scriptures assuring me that God will never break His covenant with His children—as long as dawn stretches across the eastern skies every morning, as long as there is rain in early spring! Folks, that's a long, long time. It's forever! God will never break His promises to us.

I think this must mean if God promised that the sun is going to come up every day, then when you and I cry out to Him, He has to respond to us. He won't stop the rains in early spring. He won't stop the dawn. And He won't stop hearing our cries for help.

So when you cry out to God, there is nothing you can do to stop Him from responding to you. Isn't that a blessing!

❧❧

Lord, I want to know You. I press on to know You. I need to know You more every day. I know that as I draw near to You, You will draw near to me and respond to my cry.

God's Not Deaf

Listen now! The Lord isn't too weak to save you. And he isn't getting deaf! He can hear you when you call!

—Isaiah 59:1

God never changes. He's always the same. Just like the scripture says, He is not getting deaf. We may lose a little of our ability to hear as we grow older, but we don't have to. God doesn't, and we're made in His image, so why should we?

He is always there to save you and hear your prayers. So cry out to God, and don't be surprised when He answers you!

❀

Thank You for hearing me when I call out to You, Lord, for help. Your faithfulness is wonderful. You are mighty to save and mighty to deliver me in every circumstance. I call out to You now for the situation I am facing, and I know You will give me the right answer to overcome it in Jesus' name.

How Persistent Are You?

"And so it is with prayer—keep on asking and you will keep on getting; keep on looking and you will keep on finding; knock and the door will be opened."

—Luke 11:9

When our middle daughter, Tamara, was about ten years old, she came to John and said, "Daddy, I want a rabbit." John said, "Honey, we've got a house full of kids. Forget it. You are not going to have a rabbit."

She came back to her daddy day after day only to hear him say, "Please stop talking to me about this rabbit." Finally, Tamara said, "You said in your book *Miracle in Your Mouth* that we can have what we say, and I want a rabbit."

John tried to reason with her. First he told her she had no place to keep a rabbit, but she had worked out a plan with her brother Paul about that. Next he said he'd never heard of a rabbit being for sale in Humble, Texas where we lived. To that remark she responded, "I saw a sign!"

This child was so persistent. She was determined to have a rabbit. Guess what? John and Tamara got in the car to go look for the sign she insisted she'd seen. Sure enough, there was a little bitty sign, "Rabbits For Sale." She got two!

This kind of persistence is what Jesus talked about in Luke 11:9—shameless persistence that won't give up. How great is your desire to be faithful? How much do you want to please Jesus? How big is your desire to be a strong soldier of Jesus Christ? If you will ask and keep on asking, seek and keep on seeking, you will receive from God.

Father God, I want to have persistent faith. When I see a promise in Your Word, I determine in my heart that I will pursue that promise with shameless persistence until I receive what You have promised me. I won't take "no" for an answer. I want my faith to please You.

Take Time to Pray for Others

For I was...sick...and you visited me.
—Matthew 25:36

We take time to pray for the sick because we know the power of God to heal. And we advertise it! Members of our church have bumper stickers on their cars announcing "We're here for you."

One of our members and her friend had an interesting experience because of that bumper sticker. As she and a friend were getting out of their car, a lady stopped them and said, "I am on my way to make amends with a family member with whom there's been a misunderstanding. I saw your bumper sticker and know that the people at your church pray. I need prayer for this relationship to be healed."

These ladies stood in pouring rain and prayed for the lady. Their hair was dripping before they were finished, but God worked everything out.

If you don't know how to pray, just talk to God from your heart. He will hear you and answer your prayers.

❈

Teach me to pray, Father, that I might be a blessing and comfort to those who are troubled. Give me a discerning heart to take time to pray for others even if I'm in a parking lot.

Do Your Best to Do God's Will

... *"O Lord God of Israel, there is no god like you in heaven or
earth, for you are loving and kind and you keep your promises to
your people if they do their best to do your will."*

—1 Kings 8:22,23

*K*ing Solomon lifted up his hands before the people and made this
declaration. He wanted the people to know that God's Word was good—
that He always does His part if we do our best to do our part.

God is loving and kind to His people. All He asks of us is our best. Now,
sometimes we may miss it and make mistakes. But if those mistakes are from the
mind and not from the heart, He gives us credit for doing our best anyway
because He's a God of mercy.

Let's try to do even better starting today. You can find out more about God's
best by reading His Word, praying, studying, and hearing the Word over and over
again. When you develop the habit of starting your day with God, you'll begin to
see His best coming out in you! Have a really great day!

❧

*Thank You, Lord, for Your love and kindness toward me when I do my best to
do Your will. Even when I make honest mistakes, You keep Your promises because
You are a God of mercy. Thank You for bringing out Your best in me.*

God Heals All Our Diseases!

Bless the Lord, O my soul: and all that is within me, bless his holy name. Bless the Lord, O my soul, and forget not all his benefits: who forgiveth all thine iniquities; who healeth all thy diseases.
—Psalm 103:1-3 KJV

It's not all that hard for us to believe that God will forgive our sins. It isn't so difficult to accept that Jesus will forgive us when we accept Him in our heart, is it? Then why don't we believe the next little phrase that follows—"who healeth all thy diseases?"

God wants to heal you. He hasn't changed. If you don't understand that God heals today...you need to, because He most assuredly does. I am living proof. I have walked in supernatural health and wholeness since God healed me of cancer in 1981!

I am so thankful to be alive and well today, and I believe that God will heal you too. Bless the Lord and don't forget the benefits He has made available to you.

Lord God, I know that You've healed others, and I believe that You will heal me too. Help me to receive all the benefits that You have provided for me.

Jesus Wants to Heal You

And there came a leper to him, beseeching him, and kneeling down to him, and saying unto him, If thou wilt, thou canst make me clean. And Jesus, moved with compassion, put forth his hand, and touched him, and saith unto him, I will; be thou clean. And as soon as he had spoken, immediately the leprosy departed from him, and he was cleansed.

—Mark 1:40-42 KJV

*S*ome people really don't know that they are held captive by a thought. They don't know that it's God's will for them to be healed or to lead a prosperous life. They may be just one step away from receiving all that God has for them.

When the leper came to Jesus, he said, "If you will, you can make me clean." He knew that Jesus could heal him, but he didn't know if it was Jesus' will to heal him. Jesus answered with two simple words, "I will."

If you need healing today, you must believe that God can heal you—but you also must believe that it is His will to heal you. And the same thing is true for the other needs in your life. It is always God's will to provide the best for you. So believe and receive!

❧

I come to You today, Lord Jesus, like the leper who came to You two thousand years ago, believing You are the Healer. I believe You are my Healer because I'm convinced it is Your will to heal me, according to Your Word. I am asking You to heal me today, and I am thanking You in advance for cleansing me from all sickness and disease and making me whole.

Touch Jesus, and He'll Touch You

As they went a woman who wanted to be healed came up
behind and touched him [Jesus], for she had been slowly bleeding
for twelve years, and could find no cure (though she had spent
everything she had on doctors). But the instant she touched the
edge of his robe, the bleeding stopped.

—Luke 8:43,44

Remember when Jesus was asked to go to Jairus's house because his daughter was so sick? As He was on the way to his house, a little lady with an issue of blood came up to Jesus and touched the hem of His garment. That is so precious to me because of the boldness of this quiet little lady.

Jesus immediately knew that someone had touched Him, and He said, "Someone deliberately touched me."

Have you ever *deliberately* touched Jesus? I have. Of course, I wasn't able to physically touch him. I wish He'd been there for me to touch physically, but He wasn't. I did deliberately touch Him though when I believed His Word. I believed that He could heal me of cancer, and He did.

If you need Jesus to touch you, I encourage you to touch Him. Don't just pick up a Bible and read a scripture that doesn't speak to your particular need. Find a promise in His Word that applies to your situation, and deliberately touch Jesus. He will, in turn, touch you.

Jesus, like the lady with the issue of blood, I press toward You. I deliberately reach out and touch the hem of Your garment with my faith. I believe that I am receiving a touch from You right now that will calm my fears, eliminate sickness and disease from my body, and restore me to complete wholeness. I give You thanks for doing it just because I am reaching out to You.

Jesus Heals the Most Advanced Cases

One day in a certain village he was visiting, there was a man with an advanced case of leprosy. When he saw Jesus he fell to the ground before him, face downward in the dust, begging to be healed. "Sir," he said, "if you only will, you can clear me of every trace of my disease." Jesus reached out and touched the man and said, "Of course I will. Be healed." And the leprosy left him instantly!

—Luke 5:12,13

This man did not have just a case of leprosy—he had an *advanced* case of leprosy.

We receive many letters in the mail from people who have advanced cases of cancer, AIDS, and other diseases that the medical world has labeled as terminal.

I want you to know that Jesus can heal even the most advanced cases. He is no respecter of persons, and when you believe that it is His will to heal you, then He will do it no matter how sick you are...because He loves you and wants you well.

Be encouraged today to hold fast to the truth that you know. There is a Healer in your house today. His name is Jesus, and it is His good pleasure to make you whole!

Jesus, I thank You that no disease is too advanced for You to heal. Just as it was Your will to heal the leper, I know it is Your will to heal me because You love me. Thank You, Jesus, for healing me today.

Jesus Has Compassion on the Sick

Two blind men were sitting beside the road and when they heard that Jesus was coming that way, they began shouting, "Sir, King David's Son, have mercy on us!" The crowd told them to be quiet, but they only yelled the louder. When Jesus came to the place where they were he stopped in the road and called, "What do you want me to do for you?" "Sir," they said, "we want to see!" Jesus was moved with pity for them and touched their eyes. And instantly they could see, and followed him.

—Matthew 20:30-34

The Bible also says in Hebrews 13:8 that Jesus doesn't change. That means that what He did in the Bible, He'll still do today. Notice in the Matthew 20 passage that Jesus was moved with compassion for these two blind men. So that means if you have anything wrong with your health today, Jesus is moved with compassion for you. All you have to do is say, "Jesus, I need Your help."

Many times I've shouted, "Jesus, I need Your help!" And He's always had compassion and met my need. And He'll do the same for you. When you cry out to Him, He is moved with compassion just as He was that day for those blind men—and He'll touch you and make you whole.

❧

Jesus, I cry out to You now, and ask You to heal me and do what men cannot do. Thank You for hearing me and for healing me today.

God Gives Mercy to All

O Lord, you are so good and kind, so ready to forgive; so full of mercy for all who ask your aid.

—Psalm 86:5

*P*eople ask God for help and He helps them. They ask for forgiveness, and they are forgiven. Others ask for healing when disease comes against their bodies, and they are healed. He is good—kind *and* ready to forgive.

But we can ask God for anything because He really does give mercy to all. The AIDS victims came to my mind as I pondered this scripture from the Psalms—*...so full of mercy for all who ask for aid.* And I thought, *There is mercy from God for all who have this disease called AIDS—not just for those who ask for aid.*

If you have the AIDS virus, I want you to know that God loves you and wants to heal you. If you know anyone who has AIDS, tell them that God is bigger than AIDS and that He wants to heal their body.

❦

Father, I thank You because You are good and kind and because Your mercy is extended to all. I praise You because Your healing power is greater than any disease—even cancer and AIDS. Right now we pray for those who have AIDS and ask You to demonstrate Your goodness by healing them through Your love and mercy.

You Will Live a Long Life

With long life I will satisfy him, and show him My salvation.
—Psalm 91:16 NKJV

I simply love every word of Psalm 91, but verse 16 is particularly special to me. When I was struggling with cancer, that verse really ministered to me.

Anyone who has read my book, *Healed of Cancer,* knows that I didn't spend a lot of time in bed or giving in to my feelings. My flesh wanted to, but I had to work hard—fight hard—for my healing. From the time John and I prayed, my family believed that I was healed and treated me accordingly. Sometimes I asked them to do things in the house, but because they believed I was healed, they insisted that I could do them.

It was good for them to treat me normally, because I was tempted to have pity parties. They wouldn't allow me to feel sorry for myself. I thank God that they have been grounded in the Word.

At the time, John and I lived 24 miles from the church. As we drove to the church to work almost every day, we passed two cemeteries off the freeway. Just as we'd first glimpse those cemeteries coming up, we would personalize Psalm 91:16 and say out loud, "With long life God satisfies me and shows me His salvation." I still do it today!

Don't sit around feeling sorry for yourself. Pity never wins! I commanded my body to come in line with the Word of God, and it did! Yours will too! God wants you to be well!

Father, I will be satisfied with long life because You love me and have provided abundant life for me. Through Your Word I can defeat the enemy of my soul. I resist pity parties in Jesus' name. I am the healed of the Lord, and I say so!

Heaven's Storehouse is Fully Stocked

And it is he who will supply all your needs from his riches in glory, because of what Christ Jesus has done for us.
—Philippians 4:19

*E*very week department stores advertise upcoming sales events in the newspapers and on television. We often go shopping just to catch these advertised sales. And I have found that when something I wanted to buy at the sale price is out of stock, the store will usually give me a "rain check." This means when the store has that item in stock again, I can go in and buy it at the sale price even though the sale is over. But what happens if I need that item immediately?

God doesn't need rain checks because He is never in short supply. All of His promises are "yes" and "amen," and they are available right now. We don't have to wait for anything that God promises in His Word.

Whatever you need—whether salvation, freedom from fear, protection, or anything else—go to God's Word and discover what He has promised to you. What He advertises, He can deliver...now!

❧

Thank You, O Father, that Your storehouse is always full of everything I need. You always supply my needs because Jesus has already paid the price for my needs to be met. You always supply my needs in abundance!

An Open Mind Can Understand God's Word

My words are plain and clear to anyone with half a mind—if it is only open.

—Proverbs 8:9

For years and years, I have heard people say they don't read the Bible because they can't understand it. Then I found this scripture that says anyone who has an open mind can understand God's Word.

Have you ever said you didn't understand the Bible so you weren't going to read it? Then your mind must not be open. You could be the most intelligent person in the world and read the Bible with a closed mind and not understand it.

On the other hand, you could be the most uneducated person in the world, but if you open your mind to God's Word, you could understand every word.

There is no excuse for people to say they can't understand the Bible, because they can if they purpose in their hearts to have an open mind to its truths. Dig into the Word today with an open mind and let the life-changing revelations begin!

As I read Your Word today, Lord, I open my mind and ask You to help me understand the truth of Your Word. Make Your words plain and clear and speak to my heart as I am reading. Give me eyes to see, ears to hear, and a heart to understand Your truths.

God's Word Takes Hold of Your Heart

So get rid of all that is wrong in your life, both inside and outside, and humbly be glad for the wonderful message we have received, for it is able to save our souls as it takes hold of our hearts. And remember, it is a message to obey, not just to listen to....

—James 1:21,22

*D*o you realize that God's Word can take hold of your heart? It can, and when it does, you'll find that you want to clean up on the inside and the outside too. You will no longer be satisfied with just hearing God's Word once a week or so, commenting on how great it was, and then going on about your life as usual. You'll want to *obey* the Word when it takes hold of you. You will have a desire to know more about what it says regarding situations in your own life.

When you hear and obey the Word and allow its message of love to take hold of your heart, you'll be happy and have God's peace that passes all understanding.

❧

Father, I surrender my will to You completely today. I want Your Word to take hold of my heart. Most of all, I want to obey You and please You in all that I do. I will not just listen to Your Word, but I will obey it too. In Jesus' name.

Stand Firm on the Word of God

Know what [God's] Word says and means....God's truth stands
firm like a great rock, and nothing can shake it....
—2 Timothy 2:15,19

*I*f you want God's truth to stand like a great rock that cannot be shaken, then you have to know it. You must know what it says and make up your mind that no matter what happens to you, God's Word is unshakeable. It cannot be moved. It does not change—now or ever!

When you stand on the truth of God's Word in the challenging times that you face, you will still be standing when it's all over. Isn't that good news?

Take time today to stand like a rock on the Word of God and grow strong in His knowledge, because taking that stand will cause us to become unshakeable.

❀

How I thank You, God, for causing me to stand like a rock on Your Word.
I believe that nothing can shake the truth of Your Word—it is the foundation of
my life. Help me to continually grow strong in the knowledge of You.

Learn Well from Your Teacher

For the Preacher was not only a wise man, but a good teacher;
he not only taught what he knew to the people, but taught them in
an interesting manner. The wise man's words are like goads that
spur to action. They nail down important truths. Students are wise
who master what their teachers tell them.

—Ecclesiastes 12:10,11

This scripture reminds me so much of my husband. He was a wise man and a good teacher. He taught people what he knew in an interesting manner. And those good characteristics continued to grow during his 60 years in the ministry.

His words also spurred us to action. You know what happens when you spur a horse—it will just take off and go. Well, that's what good teaching should do to us. When God spurs us on, we need to go and do what He says to do. We need to be doers of the Word and not hearers only, according to James 1:22.

I encourage you to appreciate the good and interesting teachers who have brought messages that have helped you and spurred you on to do God's will and God's work.

❦

God, I do appreciate the good teaching I have received from interesting and motivating teachers. Continue to give Your teachers wisdom, strength, and integrity, Father, to nail down important truths. Help me to be wise and not only learn but also do what Your Word says to do.

God Is Well Able to Do What He Promised

He [Abraham] was completely sure that God was well able to do anything he promised.

—Romans 4:21

I love to hear teaching on Abraham and Sarah because of their strong beliefs. Even though they were old and all reasonable hope was long gone with regard to becoming parents, they judged God faithful because He had promised. God had said it, they believed it, and that's all there was to it. They knew that He was fully able to do everything that He had promised. They had faith.

If you don't have faith, you can get faith to come to you and live in your heart. Where does faith come from? Faith comes by hearing the Word of God. You cannot see God work without faith, for without faith, it is impossible to please Him.

Find some Scriptures that apply to your life and the situation you find yourself in right now. Remember—just like Abraham and Sarah—God is well able to do what He promised if you keep on believing.

Father, help me to be as steadfast and unmovable as Abraham and Sarah. I know You will do what You have promised because You are faithful. I thank You because I know You will fulfill Your Word in my life.

Never Lay Aside God's Laws

I will never lay aside your laws, for you have used them to restore my joy and health.

—Psalm 119:93

*H*ave you had your health restored because of the Word of God...because of Jesus and His goodness? I have. Therefore, I will never lay aside God's laws. I need them in order to live every day. You need them to live every day too.

You need the Word of God to keep you from harm, to keep you well, to keep you safe, to show you how to live, and to keep you from getting into trouble.

So, whenever you have the Word of God in you, then you have the joy that the Holy Ghost gives. He will help you to have good health if you walk in the knowledge of the Lord Jesus and believe that He can heal and make you whole.

Jesus did that for me—He made me whole. He spared my life in 1981, when I was dying of cancer. I will never lay aside His laws, because they are my life, my health, and my joy.

Lord, I need Your laws to know how to live my life in health and joy. I ask You to please teach me through Your Word and through Your precious Holy Spirit.

Jesus Heals Fragmented Lives

"Now gather the scraps," Jesus told his disciples, "so that nothing is wasted."

—John 6:12

The King James Version uses the word, "fragments," instead of "scraps" when describing Jesus' directive to pick up the leftovers after He had fed more than 5,000 people from the fishes and loaves of a small boy's lunch basket.

Perhaps you feel fragmented today. You may have a smile on your face, but there's a frown in your heart. You may have abundant material possessions...yet your heart is empty. If people around you knew what battles you were fighting—the broken heart, the broken dreams—they'd be amazed. People around you may not have a clue about what's really going on with you.

But Jesus knows...and cares. He is great at taking fragmented lives—broken in every area—picking them up, replacing the negatives with positives, mending the broken and shattered dreams, and creating a purpose for them.

Jesus will never fail you. He lifts you up when you are down. He forgives you when you sin. He gives you mercy when you've done wrong. Oh, what a Savior—what an ally Jesus is to the weary and bruised.

Let Him have the fragments in your life because He can change every situation and make your fragmented life whole again.

Thank You, Jesus, for taking the fragments in my life and miraculously transforming them into something useful for You. I believe in You as my Miracle Worker today. Continue to strengthen me and help me be all that You have called me to be. I want my life to count for You. & & pray matter 2 others 2 some one, some man special

Feeling Out of Joint?

My God, My God, why have you forsaken me? Why do you refuse to help me or even to listen to my groans? Day and night I keep on weeping, crying for your help, but there is no reply....
—Psalm 22:1,2

*P*salm 22 is a picture of the cross. It tells all about how Jesus' hands and feet were pierced. In the midst of all this agonizing pain, Jesus no doubt quoted this whole Psalm. Verse 14 (KJV) goes on to say, *I am poured out like water, and all my bones are out of joint....*

At times you may really be experiencing physical pain as Jesus was. What was Jesus really saying here? He was saying, "I'm paying the price for every one of My children who get out of joint. I'm the only one who can put you back in joint. I'm willing to suffer, bleed, die, and rise again—not only so you can be saved, but so you can be restored when you slip and fall!"

You can get set back in place when you're feeling disjointed. Jesus paid the price for every bone in your body to be put back in place. Even if you've turned your back on God, you don't have to stay "out of joint." Jesus paid the price so you could be brought back to your place of right standing with Him. Repent and ask for His help today. You don't have to feel "out of joint" any more.

Thank You, My Father, for putting me back together when I feel out of joint. Jesus, it is Your redeeming love that sustains me through every trial of life. When times are tough, I'll remember what You suffered on the cross for me. I give You thanks that You paid the price for me to be whole again.

He's the God of Second Chances

Then at last he came to his senses and cried out humbly to God for help. And the Lord listened, and answered his plea by returning him to Jerusalem and to his kingdom! At that point Manasseh finally realized that the Lord was really God!

—2 Chronicles 33:12,13

I want to tell you a little about Manasseh. He was a bad king who began his reign at the age of twelve. He constructed idols in the temple and chose to ignore all the warnings of the Lord, so evil came upon him. The Assyrian armies came, seized him with hooks, bound him with chains, and carted him off to Babylon.

But the Bible tells us in 2 Chronicles 33 that he finally came to his senses and realized that the Lord was truly God!

Many people mistakenly believe their disobedience will cause God to reject them entirely. That's not true! Just as He did with Manasseh—returning him to his throne after he humbled himself and acknowledged God as God—He will mercifully give you another chance.

When you repent of whatever it is that has separated you from your heavenly Father and truly desire to change, God will restore all you have lost. He loves you that much!

❀

Lord, when I've strayed from You and things aren't going well, help me to come to my senses and humbly ask for Your help. I thank You for being God, and for loving me and giving me another chance.

Obey Jesus

*When Jesus saw him and knew how long he had been ill, he
asked him, "Would you like to get well?" "I can't," the sick man
said, "for I have no one to help me into the pool at the movement
of the water. While I am trying to get there, someone else always gets
in ahead of me." Jesus told him, "Stand up, roll up your sleeping
mat and go on home!" Instantly, the man was healed! He rolled up
the mat and began walking!*

—John 5:6-9

The man at the pool of Bethesda had been sick for 38 years. When Jesus
told him to stand up, roll up his sleeping mat, and go on home, he was instantly
healed. He rolled up his mat and began walking.

The Jewish leaders saw the healed man carrying his mat and reprimanded
him for working on the Sabbath. They said it was illegal for him to carry his mat
home! He told the church leaders that he was obeying the man who healed him.
I like that.

When the man who heals or saves you tells you to do something, do it
immediately. Be just like that man at the Bethesda pool—whether it's on the
Sabbath or not, do it. When Jesus speaks to you to do something, be obedient
like this man.

❦

*Father, You are Lord of my life. I want to always be quick to obey You in every
situation. I realize that sometimes my life and health may depend on it!*

God Washes Our Sins Away

Come, let's talk this over! says the Lord; no matter how deep the stain of your sins, I can take it out and make you as clean as freshly fallen snow. Even if you are stained as red as crimson, I can make you white as wool!

—Isaiah 1:18

Sadly, many people don't have joy because they're haunted by their past—things that happened before they got saved and began to serve the Lord. It's difficult for them to believe that God has forgiven them. They've listened to the lies of the devil instead of meditating on the promises of God.

This scripture in Isaiah is so encouraging and appropriate to the situation. If past sins are weighing you down, just remind yourself of how beautiful newly fallen snow is when no one has walked on it yet. That's exactly what we look like to God after He has washed our sins away.

When He cleanses you, He doesn't see or remember your sins. And if He doesn't remember them, you don't need to remember them either. Talk it over with the Lord and get on with your life. You were forgiven the instant you repented of your past sins. Now live your life for Jesus, and, like Him, see yourself as white as wool fit for the Master's use.

Thank You, mighty God, for the joy that lives in my heart since I gave You my life. Though I was stained as red as crimson, You have made me white as wool. You have been so faithful in Your promises to me. You have made me as spotless as freshly fallen snow. I praise You!

A Life of Joy Does Not Embarrass God

*We talked to you as a father to his own children—don't
you remember?—pleading with you, encouraging you and even
demanding that your daily lives should not embarrass God, but
bring joy to him who invited you into his kingdom to share in
his glory.*

—1 Thessalonians 2:11,12

$\mathcal{S}$ometimes we do things unintentionally that embarrass God. I know I have
done it a lot of times, but we ought to live joy-filled lives that never embarrass God,
because people are watching us. Some people will not go to church, and our lives
are a testimony to them.

We need to be careful not to embarrass God, but to be a joy to Him because
He's invited us into His kingdom to share in His glory.

❧

*Father, I don't mean to do things that would embarrass You or bring shame to
Your kingdom. I know people are watching me, and I want my life to bring joy to
You and glory to Your Kingdom.*

You Can Walk in Delightful Paths

> *Make me walk along the right paths for I know how delightful they really are.*
>
> —Psalm 119:35

*W*hen we are obedient to God, we truly walk on a delightful path. If we refuse to be obedient, however, we'll never come to know how completely delightful God's paths are.

I want to experience God's delightful paths in my own life. How about you? Aren't you weary of doing things your own way—tired of trying and failing at things you only thought would make you happy?

Just make up your mind today to try God. He won't do you any harm—and who knows?—perhaps you will find His paths a delightful contrast to those you've chosen for yourself.

❧

Father, I am weary of doing things my own way. I turn all of my projects and plans over to You. I want to experience Your delightful paths every day.

August 18

Give God First Place in Your Life

*"So don't worry at all about having enough food and clothing.
...your heavenly Father already knows perfectly well that you need
them, and he will give them to you if you give him first place in your
life and live as he wants you to."*

—Matthew 6:31-33

*M*any people today struggle because of all the demands on their resources. For many, it seems there is too much month left at the end of the money, with little or nothing left for some of life's necessities. For others, the need may be family problems or lack of health. Whatever your need, be assured by this promise in Matthew.

If you give God first place in your life and live as He wants you to live, then He has promised that you don't have to be anxious about tomorrow...regardless of your need. He will take care of you when you put first things first.

God wants to meet our needs. His desire is that we be at peace with Him and with ourselves. He wants us to be totally free from worry and fear. But He requires something on our end—He'll supply our every need if we will only order our priorities to place Him at the top of our list.

❦

Heavenly Father, Jesus said You would provide for all my needs and wants when I put You first place in my life and live right. So today I again give You first place, and I refuse to worry about anything. I know You will continue to supply whatever I need because You promised You would in Your Word.

Never Forget God

> *"And you, his successor, O Belshazzar—you knew all this, yet*
> *you have not been humble. For you have defied the Lord of Heaven,*
> *and brought here these cups from his Temple; and you and your*
> *officers and wives and concubines have been drinking wine from*
> *them while praising gods of silver, gold, brass, iron, wood, and*
> *stone—gods that neither see nor hear, nor know anything at all.*
> *But you have not praised the God who gives you the breath of life*
> *and controls your destiny!*
>
> —Daniel 5.22,23

The story of Belshazzar, son of King Nebuchadnezzar, is a good lesson about what can happen when we become proud and forget God. When he became king, Belshazzar forgot God just as his father had. He brought in idols of silver, gold, and wood.

On the last night of his reign, at a great banquet, mysterious handwriting appeared on the wall, which no one could decipher. Belshazzar sent for Daniel the prophet, and Daniel humbly confronted the king with the ominous meaning of the message that God had ended his kingdom and divided it.

Belshazzar was killed, and the Babylonian Empire fell to the Persians that night. When the Persians took over, Daniel held a prominent position under the new king. Later, Daniel wrote a series of striking visions about the future of Israel. He never, ever forgot the God he served.

Although evil seems to prevail in our world today, you and I don't have to participate in it. We need to remain close to God and entrust our destiny to Him.

Lord, I choose to walk humbly before You. You are the God who sees and knows all things. I will never forget You and all Your wonderful ways. I praise You for giving me life and controlling my destiny.

Don't Cause the Holy Spirit Sorrow

Don't cause the Holy Spirit sorrow by the way you live.
Remember, he is the one who marks you to be present on that
day when salvation from sin will be complete.

—Ephesians 4:30

*T*hese are difficult days, so be careful how you act. I encourage you to make the most of every opportunity you have for doing good. Don't act thoughtlessly or selfishly, but try to find out and do whatever the Lord wants you to do.

This is an hour in which you are repeatedly urged by the negative influences around you to "do your own thing," or to "just do it" because it feels good. That kind of direction doesn't bring lasting happiness, and it saddens the Holy Spirit.

If you've been "doing your own thing" and found that it hasn't brought you the contentment it promised, then allow the Holy Spirit to lead you...beginning today. He will never cause you sorrow. He wants you to have a good and happy life, both now and in eternity.

❧

Forgive me, my Father, for ever causing the Holy Spirit sorrow by the way I live. I want my life to please You so I can stand before You unashamed on that day when I see You face to face.

Be Careful Not to Forget God

> *"You must obey all the commandments I give you today. If you do, you will not only live, you will multiply and will go in and take over the land promised to your fathers by the Lord.... But that is the time to be careful! Beware that in your plenty you don't forget the Lord your God and begin to disobey him. For when you have become full and prosperous and have built fine homes to live in, and when your flocks and herds have become very large, and your silver and gold have multiplied, that is the time to watch out that you don't become proud, and forget the Lord your God who brought you out of your slavery in the land of Egypt."*
>
> —Deuteronomy 8:1,11-14

*W*hen God helped the Israelites through the wilderness, He gave them everything they needed. He directed them to a land filled with milk and honey with a warning, "When you get there, don't forget Me." Why? Because God knew that when they had all that they needed, they would think they no longer needed Him.

You can't stop being obedient to God when you have everything you need. You must be obedient whether you have everything you need or nothing at all.

Be obedient to God because that's where He wants you. Be careful that you don't get rich and forget God.

❦

Father, I cannot imagine forgetting You or feeling as though I don't need You in my life. You have blessed me in every area, and I'll always love and obey You. Thank You for Your abundant provision and supply.

Who Can Compare to the Holy One?

"With whom will you compare me? Who is my equal?" asks the Holy One.

—Isaiah 40:25

Isaiah 40 elaborates on the awesomeness of God, pointing out that He held the oceans in His hands and measured off the heavens with His ruler. He knows the weight of the earth...and picks up islands as if they had no weight at all. He created the stars and the planets. Verse 16 says, *All of Lebanon's forests do not contain sufficient fuel to consume a sacrifice large enough to honor him, nor are all its animals enough to offer to our God.*

But even more awesome than all of this is the fact that He loves us and is concerned about our problems. He loves us with an everlasting love, and He wants us to understand that no one else can do for us what He can do. Too often we turn to other people for help when we have a problem, but Proverbs 18:24 tells us that Jesus is a friend who sticks closer than a brother.

Recognize that no one can compare with Him, and put your full trust in Him today.

❀

Lord, thank You for Your greatness and Your holiness. I realize that no one loves and cares for me as much as You do...nor can anyone else offer the divine provisions you have for me. I offer You a sacrifice of praise today. You are an awesome God!

God's Love Is Steadfast

The Lord says: Let not the wise man bask in his wisdom, nor the mighty man in his might, nor the rich man in his riches. Let them boast in this alone: That they truly know me, and understand that I am the Lord of justice and of righteousness whose love is steadfast; and that I love to be this way.

—Jeremiah 9:23,24

No matter how wise you are...how great...or how much money you have, if you don't know Jesus, you don't have anything.

God tells us that we only have one thing to boast about and be proud of: the fact that we know Him and believe that He is just and righteous in His dealings with us. We can boast of His steadfast love and of the fact that He is just and righteous because He loves to be that way!

Some people think God is mean and only wants to punish us. But He doesn't want to do that. He wants to love us. His love is steadfast—never-ending. And He wants us to know that He loves being all that we will ever need.

❧

God, You are just and true, and I depend on Your love and mercy toward me. Thank You for expressing Your heart in Your Word so I can know and understand how much You love me.

Having Christ Is What Matters

In this new life one's nationality or race or education or social position is unimportant; such things mean nothing. Whether a person has Christ is what matters, and he is equally available to all.
—Colossians 3:11

*W*e are new creatures when we accept Jesus into our hearts. Everything about us is brand new. We have received a fresh start! Social position isn't important. The level of your education doesn't matter. Whether you're red, yellow, black, brown or white is meaningless. All that matters is that Jesus lives in your heart. He is equally accessible to everyone. He has known you since you were formed in your mother's womb. He knows all about you, and He's just been waiting for you to want to get to know Him.

Don't wait—get to know my Jesus. He's exactly what He says He is—ready to be closer to you than any brother.

❧❧

Father, I thank You that having Jesus in my heart is what really matters. That is what determines success in life. You are always there for me day or night whenever I need a friend and counselor.

A Shield of Protection

What a God He is! How perfect in every way! All his promises prove true. He is a shield for everyone who hides behind him...He fills me with strength and protects me wherever I go...God is alive! Praise him who is the great rock of protection.

—Psalm 18:30,32,46

Ps 139:5

Doesn't that passage of scripture bless you? In this day and time, we need God's protection. Never in history has there been a time when we needed God's protection more. And do you know what else I like about these scriptures? He is a shield for everyone who hides behind Him! When you're out somewhere and it's dark, or you feel fear, remember, God is right there with you as a shield. And when you're walking right behind Him, nothing can hurt you. Nothing—because He is your great shield of protection.

❀

Lord God, You are perfect in every way, and all Your promises are true. Thank You for Your promise to give me strength and protect me wherever I go. You are alive, and I do not have to fear because I can hide behind You! You are my great rock and shield of protection.

God Will Invade Your Storm

*O God, have pity, for I am trusting You! I will hide beneath
the shadow of your wings until this storm is past.*

—Psalm 57:1

*G*od does not send you storms, but He will invade your storms. And when
He does that, the storms will turn into nothing more than mere showers.

The dictionary describes the word *invade* as "to enter by force to conquer;
to encroach upon; to overrun as if by invading; to enter and spread harm
through." Storms come in and rip up and tear up, but showers bring freshness
and renewed growth. I'm sure you have noticed how calm and peaceful it is after
a storm has passed.

You may be going through a storm in your life right now, but God did not
send that storm. Just as there's a God...there's also a devil. He's evil, and his only
job is to try to steal, kill, and destroy you (see John 10:10).

But God will invade the storm the devil has sent your way if you ask Him.
I love Psalm 56:9, which says, *The very day I call for help, the tide of battle turns....*
Begin to thank Him right now for invading your storm and replacing it with peace.

❧

*I thank You, Father, that You do not send storms into my life, but You invade
them and cause them to dissipate. I call upon You to bring Your peace into every
situation I may face today. I hide beneath the shadow of Your wings, and I put my
trust in You.*

God Brings Us Safely through Troubles

Though I am surrounded by troubles, you will bring me safely through them.

—Psalm 138:7

People in the world are going to have troubles—that's all there is to it. We don't want troubles, but they just seem to pounce on us sometimes. We don't know from one day to the next what we may have to face. Even though troubles seem to be everywhere, if our trust is in the Lord Jesus Christ, then we can be assured that He will bring us safely through them.

I encourage you to put your trust in Jesus. He is the only one who can help you. He is the only one who can bring you peace and safely usher you through troubling times.

❧

O God, today I declare that You will bring me safely through all the troubles I may encounter. Even if I am surrounded by troubles, I will keep Your peace in my heart and my trust in You.

Run to God in Times of Trouble

The Lord is good. When trouble comes, he is the place to go!
And he knows everyone who trusts in him!

—Nahum 1:7

*G*od is good all the time, but when trouble comes, I don't know what I would do without Him. Do you run to God in times of trouble, or do you try to figure out what to do, fretting and worrying over things that you can usually do nothing about?

I like knowing that God knows everyone who trusts in Him. I have trusted God in times of trouble as well as in the good times, and He has never let me down. Today I encourage you to open the rooms of your heart and mind to our good God. Let Him take over every area of your life.

In good times and bad, O Lord, You are my shelter. I thank You because You know me and You are good. I'm glad that in times of trouble, I can run to You with full confidence that You will help me. I can always trust in You.

Call on Jesus in the Time of Trouble

...He does not ignore the prayers of men in trouble when they call to him for help.

—Psalm 9:12

*I*f you're in trouble today—perhaps facing some problem that seems insurmountable to you—it is important for you to know that you can call on Jesus. He will never ignore you. In fact, He wants to help. He is just waiting for you to let Him.

Jesus will never interfere where He isn't welcome. So why don't you take a moment right now and invite Jesus to help you in your troubles. Ask Him what direction He would have you to take, and then seek His peace in that situation. God's Word promises that He is beautiful for situation, the joy of the whole earth (Psalm 48:2 KJV).

※

O Jesus, I'm in trouble. I don't know what to do. I really need Your help with this situation. Help me to allow Your peace to overtake me in the midst of this storm. Thank You for loving me so much and being so willing to help me overcome every challenge in life.

God Helps Those Who Call on Him

All those who know your mercy, Lord, will count on you for
help. For you have never yet forsaken those who trust in you.
—Psalm 9:10

*Y*ou know that God will hear you when you call on Him in the time of trouble. He'll even hear you if you're not in trouble. Whether or not you're facing a challenging day today, call on the God of mercy because He wants to help you.

He delights in answering the prayers of those who believe He will help them. Please let Him help you—don't put it off until another time. God wants to hear from You today.

Merciful God! Thank You for being so close that I can always count on You to help me. You never leave me nor forsake me. I put my trust in You. Thank You that Your mercies are new every morning. I need all the help I can get! With You beside me, I will be able to face any challenge that comes my way today in Jesus' name.

Don't Doubt in Your Heart

So Jesus answered and said to them, "Have faith in God. For
assuredly, I say to you, whoever says to this mountain, 'Be removed
and be cast into the sea,' and does not doubt in his heart, but
believes that those things he says will come to pass, he will have
whatever he says."

—Mark 11:22,23 NKJV

Why do we spend so much time and effort trying to figure out what's
going to happen when we get into a situation that requires mountain-moving
faith? We know that He is greater than any situation we'll ever face, yet we worry,
doubt, and fret. *His Word   Ps 138:2*

We need to develop an unshakeable confidence in God—allowing no doubt
to penetrate our hearts. Confidence is faith. It means we have assurance deep
down in our hearts that God will cause everything to turn out all right. *Gen 50:20*

When we do not doubt God's willingness and ability to help us triumph over
situations, we can believe that whatever He says will happen. *138:2*

If you're worried about something right now—your spouse, children, business,
something going on at church—hold on to your joy, smile, and confess: "God *1 Cor 2:16*
always causes me to triumph, He causes everything I put my hand to to prosper. *Ps ?*
God's going to save my entire household. Greater Is He that Is In me than he that *Deul 28*
is in the world." *1 Jo 4:17, 4:4, 5:18   3 Jo 2   Ps 5, 90:12*

Trust God in times of trouble. He'll always see you through. *91, 92,*
103, 105:
35

※

Father, Your Word says if I only have faith in You, I can speak to the
mountain of circumstances I'm facing, and it has to obey me. I believe and speak *Ps 48:*
Your Word in faith today, with no doubt in my heart, believing that Your Word *8*
will come to pass. *55:11*
knowg   Ps 138:2 *61:1?*

Jesus Is the Messiah

The disciples of John the Baptist soon heard of all that Jesus was doing. When they told John about it, he sent two of his disciples to Jesus to ask him, "Are you really the Messiah? Or shall we keep on looking for him?"

—Luke 7:18,19

*P*eople still wonder today if Jesus is truly the promised Messiah. When John sent two of his followers to see what Jesus had to say about himself, John wanted his disciples to have confirmation of what he already suspected was true.

In the meantime, the two men witnessed Jesus opening blind eyes and healing the lame and lepers. To us it seems obvious that He was the Son of God. Yet they asked Him if He was the Messiah. Jesus told them to go and tell John what they had seen and heard, and that those who did not lose faith in Him would be blessed.

We are blessed today because we have not lost faith in Him. We know who Jesus was and is. We realize that He is the promised Messiah. If you need a miracle, Jesus is the only One who has the power to give it to you. Won't you call on Him today?

❦

Jesus, I believe You are the Messiah, the one God sent to show His compassion for suffering humanity. I thank You that You are the true God who is the same yesterday, today, and forever. You never change, and You still heal those who come to You.

Trust in the Lord

Those who trust in the Lord are steady as Mount Zion, unmoved by any circumstance.

—Psalm 125:1

If you have ever been to Israel and seen Mount Zion, you know it's big. There is no way it could move unless God himself would cause the earth to quake and break it apart or cause it to fall down.

God's Word says those who trust in the Lord are as steady as that great big mountain in Israel. That's you—steady as you go through the storms of life. You are unmoved by circumstances that would break or even destroy someone who doesn't know God and the power of His might. *His Word*

Today I encourage you to keep your mind and heart stayed on God, and purpose to be unmoved by any circumstance that attempts to hinder your *Is 26:3* progress. Begin to see yourself as the overcomer you are!

Lord God, one of the things I desire most in life is to be balanced and steady— unmoved by the circumstances around me. I don't want to be up one day and down the next. Therefore, I trust in You with my whole heart and ask You to establish me in all my ways.

Try Trusting God

Then the Lord said to Moses, "When did I become weak? Now you shall see whether my word comes true or not!"

—Numbers 11:23

The Israelites were always complaining to Moses about something during their wilderness journey. They just complained about everything that God did for them!

Finally Moses went to God and asked why he had to put up with these people? And God said to Moses, "When did I become weak? Now you shall see whether My word comes true or not." The Lord wanted Moses to know that He had not changed and that His Word would be fulfilled.

It is still true today. God hasn't changed. Jesus is the same. God and Jesus haven't become weak, and God's Word hasn't changed either. So if you have problems trusting people—like the Israelites thought they couldn't trust Moses—then just try trusting God. He hasn't become weak like we humans are weak. He is strong, and He wants to fulfill His Word in your life. So just trust Him, and He will help you.

❦

Lord, I repent for sometimes complaining about my circumstances. You have not become weak, and nothing is impossible with You. I know Your Word is true, and I appreciate Your abundant provision in my life. I recommit my trust in You now to fulfill Your Word in my life.

Be Not Dismayed

Because the Lord God helps me, I will not be dismayed;
therefore, I have set my face like flint to do his will, and I know
that I will triumph.

—Isaiah 50:7

*W*e don't have to be dismayed when troubles try to overwhelm us. The word *dismayed* means "filled with fear or dread so that one is not sure what to do; loss of courage or confidence when faced with trouble or danger."

When you remain full of confidence in God at the onset of trouble and refuse to be afraid, you will triumph in troublesome situations because you know that God is on your side. He will help you because you are trusting in Him.

In Psalm 42:11, David said, *But O my soul, don't be discouraged. Don't be upset. Expect God to act! For I know that I shall again have plenty of reason to praise him for all that he will do. He is my help! He is my God!*

Put your faith in God today. Trust Him and watch Him display plenty of reasons for you to praise His holy name!

✤

Father, I will not be dismayed today. I expect You to act in my behalf. Because You help me, I have set my face like flint to do Your will. I know You will cause me to triumph over every situation. And I praise Your holy name!

God Can Do What Men Cannot

"God can do what men can't!"
—Luke 18:27

There comes a time in all of our lives when we have to look to God, because nobody else can do for us what He can do. That time came for me in 1981 when doctors could do nothing to help me deal with their diagnosis of liver cancer. I had to trust in Jesus completely because only God could do what these wonderful, talented, educated men could not. They were completely helpless to offer me any solution to my problem, but God could...and He did.

God has not changed—He can still do what seems impossible. Don't wait to trust in God until you've exhausted all possibilities of help on earth. Remember—He can do things that men cannot.

❦

Oh God, in You alone, I place my trust. I know You can do things that I cannot do. You can do what men cannot. In fact, nothing is impossible with You!

September 6

How Do We Describe God?

How can we describe God? With what can we compare him?
—Isaiah 40:18

How do we describe God? As Christians, we say God is love, mercy, and compassion. He's awesome. He is a healer. He's a saving God, a deliverer, a lover, a protector. He is anything you need.   My ABBA, – King & Creator of –

Just how do you describe Him? Who is God to you? Words are not adequate ^(Whole) enough for us to describe God, and there is no one else with whom we can compare ^(everything) Him. He's everything and anything we need...and He's always there for us. ^(& everyone)

Describe God? There's no way! But we can let Him know how awesome He is to us by loving Him and serving Him. What a mighty God we serve!

❧

Father, words are just not adequate to describe what a truly wonderful God You are. I'm so glad You are everything to me and You are always here for me. You are the all-powerful, all-knowing Creator and Ruler of the universe, and I will always love and serve You.

No Other God Can Do What Our God Can Do

"...For no other God can do what this one does."
—Daniel 3:29

Most all of us know that we serve a God who can do anything, but this verse from the book of Daniel literally proves it. It is a quote of Babylon's King Nebuchadnezzar, who had just witnessed God's amazing rescue of Shadrach, Meshach, and Abednego from the fiery furnace execution to which he had sentenced them for rebelling against his orders.

Although the king acknowledged God, he believed in many gods and considered himself the top spiritual authority in Babylon. However, after seeing with his own eyes the power of the Most High God, even this ungodly king could see that our God can do things that no other can.

And I just say, "Amen!" to that. Never let anyone tell you that someone can do for you what only God can.

❧

Oh God, You are the only true and living God. There is no other God like You. You will rescue me out of every situation because You are the Most High God, and You are my God!

Change Your Mind and Attitude toward God

Now change your mind and attitude to God and turn to him so he can cleanse away your sins and send you wonderful times of refreshment from the presence of the Lord.

—Acts 3:19

When Peter and John healed the lame man and told him to rise up in the name of Jesus, Peter saw it as an opportunity to witness to the people. He told them that crucifying Jesus had been wrong. Of course, it was part of God's plan, but Peter said they had murdered Jesus because of their ignorance. They didn't know who He was.

Then Peter told them to change their mind and attitude toward God and let Him cleanse them and send them wonderful times of refreshment.

You may not believe that Jesus can still do miracles today. You may not have a good attitude toward God. But I encourage you to change your mind and let Him give you times of refreshment. Invite Jesus into your day and see for yourself what a difference He makes in it.

Lord, I want thoughts and attitudes that are acceptable in Your sight. I rejoice that You cleanse and refresh me in Your presence. I'm so grateful that You provide times of refreshing. I praise You for being so good to me.

God Requires Loyalty and Devotion

For you must worship no other gods, but only Jehovah, for he is a God who claims absolute loyalty and exclusive devotion.

—Exodus 34:14

This scripture applies to us today as well as to the Israelites as Moses led them through the wilderness toward the Promised Land. There is no other God. People make other gods, but there is only one true God—Jehovah—and He requires our loyalty and exclusive devotion.

The word *loyalty* means "firm in allegiance to one's government, homeland, or sovereign; faithful to a person, custom, or ideal." *Devoted* means "to give one's time, attention, self entirely to a particular activity or cause."

When we give ourselves entirely to the cause of Christ and are loyal to Him, we will have happiness in this world, where there isn't any real happiness without God.

I worship You, my Father, and no other. You are worthy of absolute loyalty and exclusive devotion. I'm yours, Lord—everything I am and am not, all belongs to You. You are my God, and my happiness is in knowing You.

Be Loyal to God

Oh, love the Lord, all of you who are his people; for the Lord protects those who are loyal to him....

—Psalm 31:23

*P*ay attention to this one little phrase: *...for the Lord protects those who are loyal to Him.* Now, if you want protection, then, obviously, you have to be loyal to God. Loyalty is all that God asks in exchange for His protection.

The word *loyal* is similar in meaning to loyalty. The dictionary defines *loyal* as "firm allegiance or faithfulness to a person, custom, or ideal." Being loyal to God means godly living Monday through Saturday as well as on Sunday in the presence of other Christians.

The word *protection* means "to keep from harm, attack, or injury; to guard." I like the feeling that someone as important as God is keeping harm, attack, and injury away from me!

As a committed Christian since my early teens, it isn't difficult for me to be loyal to God. I have no desire to split my allegiance between God and the devil.

I realize it isn't that easy for everyone. Some Christians still have one foot in the devil's kingdom and one foot in God's kingdom. They're riding a fence named *lukewarm.* Jesus warned us against that in Revelation 3:16. He said he would spit lukewarm Christians out of His mouth! You don't want to be in that group!

Recharge your spiritual battery. Get excited again about God! Display your loyalty to Him, and let Him surround you with His protection!

❦

I give You my loyalty, God, and thank you for Your protection. I pledge my faithfulness to You. I never want to be a lukewarm Christian that You spit out of Your mouth. Thank You for keeping me from all harm, attack, and injury. I will live godly to demonstrate my love for You.

Turn Your Thoughts Toward God

He will keep in perfect peace all those who trust in him, whose thoughts turn often to the Lord!

—Isaiah 26:3

*I*n the chaos of today's fast-paced world, it is difficult to find quiet moments for meditation. We get so caught up in the "busyness" of all our commitments that we sometimes become weary, stressed, and out of sorts. But God has the remedy. This passage in Isaiah says, He will give us *perfect peace* when our thoughts are turned *often* toward the Lord—not just once in a while or sometimes, but often.

If you want to have peace in this world, you must be determined to keep your thoughts focused on God. Focusing on God and the good things of God *all the time* is even better than doing it often, because He'll always be good to you—He doesn't know how to be any other way. Isn't that a comforting thought?

❧

Lord God, I choose to keep my thoughts focused on You today. Because I trust in You, You will give me Your perfect peace even in the presence of the distractions of the world around me. I choose to walk in Your peace all day long.

September 12

God's Promises Are Kind

O Lord God of Israel, there is no God like you in all of heaven and earth. You are the God who keeps His kind promises to all those who obey you and who are anxious to do your will.

—2 Chronicles 6:14

God's promises to you are kind because He is a good and merciful God. He is just naturally compassionate and kind. When we are eager to obey God and do His will, He is happy to keep His kind promises to us.

God always fulfills His promises, so look up some of them today. When you obey God's Word and His will, you'll find a firm foundation on which to build your life.

❧

Oh God, there is truly no God like you. You always keep Your promises because You are kind. I am eager to obey You and do Your will. You are my firm foundation!

Do Something for Somebody Else

"Send this word to Ebed-melech the Ethiopian: The Lord of Hosts, the God of Israel, says: I will do to this city everything I threatened; I will destroy it before your eyes, but I will deliver you. You shall not be killed by those you fear so much. As a reward for trusting me, I will preserve your life and keep you safe."

—Jeremiah 39:16-18

God will always reward you for whatever you do for anyone else. Even if it's giving someone a cup of cold water, He said He will reward you for it.

King Zedekiah was angry with Jeremiah for prophesying that God was going to destroy Jerusalem, so the king's men lowered Jeremiah into a pit.

When an important palace official by the name of Ebed-melech heard about Jeremiah's fate, he tied together a bunch of rags to make a rope that was thrown into the pit so Jeremiah could climb out.

Now, God was about to destroy the city, but Jeremiah said, "Okay, but don't destroy my servant who got me out of that pit." So God spared Ebed-melech to reward him for rescuing His great prophet, Jeremiah, from the pit.

I encourage you to do something for somebody today. Whatever you do, God will reward you, preserve your life, and take care of you when you are considerate of others.

❦

O God, I thank You for opportunities to do something good for someone today. As I help others in their time of need, You will help me in my time of need. You reward me for trusting You by preserving my life and keeping me safe.

God Takes Care of Us from Birth to Old Age

"Listen to me, all Israel who are left; I have created you and cared for you since you were born. I will be your God through all your lifetime, yes, even when your hair is white with age. I made you and I will care for you. I will carry you along and be your Savior."

—Isaiah 46.3,4

It is reassuring to know that God cares for you throughout your life. He made you, and He'll care for you no matter how young or old you are—whether your hair is light, dark, gray, or white. No matter what happens, God has committed himself to your care from the beginning of your life to the end—and beyond. He's even covered eternity just for you!

God is going to carry you along life's journey. Remember that He loves you with an everlasting love. There's not one thing you can do to keep Him from loving and caring for you.

Your love, God, is something to rejoice about. I praise You that nothing I do can keep You from caring for me and carrying me along life's journey. I thank You that You are my Savior.

The Power of the Tongue

Righteous lips are the delight of kings; and they love him that speaketh right.

—Proverbs 16:13 KJV

*W*e create our own world by the words we say. And many times we're our own worst enemy. We talk poverty, for example, and then complain because we don't have wealth. We talk sickness and wonder why we don't have health. We talk defeat and wonder why we don't have victory.

There is power in our words! Even psychologists say that our bodies listen to our words.

When my husband and I learned about the importance of words, we wouldn't let each other say anything negative. If I said, "I think I'm getting a headache," John said, "Now, don't you say that." If he said, "I'm feeling kind of bad," I'd say, "Don't say that!"

Now, God didn't mean for us to call the things that *are* as though they're *not*. Instead, He wants us to call the things that are *not* as though they *were*. If you have sickness, don't say, "I'm not sick." Rather, say, "According to 1 Peter 2:24, by the stripes of Jesus I am healed. I call what is not—healing—to come to my body now. God's Word says I am healed." You need to find and claim the scriptures in the Bible that pertain to you, as a believer.

We will change our world when we change our words!

❧

Father, thank You that You make my lips righteous as I speak Your words. Your Word in my mouth is powerful, and I will speak Your truth today over my life in strong faith. I will say what You have said in Your Word about my situation, because You watch over Your Word to perform it in my behalf!

The Word is God-breathed

Every Scripture is God-breathed (given by His inspiration) and profitable for instruction, for reproof and conviction of sin, for correction of error and discipline in obedience, [and] for training in righteousness (in holy living, in conformity to God's will in thought, purpose, and action).

—2 Timothy 3:16 AMP

The breath of God is in His book. This means the Bible came out of the inside of God—He breathed the Bible to life. The words that are printed in the Bible may look just like words you see in magazines, newspapers, and other books, but they are very different. The life of God is contained in His Word.

God said that all Scripture benefits us for instruction or teaching, for being convicted of sin, and for correction, so we can become spiritually mature and thoroughly prepared to do good works. Good works advance God's kingdom. When the kingdom advances to the place that everyone has heard the Good News, Jesus can come back and take us home to live with Him in heaven.

You can overcome all the battles of life with the Word of God. The Word will give you the faith you need to lay hands on the sick and see them recover, cast out devils and see people delivered, see and recognize miracles, signs, and wonders, and just fall deeper and deeper in love with Jesus, your Savior and your King.

As you read your Bible every day, you treat yourself to its God-breathed truths. You'll be forever glad you did.

❧

Thank You, Lord, for breathing Your truth into the Bible. I treasure the Scripture as my instruction, reproof, correction, and conviction of sin, and for discipline to obey Your will. As I read Your Word and act on it, I will see Your life flow out of me in good works that will advance Your kingdom in the earth.

Stirred by God's Word

So mightily grew the word of God and prevailed.
—Acts 19:20 KJV

The Word of God is strong and powerful. We need to read it, meditate on it, and digest it. We need to walk in the light of it and confess it. How do we do that?

We put it in our mouths and in our hearts. We have to do that ourselves. Then we won't have to run to someone like our pastor or write a letter to the TV preacher and ask him or her where to find something in the Word when we're in trouble. We have to be stirred by the Word for ourselves.

When we find out what the Word has to say about everything—and it pretty clearly says something about every problem that has ever come up in our family—then the Word will grow mightily in us, and we will prevail.

Maybe you're in trouble today. You may be dealing with sorrow and despair, but if the Word of God is on the inside of you, you have life. Trouble, sorrow, and despair are a part of death, but you have life—and life always overcomes death, according to the Word. Get stirred up on the inside. See and feel the power of God in you. You can and will prevail.

In fact, great things are about to start happening for you today as you are stirred by the Word!

Father, I am stirred by the power of Your Word that is alive in me. As I meditate on Your Word day and night, it is growing mightily in me. I believe as Your Word grows inside me, it will prevail and overcome every obstacle in my life.

When Nothing Seems to Work

I will lift up mine eyes unto the hills, from whence cometh my help.

—Psalm 121:1 KJV

*H*as it ever seemed to you as though everybody else is on the mountaintop and you're living in the valley? Did it seem as though nothing would work for you? Did you think about lifting your eyes toward the mountaintop? If you had, you'd have seen Jesus, waiting and ready to help.

We find Jesus in His Word, where He reveals the way out of the valley. He says, *I am the way, the truth, and the life...* (John 14:6 KJV).

Let Jesus show you where you lost your way. God's Word works! If nothing is working out for you, you just might want to give yourself a reality check. Ask yourself:

1. Is there anything I need to make right with another person?
2. Have I neglected to claim God's promises for my situation?
3. Am I being positive and confessing God's Word over my life?
4. Am I trying to figure out what's wrong and seeking answers?
5. Am I in fellowship with people of faith?
6. Am I obeying the scriptures that will bring me the victory?
7. Am I praising God before I see my answer?

God's Word never fails. Jesus will never fail you. Put your confidence in Him. He's the only answer when nothing seems to be working.

❧

Jesus, show me how to get back on track. Show me if I've offended anyone or failed to stand on Your promises. Show me if I fail to confess Your Word. Help me to walk with others of faith and stay in obedience to Your Word. I praise You that Your answer is coming to me now.

"*I Believe I Receive*"

*And we are sure of this, that he will listen to us whenever we
ask him for anything in line with his will. And if we really know
he is listening when we talk to him and make our requests, then we
can be sure that he will answer us.*

—1 John 5:14,15

The devil will always try to shake your confidence in God and His Word between the time you confess with your mouth, "I believe I receive," and the time you see the manifestation and can say, "It is mine!"

Now, you rarely have an instant manifestation of something you're praying for. So during the waiting time, you must make up your mind whether you have confidence in God and His Word or not.

God assures us that He listens to us, and it pleases and honors Him when we demonstrate our confidence in Him.

Confidence in God has a great recompense of reward. He can save your life, your business, your family, your marriage, your health, and more! Hebrews 10:35,36 says we are not to let our trust die away, no matter what happens.

We must believe that God's promises are our very own. Faith is not an emotion—it is acting on a legal contract. Begin now to exercise your faith in God by confessing that you believe and receive and by thanking Him every day until you see the manifestation of what you're believing Him for. Your answer is on the way!

Lord, I have great confidence in You and in Your Word. Your Word is a legal, irrevocable contract with me that promises that You will meet every one of my needs. Your Word is Your guarantee that the things I have asked You for are on the way. I believe I receive them now in Jesus' name!

Choosing Life—One Day At A Time

Confess the Truth Constantly

Nothing is perfect except your words. Oh, how I love them.
I think about them all day long. They make me wiser than my
enemies, because they are my constant guide. ~~Ps 19~~

—Psalm 119:96-98

It is important for us to know that we should never allow our mouths to speak anything that is contrary to God's Word. We need to confess the truth *God's Word* constantly because nothing is perfect except the Word of God.

Confess that the Word of God is your meditation day and night. Psalm 19:14 KJV says, *Let the words of my mouth, and the meditation of my heart, be acceptable in thy sight, O Lord, my strength, and my redeemer.*

Confess this from Psalm 1: "Lord, because I meditate on Your Word day and night, Your Word says that I am like a tree—a strong tree. *healthy* My roots go down deep, Lord God, and reach the sustenance and the power of the Water of life that *Word* the world knows nothing about. I am like a tree planted by the rivers of water. I confess Your truth constantly!"

Rejoice that you are blessed as a result of confessing God's Word. Confess that *thinks & prayers* all of your needs are met. Find scriptures that build you up on the inside. And if you have trouble believing that a good, positive confession will help to change the circumstances in your life, just remember that they work for me. Then you can confess, "Confessing Your Word worked for Dodie Osteen, Lord Jesus, and it will work for me!" Glory to God!

Is 53:5 54:17 41:12 Is 58, 61, 66
Is 32 Is 62
Phil 4:19, Ps 23:5, 6

Father, I confess You today as my Strength and my Redeemer. I'm glad Your words are perfect. Your wisdom in me today will make me wiser than my enemies. I have hidden Your Words in my heart to guide me. Thank You, Lord, that I can count on Your Word constantly.

September 21

Let God's Word Abide in You

If ye abide in me, and my words abide in you, ye shall ask what ye will, and it shall be done unto you.

—John 15:7 KJV

This scripture is so important. Unless you ask according to the will of God, you really don't know how to ask for the things you need. So, in order for your prayers to be answered, you need God's words to abide in you.

The best way to get His words in you is found in another scripture that may be familiar to you. Romans 10:17 KJV says, *So then faith cometh by hearing, and hearing by the word of God.* Faith comes by hearing and hearing and hearing, over and over again. That's what you need. Whether it's through a sermon, tapes, or reading scripture to yourself, keep the Word of God going into your spirit until His words abide in you.

Then when you ask God for the things you need, your prayers will be answered because you are asking according to His Word, which is His will.

I challenge you to hold on to the Word of God and trust Him in every circumstance. In any situation, know that God can see you through. He's on the throne. He's directing your path. Lift up your hands and praise Him that His Word abides in you!

❧

Father, I praise You that Your Word abides in me and I abide in You. I have what I need because I ask You for the things I need, according to Your Word. Thank You, Lord, for meeting all my needs.

Fear the Lord and You Will Succeed

Tackle every task that comes along, and if you fear God you can expect his blessing.

—Ecclesiastes 7:18

*I*f you've been in church most of your life, I know you have repeatedly heard the familiar expression, "the fear of the Lord." That terminology can be very confusing to unbelievers and sometimes to believers too.

The "fear of the Lord" does not mean that you're supposed to be afraid of Him. We're talking about revering God. The word *revere* means "to regard with profound awe, great respect, love or devotion." It means we are to love Him with such holy reverence that it raises Him to a level above anyone on earth.

In the fear of the Lord, you can ask for His direction and tackle any task with the knowledge that God is going to cause you to succeed because your love and respect for Him is undeniable, unquestionable, and boundless!

You can expect the blessings of God when you truly fear God because He loves you, and He loves how you love Him!

Father, I reverence You with all my heart. Truly, there is none like You. Help me to tackle every task I face in Your strength. I expect Your blessings because I keep You first place in my life.

Don't Despise Small Beginnings

Do not despise this small beginning, for the eyes of the Lord rejoice to see the work begin....

—Zechariah 4:10

$\mathscr{I}$f you have ever started a church or helped someone start a church, you know the feeling of frustration that can come along to discourage you during the growing process. Don't allow yourself to be discouraged. If God has inspired the work, it will grow.

My husband and I started our church in a little building with less than ninety people, but God blessed it and caused it to grow to a level that we couldn't have possibly imagined in the beginning.

We occasionally experienced frustration, but we learned not to despise what seemed like a tiny beginning. We learned to just go on and do what God told us to do. We found that God rejoiced in the work because of our obedience unto Him.

Maybe you have started a business, or have plans to start something that is new to you—something you have never done before. Maybe you're purchasing your first car or home. It's wise to start small and see how things go before making larger investments. God gives us dreams that only He can fulfill! You may grow discouraged from time to time, but if God's in it—it will grow!

❦

Lord, cause me to be content with my present season of life and ministry. Help me to completely comprehend the wisdom of starting small and building toward the future. I want to lay a strong foundation, and I don't need everything in the beginning. Let me savor and appreciate every step of the work as it progresses day by day.

Wait on God

*For since the world began no one has seen or heard of such a
God as ours, who works for those who wait for him!*

—Isaiah 64:4

*D*o you realize that if you will wait for God and wait on Him, you won't
go ahead of Him and wind up doing everything on your own? If you wait for
Him to come on the scene, God will work for you! Isn't that what we need in
these last days—for God to work for us? Too many people wear themselves out
plunging into activities they're "sure" God would approve of, only to fall flat
because they haven't waited for God's direction.

Start listening for God's still small voice, avoid jumping out ahead of His
perfect timing, and learn to patiently and faithfully wait on Him. His guidance is
worth waiting for. It will save you lots of effort, disappointment, and might even
save you money!

❊

*Lord, deliver me from an impatient spirit. Help me to avoid stepping out
ahead of You and misunderstanding Your will in my life. Cause me to wait with
patience and trust in Your timing.*

Quit Quarreling with God

"Quit quarreling with God! Agree with him and you will have peace at last!..."

—Job 22:21

*H*ave you ever quarreled with God? Perhaps you've been angry with Him for one reason or another. I know how that feels because I've been there. But the truth is, we need to quit quarreling with God, really become acquainted with Him, and begin to agree with Him. Then we'll have the peace in our lives that we all long for.

Verse 29 says, *"If you are attacked and knocked down, you will know that there is someone who will lift you up again...."* To me, this verse means that when I fall or am knocked down, there'll be somebody [Jesus] there to lift me up when I quit quarreling with God. Now, that's my paraphrase, but doesn't it make sense?

I urge you today to make peace with God, follow His directions, and begin to enjoy your life. That may sound simple and easy to say, but try it for yourself, and see if it works! I believe it will.

❧❀❧

God, I admit that I have been quarrelsome at times. Please forgive me. I come into agreement with Your purpose for my life. I will start following Your directions so that I will have lasting peace.

Follow after Peace

*And let the peace of God rule in your hearts, to the which also
ye are called in one body; and be ye thankful.*

—Colossians 3:15 KJV

*N*ow, this verse doesn't say you should let the peace of God rule in your
pastor's heart or in your husband's heart or in your wife's heart. It says, *...let the
peace of God rule in your hearts....* When you don't have peace about a decision
you're facing, evidently, you're getting ready to make the wrong decision.

If you have unrest, then things need to change, because the peace of God
that passes all understanding will guard and guide your heart and mind if you
allow it to.

Remember to follow after peace whenever you're facing a decision. Let peace
be your umpire, and then you'll be headed in the right direction. Let God's peace
settle all questions that arise in your mind.

*My Father, I need Your help to make quality decisions. Thank You for sending
Your peace to rule my heart at all times. Even when I don't understand the direction
You are leading me, I will follow after Your peace, which passes all understanding,
and I know You will work everything out for my good in the end.*

A Quiet Spirit Quiets a Bad Temper

If the boss is angry with you, don't quit! A quiet spirit will quiet his bad temper.

—Ecclesiastes 10:4

You can really relate to this scripture if you work in today's marketplace. It may be hard to believe, but your quiet spirit will quiet the bad temper of somebody who is ranting and raving. If you just pray and ask God to give you a quiet spirit and a quiet and undisturbed mind, you'll be surprised what it will do for you and your boss or supervisor.

It's very likely that his temper tantrum will just fizzle out when he sees the peace that surrounds you—that you aren't reacting with rage or fear. It's possible that he may actually apologize. Whether he does or not is not as important as maintaining your peace in the midst of his storm. Ultimately, respect will be developed as you demonstrate godly character in his presence.

Have a great day at work today!

❧

Mighty God, I choose to remain calm on my job—especially when others are not. I let the peace of God rule in my mind and heart so that my spirit will be quiet and remain peaceful in the midst of strife.

The Spirit Inside Makes You Wise

*For those who are older are said to be wiser; but it is not mere
age that makes men wise. Rather, it is the spirit in a man, the
breath of the Almighty which makes him intelligent.*

—Job 32:7-9

*W*henever I see someone with beautiful, snow-white hair, I think of their age and the great wisdom they must have accumulated over the years. But this scripture in Job says it isn't just age that makes a person wise.

No matter how young or old you are, if you have the breath of Almighty God in your spirit, then you are a wise person. The book of Proverbs speaks a lot about wisdom. The wise person has the ability to adapt himself to God's plan for his life.

God is the source of all wisdom, so when you choose to stay on His course, you will prosper and be successful. Make the choice today to follow after wisdom, and you will begin to enjoy life on an entirely new level.

❧

Oh God, I ask You above all else to give me Your wisdom. Thank You for imparting your wisdom to my mind and my spirit so I will make wise decisions that are in line with Your Word and Your will for my life.

You Can Count on God for Help

*All those who know your mercy, Lord, will count on you for
help. For you have never yet forsaken those who trust in you.*

—Psalm 9:10

*D*o you trust God? Do you feel that you can count on Him to help you,
protect you, and keep you from making mistakes? As I read verse 10 of Psalm 9,
I wondered if anyone who knows the Lord could honestly say they have never
experienced the mercy of God? I don't think that's possible.

Whether or not you are aware of it, God protects you every day of your life.
He takes care of you and watches over you every minute of every hour. Though
you may not have *felt* anything unusual, who knows how many times God
has protected you from incidents, accidents, injuries, and troubles...even before
they happened?

You can count on God for help. You have His Word on it. Hebrews 13:5 says
He will never ever leave you or forsake you when you trust in Him!

❧

*I know your mercy, Lord, and I count on You for help. You have never
forsaken me, and You never will! I totally trust You to protect me and keep me
from making mistakes.*

You Are Safe in God's Care

> *"Even when you are chased by those who seek your life, you are safe in the care of the Lord your God, just as though you were safe inside his purse!..."*
>
> —1 Samuel 25:29

I love this scripture. It is a quote from Abigail to David. Her husband, Nabal, had insulted David, who had sworn to kill him. But Abigail was a sensible woman, and her kind words and generosity completely changed David's mind.

You probably are not being chased by a physical person, but perhaps some dreaded disease or equally serious problem has come against you and seems to be seeking your life. The Bible says you are safe in God's care just as if you were tucked inside His purse.

How about that? We usually guard our money by keeping it in a billfold. Women generally tuck their billfolds in purses, and men keep theirs in their pockets. When we have our billfolds in our pockets or purses, we usually feel pretty confident that everything is safe.

But just imagine God guarding us in a big purse that He holds close to himself, saying, "You're safe in here. You're close to My heart."

Remember that you're in safe hands because you're locked up in God's great big purse, close to His heart. He'll always take care of you.

I like knowing that I am safe with You, God. I praise You for Your continued protection from harm. I picture myself today held tightly in Your hands and close to Your heart.

The Lord Holds You with His Hand

The steps of good men are directed by the Lord. He delights in each step they take. If they fall it isn't fatal, for the Lord holds them with his hand.

—Psalm 37:23,24

*A*ll of us are trying to serve God, but we make mistakes sometimes. If you've ever made a mistake, join the club. You are not alone. But when you fall, you need to get right up and keep on going. This psalm confirms that what I'm telling you is true. It isn't fatal to make a mistake, so just take hold of the Lord's hand and keep trying to live right and do good.

I may fall from time to time, but when I hold on to Jesus, He knows I'm trying, and He helps me. He'll help you in the same way because He is no respecter of persons. What He's done for me, He will do for you...when you let Him. Don't allow guilt to control you. As a blood-bought child of God, your sin debt is cancelled. Guilt has no place in your life. It is time you let go of self-condemnation and let God take control of your life.

❦

Lord, thank You that my steps are directed by You. I appreciate You for helping me up when I fall...and for holding me with Your mighty hand.

Take Hold of God's Strength

*...let him take hold of my strength, that he may make peace
with me; and he shall make peace with me.*

—Isaiah 27:5 KJV

*E*verybody's busy. Anytime you ask someone how he or she is, they nearly
always say, "I'm busy!" We're all going in different directions—mothers are rushing
home from a day at work to care for their families. Fathers are hurrying to get to
the kids' ball games after a long, hard day at work. We need strength!

There is strength in the Word of God. When you get tired, go to the Word
and find the scriptures on strength. There is usually a Concordance in the back of
the Bible and it lists key words and where to find them. Look up these verses and
repeat them to yourself.

Then raise up your hands like a little child and say, "Now, God, I need Your
strength." You will actually sense strength flowing into your body.

Another scripture that blesses me is Psalm 68:35 KJV, *...the God of Israel is he
that giveth strength and power unto his people. Blessed be God.*

You know who will give you strength and power. All you have to do is ask Him.

*Lord God, I lift up my hands to You like a little child because I need Your
strength today. I take hold of Your power that gives me peace and strength when I
am weary. When my schedule gets too busy, Lord, remind me to stop and lift my
hands to You. Then I will receive Your mighty strength to do all I need to do each
day. And I'll have Your peace.*

Jesus Will Never Disappoint You

...the Scriptures tell us that no one who believes in Christ will ever be disappointed.

—Romans 10:11

*I*sn't that good news? Hallelujah! If you believe in Christ, then you don't ever have to be disappointed in Him. Now, people will fail you because they are human beings. There are insensitive people all around you every day that will disappoint you. Sometimes your spouse or your children will let you down, and when it happens, you'll be disappointed in them. But not so with Jesus—He will never give you cause to be disappointed in Him. He is the only One who is perfect, and He loves you with an everlasting love. When you need to trust in somebody, trust in Jesus. You won't be disappointed!

❧

God, I thank You today that because I believe in Jesus Christ, I will never have occasion to be disappointed in Him. Your promises are always "Yes!" and "Amen!" and I put my trust in You.

God Will Rescue Us

*The Commander of the armies of heaven is here among us. He,
the God of Jacob, has come to rescue us.*

—Psalm 46:7

*W*e went through a brief war several years ago called Desert Storm.
Morning, noon, and night, we actually saw this war fought on television! TV,
newspapers, and magazines featured articles on the tactical maneuvers developed
by the great generals and commanders in charge of implementing a victory for
our army.

But God is the great Commander of the armies of heaven, and He is here to
rescue us.

Do you need to be rescued? I have often needed Him to rescue me in times
of trouble—with a lot of things that were going on in my life, our family, our
church, our city, and our nation.

If you need someone to rescue you today, call on the Commander of heaven
and earth. He's just waiting for you to seek His direction.

❧

*I call upon You Lord, as my Commander-in-Chief, to dispatch help from heaven
today and rescue me from any destruction the devil had planned for me. I put my
trust in You and thank You for rescuing me out of the hand of the enemy.*

Encourage Yourself in the Lord

...but David encouraged himself in the Lord his God.
—1 Samuel 30:6 KJV

This is an hour in which we can get dismayed fairly easily. But God's Word says that David encouraged himself whenever he was down. When we get discouraged, we have to encourage ourselves. And if we do that—setting our faces like flint to worship God, to serve Him, and to do His will—then we know that we will triumph.

If you are having trouble—if you're dismayed—you can just change things around by saying, "I am not going to be dismayed. I am going to worship You, Jesus. I am going to praise You, Jesus. I am going to believe that You are helping me. I will set my face like flint to serve You and to do Your will. I know that You will cause me to triumph because You will tread down my enemies."

❧

Father, I will not be dismayed, but I will encourage myself in You like David did. I set my face like flint to serve You in righteousness and in truth. Thank You that You always cause me to triumph!

A Crooked Arrow Misses the Target

> *They turned back from entering the Promised Land and disobeyed as their fathers had. Like a crooked arrow, they missed the target of God's will.*
>
> —Psalm 78:57

Maybe you once knew God, but like the Israelites in the wilderness, you've been sidetracked and turned back. Maybe something came along in your life to distract you. Maybe you haven't been as appreciative of God as you could have been or you haven't always been obedient and, like a crooked arrow, you're missing the center of God's will.

It's time to line up, turn our hearts toward heaven and home, and get right in the center of God's will for these last days.

And these are the last days. The signs of the times demonstrate exactly the events foretold in Scripture. We need to be our best for Jesus in these times of increased wickedness, love of self and money, disobedience and ungratefulness, troublemaking, lying, betrayal, pride, immorality, and more (see 2 Timothy 3:1-5).

Keep listening and believing in godly teaching. Remember, the Bible was inspired by God to teach us the truth and to help us do what is right.

Stay on course, keep your arrow headed straight toward the target—abundant life on earth and eternal life in heaven. God's good plan includes you!

Father, I commit to following Your path for my life today. I want my life to be like a straight arrow headed for the bull's-eye, in the center of Your will. I will obey Your Word and enter the Promised Land of abundant and eternal life. I will not miss the target of walking in Your perfect will.

Listen to God's Voice Today

But now is the time. Never forget the warning, "Today if you hear God's voice speaking to you, do not harden your hearts against him, as the people of Israel did when they rebelled against him in the desert."

—Hebrews 3:15

Have you ever taken God for granted? It really isn't that hard to do. You get caught up in the busyness of life these days and, first thing you know, you miss church one Sunday "just to rest," and then next Sunday the lawn needs mowing because it rained all week...and on and on it goes.

For example, the story of a family who admitted that they had "put God on the back burner"...until tragedy struck.

It came "out of the blue," so to speak, as most tragedies do. The husband suffered a cardiac arrest on a parking lot. Paramedics worked with him and brought him back to life, but they said he would have brain damage.

The family rallied around God in their time of crisis, and today this man's brain is not damaged. In fact, he's perfectly well. He's in church every week and faithfully serves God.

Sometimes we think we don't need God right now. We think we can wait until later in life. But you never know how long "later" will be or how much time you have.

Don't wait until tragedy strikes. Serve Jesus now and for the rest of your life— then if tragedy comes, you'll be ready for it. Meditate on and speak God's Word every day, and act on what God tells you to do as you listen to His voice.

❀

Father, I confess that Jesus is Lord of my life. I refuse thoughts that tempt me to harden my heart against You. I won't wait until tragedy strikes to seek You, and I will never take You for granted. I will obey You when You speak to me.

God's Grace Is With You

But whatever I am now it is all because God poured out such kindness and grace upon me—and not without results: for I have worked harder than all the other apostles, yet actually I wasn't doing it, but God working in me, to bless me.

—1 Corinthians 15:10

*S*ometimes we think that everything depends entirely upon us and what we can do. But that only results in frustration and disappointment. In this powerful scripture, the apostle Paul confessed to the Corinthian church that though he considered himself the least among them because he had persecuted the church, he had nothing to be ashamed of. Still, he would never boast in himself.

If he had considered his past, Paul would have been very discouraged and ashamed. But he knew all about God's grace and was able to say, "By the grace of God, I am what I am!"

Grace is the foundation of the Christian life. The Old Testament mentions the word *grace* forty times and one hundred fifty times in the New Testament. *Grace* means "undeserved favor."

God has given every man and woman the power to choose. God gave Adam a free choice in the garden, but when Adam made the wrong choice, God's great love began to act on behalf of all mankind.

Accept God's gift of grace. Stop working for God's (and man's) approval, and receive grace. When your situation seems impossible, if you will believe, you will see the grace of God manifested for you!

❦

Thank You, Father, for pouring out Your grace and kindness upon my life. Although I don't deserve Your favor, You give it to me anyway. Thank You for loving and accepting me just as I am.

Humility Brings Rewards

True humility and respect for the Lord lead a man to riches, honor and long life.

—Proverbs 22:4

*G*od greatly rewards those who live lives of humility. Humility is not a weakness. It is a total dependence on God's ability, coupled with a total lack of confidence in our own ability without Him.

Walking in the spirit of humility is a very important attitude that all Christians should practice. Many people are used of God for a short time, but the key to continual usefulness is humility.

It is not so difficult to be humble when you realize that all blessings come from God. All that we are and all that we have is a result of God's grace in our lives. We are continually aware of the fact that all the good that is done through us is the result of the work of the Holy Spirit.

We should always hold one another in high esteem because God has a special work for each of us. Pride destroys the flow of God in our lives. God resists the proud but gives grace to the humble.

I need all the grace I can get. Christ is our sufficiency—the source of life for you and me. And humility is the key to being used by God to be a blessing to others. Humility is *not* a weakness—it's a strength!

❧

Father, Your Word says that true humility and respect for the Lord lead a man to riches, honor, and long life. Therefore I reject pride and arrogance in my life today and humble myself before You at Your throne of grace. Help me to serve and bless others in Your name.

Kings of Life Because of Jesus Christ

The sin of this one man, Adam, caused death to be king over all, but all who will take God's gift of forgiveness and acquittal are kings of life because of this one man, Jesus Christ.

—Romans 5:17

The apostle Paul's letter to the Romans said that death reigned in life through Adam's offense, but those who have received the abundance of grace and the gift of righteousness are to reign in life through Jesus Christ.

God says we are to reign in the midst of trials, tribulations, the uncertainties that come with our jobs and raising a family, problems that are hurled at us, and even tragedies. We are to live above the circumstances—never under them!

When we don't see anything good happening, God says, "You'll see it!"

When we don't think we can make it, God says, "You are going to make it!"

When we don't understand what's going on, God says, "You will understand soon."

You can reign victoriously over the greatest of hardships. God has good things to say to you and about you. Start agreeing with what He says and begin to enjoy life!

❀

Thank You, Father, for helping me to reign over every trial and tribulation through Your gracious gift of righteousness. Because of Jesus' loving sacrifice, death no longer reigns in my life. I not only am forgiven, but You have also declared me not guilty. Therefore, I hold my head high and walk as a king in this life!

God Just Wants our True Thanks

No, I don't need your sacrifices of flesh and blood. What I want from you is your true thanks; I want your promises fulfilled. I want you to trust me in your times of trouble, so I can rescue you, and you can give me glory.

—Psalm 50:13-15

Since Jesus came, we have a new covenant. We no longer have to bring blood sacrifices to the temple as they did in Old Testament times. But even in this Old Testament Psalm, God tells us that He desires a real relationship with us. He wants to fulfill His covenant to us as we express our heartfelt thanks to Him and as we trust Him totally to rescue us in times of trouble. Then we will give Him honor and glory forever!

Aren't you grateful when you suddenly find a solution to your problem? Don't you just overflow with thanksgiving when you begin to feel better after being sick or in pain? To whom do you express your heartfelt thanks? It ought to be to Jesus, for He paid the price long ago for your total health and well being with His own blood.

Offer your true thanks to God today for His demonstrations of goodness to you. Keep your line of communication open to Him, and watch Him rescue you in times of trouble!

Jesus, I bring You thanks today for fulfilling Your many promises in my life. Thank You for rescuing me in times of trouble. Your healing and protection are demonstrations of Your goodness in my life. Thank You for always watching over me. I give You glory!

Delight Yourself in the Lord

Be delighted with the Lord. Then he will give you all your heart's desires.

—Psalm 37:4

*D*on't pay attention to people who try to discourage you. There are always those who criticize God's people and try to cause trouble. But we are told to be kind and good to others because one day the wicked will fade like grass and disappear.

King David was criticized by his own wife for dancing with joy before the Lord. Second Samuel 6:14-20 tells the story. It says she *despised* David because he so freely displayed his joy.

Despite the criticism your joy and delight in the Lord may attract from others, keep it up. We are to rejoice evermore according to 1 Thessalonians 5:16. Be happy when you speak with the Lord—enjoy your time with Him. Don't make your prayer life a ritual—sometimes just praise Him, other times you may want to talk about your work. Still other times, you may want to just fellowship with the Lord while driving in your car.

No matter what happens, God's children ought to be glad in the Lord. We have eternal life—we're on our way to heaven where there is no sighing, crying, or dying...where there's no death, pain, or sorrow. So we have every reason to delight ourselves in the Lord.

Keep the blessed hope ever before you. Delight yourself in the Lord and He will give you the desires of your heart!

I delight myself in You, oh Lord, and I praise You for Your mercy that blesses my life. I will not pay attention to those who criticize and try to discourage me. My joy and delight are in You. I enjoy my daily fellowship with You, and I thank You for giving me my heart's desires.

Our Responsibility to Jesus

Jesus traveled all through Galilee teaching in the Jewish synagogues,
everywhere preaching the Good News about the Kingdom of Heaven....
Enormous crowds followed him wherever he went....

—Matthew 4:23,25

*W*e have a responsibility to follow Jesus wherever He leads us. We are not to make up our mind as to what we want to do and where we want to go. Our main duty in life is to follow the Lord's leadings.

Why? Because God knows every obstacle and every blessing on the pathway He has planned for us. He knows ahead of time which paths are going to lead to trouble and which ones will keep us on the course He's already laid out for us.

Although we are living in a world filled with trouble, stress, and chaos, it is important for us to stay in touch with God. We must be diligent in seeking Him and following His direction for our lives.

When God calls us to a particular part of the world, we must be obedient. If we don't obey, it's not God's fault when troubles come instead of blessings.

Years ago, my husband was ministering in the Philippine Islands, when the Lord sent him back to Lakewood Church in Houston. He wasn't excited about coming back, but had he said, "No, I am not going," we would have been in a mess. Being obedient has brought many years of great blessing and harvest.

We followed where God led and were greatly blessed—and when you do that, He will pour out so many blessings on you that you literally will not be able to contain them.

Jesus, I am willing to follow You no matter where You lead me. I know I can
trust You to help me stay on the best pathway for my life. You know how to bless
me and take care of me, so I say, "Not my will, but Yours be done."

Jesus Never Changes

For I am the Lord, I change not....
—Malachi 3:6 KJV

This scripture reminds me of Hebrews 13:8, which says, *Jesus Christ is the same yesterday, today, and forever.* Do you believe that Jesus has never changed? Actually, whether you believe it or not, it's true. He will never fail you—He cannot. It isn't in Him to fail you or anyone. Some folks think He's changed just because He's not here on earth having to deal with the day-to-day issues that we face.

He doesn't have to be on earth to help us deal with those issues. The Bible says He has not changed, and that's all there is to it. He's still the same, and He loves you with an everlasting love.

Whatever your need today, just take a moment right now and say, "Jesus, I know you haven't changed. And I need Your help." Ask for His help with your specific problem, and you will see that He will come through for you because He loves you and cares for you like no one else can.

❦

Lord Jesus, Your Word says that You do not change. You are always the same. You will never fail. You love me with an everlasting love and You always will. I know that when I call upon You, You will answer me and help me.

What Do You Want from God?

When Jesus came to the place where they were he stopped in the road and called, "What do you want me to do for you?" "Sir," they said, "we want to see!" Jesus was moved with pity for them and touched their eyes. And instantly they could see, and followed him.
—Matthew 20:32-34

*T*hese verses clearly show that Jesus is approachable. We have been given the right to call out to Him when we need help. Jesus is just as interested in what's going on in our lives as He was with these two blind men sitting along the roadside. The crowd told them to be quiet—not to bother Him—but Jesus stopped when He saw them because He was moved with compassion for them.

People may tell you not to bother Jesus with your problems. They may even say Jesus can't or won't help you. That's when your faith needs to rise up big on the inside. Calling out to God is the only sure way to receive what you need from Him. Confess with your mouth, "I know God can help me. Jesus asked the blind men what they wanted from Him, and if He was interested in them, He'll be interested in me."

When you ask according to God's will, He will grant that request because He has compassion for you. According to Psalm 136, His lovingkindness continues forever.

Jesus healed the eyes of the blind men, and they became His followers. When God does something for you, don't turn the other way, but follow Him. And He'll grant you the desires of your heart.

Jesus, I thank You for coming to the place where I am right now. Thank You for Your compassion for me. I praise You, Lord, for touching me in the area of my need. I will follow You all the days of my life.

Choosing Life—One Day At A Time

The Steps of a Good Man

The steps of good men are directed by the Lord. He delights in each step they take. If they fall it isn't fatal, for the Lord holds them with his hand.

—Psalm 37:23,24

*D*o you consider yourself a good man or woman? If so, do you realize that the God of the universe directs every step you take? This is good news!

Sadly, many people don't see themselves as good. They can't imagine that God would spend any time thinking of them—let alone, ordering their every step. They've believed the lies of the devil instead of the truth of God's Word. It doesn't matter to God how bad you think you are. He still sees your potential.

When you acknowledge that you're a sinner and receive Jesus into your heart, you are changed from a sinner to a child of God in an instant. You can walk right out of darkness into the light of God's unending love when Jesus becomes your Lord and Savior.

It is great to be a child of God whose steps are directed by the Lord. You even start feeling better about yourself—immediately. See yourself as God sees you, and when your work on earth is finished, He'll welcome you to your mansion in heaven. When God directs your steps, you're being prepared for glorious things!

My Father, Your Word says that the steps of a good person are ordered by You. Just as earthly fathers delight in their toddler's first steps and are there to help them if they fall, I know that You will pick me up and strengthen me if I fall along the way—so I will walk with You today and let You hold my hand.

Jesus Is the Answer to Your Problem

"Take care to live in me, and let me live in you. For a branch can't produce fruit when severed from the vine. Nor can you be fruitful apart from me."

—John 15:4

A young lady visited our church who had been on crack cocaine since she was twelve years old. For fifteen years, she was at her rope's end. She'd been a street person and a prostitute. She didn't know anything about God. Although her life was nearly at its end, her craving for drugs did not diminish.

We laid hands on her and prayed. She screamed, "The devil's been putting me through hell, but I can feel the demons coming out of me!" That night she was saved, filled with the Holy Ghost, spoke in tongues, and was set free from the prison of her sinful lifestyle. Her desire for crack cocaine disappeared. Her little eight-year-old daughter also was saved that night in Children's Church.

A short time later, the woman said, "God has become my life. I literally live and breathe the Lord Jesus! Studies show that crack cocaine eats up your brain cells at a rapid pace, but I've started working at a good job, and I'm excelling!"

Her brain cells were not dead because God had restored them. She got a promotion with a raise! Her life has totally changed because she is careful to draw her strength from the Vine. Now she says, "I'm a living, breathing witness that the Lord Jesus Christ is, in fact, very real."

He turned this non-believer into a living miracle—and He'll do it for you too. He truly is the answer to every problem you'll ever have.

❧

Jesus, I can't live without You. Live big in me and deliver me out of the hand of my enemy, the devil. I consecrate my life to You so I can bear good fruit for Your Kingdom.

Choosing Life—One Day At A Time

God's Words Light My Path

Thy word is a lamp unto my feet, and a light unto my path.
—Psalm 119:105 KJV

*T*he Living Bible translation of this familiar psalm says, *Your words are a flashlight to light the path ahead of me, and keep me from stumbling.* I like that. It made me think about the flashlight I bought one year when a hurricane was predicted. It's the kind you keep charged up by plugging it into an electrical socket, and I keep it in the garage.

The man I purchased it from told me, "It will run for twelve to fifteen hours after being charged." His statement instantly reminded me of the Word of God. When you stay "plugged in" (getting charged up) and let the Word light your way, it will keep you going on the straight path.

But if you stop reading the Word and forget God's promises, your light will grow dim, and then it will go out. You'll lose your way, and you may stumble and fall.

Keep your "battery" charged up by setting aside time every day to read the Word of God. Let it keep you going for the twelve to fifteen hours that you have to be up and doing things, meeting with people, dealing with children, etc., and then recharge at the end of your busy day. Keep your light shining, and you'll be much less likely to trip or fall.

Thank You, Father, for the light of Your Word. As I charge my spirit today with Your Truth, show me any areas along my path that are dark and could cause me to fall. Thank You, Lord, that Your Word is a lamp to my feet and a light to my pathway. I know I will not stumble as I stay plugged into Your promises.

The House of God

... *"God lives here!"* [Jacob] *exclaimed in terror. "I've stumbled into his home! This is the awesome entrance to heaven!" The next morning he ... set his stone headrest upright as a memorial pillar.... He named the place Bethel ("House of God")....*

—Genesis 28:16-19

*W*hy did Jacob call that particular place the house of God? What constitutes a house of God? My husband once preached a great sermon on this subject. He said these were the characteristics of a genuine house of God:

1. It is a place where people can dream big dreams.

2. It is a place where heaven becomes real—this world is not all there is. In heaven there will be no pain, sorrow, tears, broken hearts, or death.

3. It is a place where sinners are welcome—a place where crippled, suffering, crying, dying, and hurting humanity can find healing.

4. It is a place that reaches out to the community, the nation, and the world, welcoming every man, woman, boy, and girl.

5. It is a place where God's voice is heard. Jacob called that special place "the house of God" because God spoke to him there!

6. It's a place where God reveals himself as a giver, a rewarder, and a good God to suffering humanity.

7. It is where major decisions are made.

Get involved in your local church and invite others to join you. Share the house of God with everyone!

Lord, I love Your house. It is a place of refuge for sinners and the brokenhearted—a place where all can listen to Your voice and respond to Your loving call.

Keep Your Confidence in God

> *"In the past you have told many a troubled soul to trust in God and have encouraged those who are weak or falling, or lie crushed upon the ground or are tempted to despair. But now, when trouble strikes, you faint and are broken. At such a time as this should not trust in God still be your confidence? Shouldn't you believe that God will care for those who are good?"*
>
> —Job 4:3-6

These verses speak of Eliphaz's exhortation to Job, who was seriously ill. Job had lost his family and everything else he ever held dear. Eliphaz reminded Job of the many times he had encouraged a troubled soul to trust in God. Eliphaz went on to remind Job that even when trouble was striking, his trust in God should still be his confidence.

This is how John and I felt when I was diagnosed with cancer many years ago. We had always preached that Jesus still heals today and assured people that our confidence was in Him. At that time, I really needed confidence in God more than ever.

In 1981, the Lord Jesus touched me and healed me. He made me whole.

My confidence is still in Him...and it always will be. I say to you today, no matter what's happened to you or come against you, maintain your confidence in God, and you will come through victoriously!

❧

My confidence is in You, Lord. When trouble strikes and I am tempted to despair, I will remember that You care for me.

Run to Jesus for Help

Then others began coming—those who were in any kind of trouble, such as being in debt, or merely discontented—until David was the leader of about four hundred men.

Run 2 God in hope t help

—1 Samuel 22:2

*D*avid ran and hid in a cave when he realized that Saul was trying to kill him. All of his brothers, family members, and others who were in any kind of trouble heard about him being there. That's why they began coming to where David was. Run 2 God in hope t help

All of us need to run to someone for help from time to time. Who can you go to for help today, unless you go to the Lord Jesus? David was, to Old Testament believers, a type and shadow of Jesus, who was yet to come. The people who were in trouble ran to David for help because the Messiah hadn't yet appeared on the scene.

Have you ever been in trouble? Have you been in debt? Have you been discontented or distressed? If you're in any of those conditions, you can run to the Lord Jesus because He's there for you.

He'll hide you under the shadow of His big wings and you'll be safe! Run to Jesus if you need help—He is the hope of the world, and He is there for you.

❦

Father, I run to you for refuge from the troubles of life. I lift up those who are in trouble and don't realize that You're standing by, just waiting to help them. Help me to lead others who are troubled to You. You are a very present help in time of trouble. mg

Only a Shepherd Boy

"...Men judge by outward appearance, but I look at a man's thoughts and intentions."

—1 Samuel 16:7

*J*esus has the power to transform your life. It doesn't matter to Him what's happened to you, whether you've been a gambler, a prostitute, a businessperson who cheated on his taxes, or if you think you've lived on "the wrong side of the tracks," have no education, or struggle to make ends meet.

When David was chosen to be Israel's king, even his own brothers said, "He's only a shepherd boy!" But God looked at him and said, "He's a king."

Let me tell you about a precious couple that attends our church. The husband was a hopeless alcoholic at one time. He was homeless and freezing to death one night in New York when he found a little shed. He climbed into that shed and said, "God, if You'll just spare my life, I'll serve You." Suddenly a big, shaggy dog came in that shed and laid down on him and saved his life!

Now he goes everywhere preaching the Good News about Jesus. He's a mighty preacher of the Gospel of the Lord Jesus Christ. People may have looked at him and thought, "Just look at that good-for-nothing beggar over there...." But God saw a preacher, and He sent a big, shaggy dog to make sure that man would live to keep his promise!

The Great Shepherd sees in you far more than you could ever imagine. Talk with Him today—you might discover exactly who you were meant to be!

❧

I thank You, Lord, that You don't judge me by my outward appearance, but You see my heart. You know my inner thoughts and motives...that I want to be my best for You. Show me Your desire and make me what You want me to be. You are my Great Shepherd, and I trust You to lead and guide me in fulfilling Your plan for my life.

My Heart Trusts in God

The LORD is my strength and my shield; my heart trusted in him, and I am helped: therefore my heart greatly rejoiceth; and with my song will I praise him.

—Psalm 28:7 KJV

*W*e serve a good God who is loving, kind, and always interested in His children and their needs. My heart truly trusts in God, and my heart rejoices because my trust is in Him. With all the things that come against us in today's world, if I didn't trust in God as my strength and shield, my heart could not rejoice.

But I have hope. You and I, as the children of the most holy God, have hope that if we have given our hearts to Jesus, we can fully trust Him and He will help us and take care of us. We don't have to be troubled in our hearts, but we will sing to Him with songs of praise.

Father, I thank You for being my strength and my shield. I praise You because Your love for me makes it easy to trust and rejoice in You.

Hold God's Victorious Right Hand

Fear not, for I am with you. Do not be dismayed. I am your God. I will strengthen you; I will help you; I will uphold you with my victorious right hand.

—Isaiah 41:10

This scripture is very helpful to us in these times in which we live— when there's so much going on and fear is so prevalent. God's right hand is victorious—and if we as His children are holding on to Him, then our right hand will be victorious also. We will be victorious because we are children of the Most High God.

Isaiah 27:5 (KJV) says, *...let him take hold of my strength....* I held on to this scripture many times during my battle with cancer. When I felt especially weak, I would reach up and say, "God, I take hold of Your strength now." By taking hold of His victorious hand, I also became victorious.

I'm glad that we're victorious through Jesus.

❧

Father, I'm so thankful that when I'm holding on to Your victorious right hand, I don't have to be dismayed or fearful, but I can draw from Your strength and be victorious too. Help me to always hold Your hand and let You help me.

He'll Bring You Safely into the Harbor

They reel and stagger like drunkards and are at their wit's end. Then they cry to the Lord in their trouble, and he saves them. He calms the storm and stills the waves. What a blessing is that stillness as he brings them safely into harbor!

—Psalm 107:27-30

Sailors who sail the seven seas—the trade routes of the world—sometimes encounter tremendous storms. They see huge waves and their ships are tossed to and fro until sometimes it seems as though they will sink. Sometimes sailors reach their wit's end and even cringe in terror.

Have you ever cringed in terror and felt like you were at your wit's end? I too have experienced that feeling. When somebody tells you that you have only a few weeks to live, you cringe in terror. In a stormy trial, you try to be strong, but you reel and stagger. You feel like the world has come to an end, just like sailors do at the peak of a raging storm.

But the Bible says when they cried to the Lord in their trouble, He saved them, calmed the storm, stilled the waves, and brought them safely into harbor. He also brought the stillness of His peace to them as He brought them into the place of safety.

He will do the same for you. Cry out to God in your storm, and let Him bring you safely into harbor.

You are my safety in times of trouble, O God. When I cry out to You for help in the storms of life, I know You will guide me to safety and calm my every fear.

Hold on to Your Confession of Faith

...for there is no question that he will do what he says.
—Hebrews 10:23

If you have a promise from God, hold fast to it. Don't give up on it. Hold on to your confession of faith like you would grasp whatever you could find to keep you from drowning.

Your mind may waver, but when you have faith in your heart, that doesn't matter. Your heart knows that God will keep His Word.

When your mind tells you that God's Word is not true or that it's not going to come to pass in your life, just say, "No! My heart knows the truth. I will hold fast the confession of my faith. I *will* not waver because He is faithful that promised and His promise will come to pass."

Father, how I praise You that I can trust You and know You are faithful to fulfill Your promises to me. I have no doubt that You will do what You say.

A Wise Person Thinks about Life and Death

...you are going to die and it is a good thing to think about it while there is still time...Yes, a wise man thinks much of death, while the fool thinks only of having a good time now.
—Ecclesiastes 7:2,4

Death may seem like a morbid subject to discuss, but the fact is that all of us are going to die someday. We are not going to live forever on this earth. That is why it is so important to think about death now and make plans for where we will spend eternity. For those who have accepted Jesus Christ as their personal Lord and Savior, death will be a joyous event because it ushers Christians into heaven, where they will live forever with Him.

Getting saved is really the best kind of insurance we could ever have, because we'll be the beneficiary!

If you are a Christian, you understand the peace of that assurance. But you may have loved ones and friends who don't have that assurance. Prayerfully ask God to provide an opportunity for you to witness to them. Then encourage them to think about where they will spend eternity, and guide them in making a wise decision that will give them eternal life!

❧

O God, thank You for salvation and the assurance that we can spend eternity with You in heaven. There we will be forever in Your presence. Help me to lead others to You so they too can be assured of a home in heaven.

Quenching the Fire of Hell Forever

The next day John seeth Jesus coming unto him, and saith,
Behold the Lamb of God, which taketh away the sin of the world.
—John 1:29 KJV

I've always been intrigued by people who fight fires for a living. There are two very well-known fire-fighting firms located here in Houston where we live. They receive calls from all over the world to help fight fires, and they're usually successful. In fact, I believe they hold a record for their innovative fire-fighting abilities and success.

But, do you know what? They can't put out the fire of hell because it can never be quenched. Their ability and wonderful methods are no match for that fire.

That place of eternal torment can only be avoided by accepting Jesus, the Lamb of God that takes away the sin of the world. Oh, what a Savior! If you haven't accepted Him and His wonderful gift, I encourage you to do so. Today is the day of salvation. If you are a Christian, I encourage you to pray for those around you who haven't yet accepted the gift of eternal life. As Jude 23 says in the Amplified Bible, *[Strive to] save others, snatching [them] out of [the] fire....*

Father, how thankful I am for Your plan of salvation. How grateful I am that because of the sacrifice of the Lamb of God, I can escape the eternal fire of hell. Thank You, Jesus, for giving Your life to take away my sins. Help me to snatch others out of the fire of hell and bring them into the joys of heaven.

The Devil Steals, Kills, and Destroys—Not God!

"The thief's purpose is to steal, kill and destroy. My purpose is to give life in all its fullness."

—John 10:10

I will never forget the couple whose child had died. Neither of them had been saved, and they both had a real spirit of grief on them. The wife requested prayer for their salvation.

While listening to my husband preach on the spirit of grief, they suddenly realized that God hadn't killed their baby. It was the devil that had come against them to steal, kill, and destroy. When they recognized the truth, they were set free!

When you are under attack or you experience a tragedy, always remember that it is not God who kills, steals, and destroys. Trust God and know that He only desires good for you. Act as though His Word is true. His Word says that it is the purpose of the devil to steal, kill, and destroy you and your family, but it is God's purpose to give you abundance in every area of your life!

It takes supernatural faith and strength to press through when the devil has stolen something from you, but if you act as though God told you the truth, your broken heart will be healed, your stolen goods will be restored, and you will rise from your sickbed and be whole. The abundant life of God is for you!

❦

I thank You, God, that Your plans for me are always good. Your good plans for my life do not include the plans Satan has for me—to steal my goods, to kill me, and to bring destruction to my life. Your purpose is to give me life in all its fullness. I praise You for giving me an abundant life!

The Spiritual World is Real

By faith—by believing God—we know that the world and the stars—in fact, all things—were made at God's command; and that they were all made from things that can't be seen.

—Hebrews 11:3

There are two worlds out there besides this one where we live. There is the wonderful, beautiful realm of spiritual reality where God reigns and Jesus and the angels live, and there is also a spiritual realm where Satan and his demons have their activities.

These two worlds are not just in our imaginations—they are real. Actually, the spirit world is more real than the physical world, because God, who is a Spirit, created the material world out of the spiritual realm.

As we walk through this life, one or the other of the two worlds constantly influences us. Satan and his forces set out to hinder us, while God and His angels are there to help us. The Lord is always there when the devil tries to discourage you, attack you, and tempt you to sin.

Don't give in to the temptations of the devil. Even when you're tempted to give in to sickness and disease, don't do it! Jesus was tempted in all points of His life, but He never once yielded to it. So follow His example!

Find out what the Word of God says about your situation...read the Word, meditate on the Word, and begin to speak God's Word. Then, just as the angels ministered to Jesus, they will come and minister to you and the devil will flee!

❧

My Father, how wonderful it is to know that everything I can see, touch, taste, or feel was spoken into existence by Your Word. Thank You for giving me Your Spirit to help me understand this natural realm and the unseen supernatural realm where You live.

The "Haunted" House

...For this purpose the Son of God was manifested, that he might destroy the works of the devil.

—1 John 3:8 KJV

*M*y husband liked to tell a story about a big, old, spooky, two-story house that he, his brother, Jack, and their friends thought was haunted. One late fall evening, Jack and John were sitting on a curb across the street from that big, old, empty house. Jack was about ten years old, and John was eight. Both were fearful, but John was growing more frightened by the minute.

Suddenly Jack just stood up and said, "I'm going in there." It was getting dark, and John remembered thinking, "I'll never see my big brother again."

Some other boys soon joined John on the curb, and they waited together while Jack investigated the "haunted" house all by himself. Pretty soon Jack showed up on the upper-story balcony and shouted down, "It's all right, fellas. I've been through this old house and there's nothing in here that can hurt us!"

That's how Jesus is when we're frightened about something. Isaiah 40:4 says He goes before us and makes crooked places straight. To me, this means He checks things out for us and lets us know if and when it's safe to proceed.

Many people fear death and dying. But Jesus marched down into the jaws of hell itself and wrestled with the principalities and powers of darkness for three days and nights. And on the third day, He came out! His cry to you and me is, "There is nothing in death to hurt you if you'll make Me your Lord and Savior!"

There is nothing to fear from anything or anyone when Jesus is your Lord!

❧

Thank You, Jesus, for delivering me from all fear. You have destroyed the works of the devil, and every fear is a lie of the enemy. Thank You for going before me and making every rough place smooth.

Rescued from Darkness

For he has rescued us out of the darkness and gloom of Satan's kingdom and brought us into the kingdom of his dear Son, who bought our freedom with his blood and forgave us all our sins.

—Colossians 1:13,14

*S*adly, many people are in bondage to the devil in these days. They literally live in the gloom of Satan's power. They long to be free, but they haven't heard the Good News. That dark kingdom spoken of in Colossians is filled with fear, torment, depression, poverty, misery, sickness, defeat—everything that hurts and destroys. But God has delivered us out of that kingdom of darkness and brought us into Jesus' kingdom. It is filled with love, joy, peace, patience, kindness, goodness, gentleness, faithfulness, and self-control—the glorious fruit of the Holy Spirit!

What a joy to tell people they don't have to remain in the devil's prison. They don't have to stay under the influence of drugs. They don't have to be prostitutes, gamblers, liars, and cheaters. They don't have to stay in that filthy life they've lived.

If you—or someone you know—are living in Satan's bondage, tell them they can be free because Satan has been defeated!

When God made a New Covenant with believers, He said, "Everything that's mine is yours! I will give you all that I have! You are my heirs and joint-heirs with my Son, Jesus Christ!" Hallelujah! We have been rescued from darkness!

❧

Thank You, my Father, for delivering me from the darkness and gloom of Satan's bondage into the freedom and kingdom of Your dear Son. Send someone across my path today that I can share Your good news with to help them out of the devil's prison. In Jesus' name. Amen.

Defeating Satan with the Word

They defeated him by the blood of the Lamb, and by their testimony; for they did not love their lives but laid them down for him.

—Revelation 12:11

We have often asked our congregation at Lakewood Church to repeat these words, "I'll overcome by the Word of God." Why?

People have a lot to deal with in these times—everywhere you look there is some kind of challenge, trouble, confusion, miscommunication, distrust—just general uneasiness. This is why it is so important for us to know and speak God's Word over every situation we face.

We can defeat the devil—the author of all dis-ease—with the Word of God.

When we started Lakewood Church, it was in a converted feedstore building that seated 234 people, and it was never full. That little church was going nowhere until we learned how to speak and confess the Word of God. Once the Word got down into our hearts, Lakewood Church began to grow, and now we're reaching the whole world with the Gospel!

We live in a world where the devil, demons, and darkness are all about us. We must get the Word of God in our hearts and learn to wield it as a sword against Satan.

Then the Word will overcome all oppression and dis-ease.

❦

Lord, I determine today that I will not be defeated, but I will defeat the devil and demons with the sword of Your Spirit. I put Your Word in my mouth, and I overcome all the oppression and dis-ease the enemy tries to bring against me through the blood of Jesus, who died for me and gave me His victory. I am more than a conqueror through Jesus. Amen!

Notorious Sinners Came to Hear Jesus

Dishonest tax collectors and other notorious sinners often came to listen to Jesus' sermons; but this caused complaints from the Jewish religious leaders and the experts on Jewish law because he was associating with such despicable people—even eating with them!

—Luke 15:1,2

*T*he dictionary defines *notorious* as someone "widely known and usually unfavorably." I like knowing that Jesus stood beside the fallen and lifted them up, took the failures and encouraged them, washed the guilty, helped all those in need, and loved even the notorious sinners! His kind and gentle heart drew them to Him.

But the religious people of the day—the Pharisees and Sadducees—stood around murmuring and complaining about Jesus inviting sinners to be with Him.

The greatest indictment against churches and Christians would be not inviting fellowship with sinners. I'm so proud of our church. We don't care who you are, we love you. We invite alcoholics and drug addicts, harlots and pimps, gamblers and drunkards. Everyone is welcome in the presence of Jesus.

Jesus went to great lengths to make sure they were comfortable in His presence. Should we do any less?

As you go out in the world this week, go out of your way to let sinners know they have a friend in Jesus.

Lord Jesus, show me opportunities to share the good news of Your love for the whole world. Help me to follow Your example of sharing Your great kindness to sinners.

Three Years That Shook the World

And a voice from heaven said, "This is my beloved Son, and I am wonderfully pleased with him."

—Matthew 3:17

One day the little virgin that Isaiah prophesied about conceived by the Holy Ghost and brought forth the child she called Jesus.

This was important to the world. We don't hear much more about Jesus until He was 30 years old, when He appeared at the Jordan River and presented himself to his cousin, John, for water baptism.

At that critical moment in time, the Spirit of God came down upon Jesus like a dove, and a voice from heaven said, *This is my beloved Son, in whom I am well pleased* (Matthew 3:17 KJV). There began three years that shook the world. And God's still shaking things up!

Jesus was merciful and kind...and went about healing the sick and driving out demons. Many people loved Him as He labored to help them.

Other people hated Jesus and conspired to destroy Him—but He couldn't be destroyed. His resurrection tells us who He really was and is.

I thank God every day for continuing to shake the world until I found Him at age thirteen and invited Him into my heart. I'm not claiming that I have arrived—but, thank God, I'm not what I used to be.

Allow the Spirit of the living God to shake things up in you until everything about you that is unlike Him has fallen away. Rejoice that you have a friend in Jesus—and what a friend He is!

Thank You, Jesus, for shaking me into repentance on the day I received You. I ask You today to continue shaking me through the conviction of Your Spirit of everything that is not like You. Purify me and help me to always please You.

Plead Guilty

If we claim we have not sinned, we are lying and calling God a liar, for he says we have sinned.

—1 John 1:10

*S*omeone once asked a preacher, "Why are you people always so happy, and our group is always so sad?"

The preacher said, "Well, I will tell you. We just plead guilty, and you people always plead your case."

That preacher was right. If you've done wrong, just say, "Father, I am guilty. Your Word says, 'If I confess my sins, You are faithful and just to forgive my sins, and to cleanse me from all unrighteousness.' I agree with that scripture. I have confessed my sins, and You have kept Your end of the bargain. Therefore I am cleansed from all unrighteousness."

No matter what you've done, if you have confessed it, you are now cleansed by the blood of Jesus from all unrighteousness.

Don't bother with pleading your case before God. He knows whether you are guilty or not anyway. If you're guilty, just say so, accept His forgiveness, and move on!

Look in the Bible at 1 John 1:9 and confess, "Your Word says it, and I agree with You—I am forgiven!"

Father, I plead guilty as charged of any sin in my life today, and I thank You for Your Word that says I am forgiven. I stop making excuses and receive Your gift of righteousness. Thank You not just for forgiving me but also for cleansing me by Your precious blood.

Plead Your Case

> *I, yes, I alone am he who blots away your sins for my own sake and will never think of them again. Oh, remind me of this promise of forgiveness, for we must talk about your sins. Plead your case for my forgiving you.*
>
> —Isaiah 43:25,26

Someone who is always conscious of his old sinful nature and is not conscious of his new righteous nature in Jesus Christ really doesn't believe in his heart that he's been forgiven. That person feels paralyzing condemnation and has no assurance that his sins have been blotted out and that God never thinks of them again.

Have you ever felt that way? Then I have a question for you. If God isn't thinking about your old sinful nature, why are you?

If you don't feel "free" from your past sins, plead your case before the throne of grace. His grace is sufficient for you—regardless of what you've done.

Until you are free from feeling unrighteous and you believe that you've been made righteous in God, you will be paralyzed in your ability to minister to people in need—which is the call of God on each of our lives.

Don't allow the devil to keep you ignorant of the truth of your righteousness through Jesus Christ. Plead your case with God. Realize that you are totally without condemnation! Jesus dearly loves you and paid a high price for your freedom!

❦

Father, I thank You for blotting away my sins and never thinking of them again. I plead my case before Your throne of grace, believing in my heart that I am forgiven. Help me to share this Good News with others that they are forgiven too.

Jesus Cleans out Your Closet

But how can I ever know what sins are lurking in my heart?
Cleanse me from these hidden faults.

—Psalm 19:12

Expect a miracle

*E*verybody has skeletons in their closets. This is a figure of speech we use to describe unpleasant things in our past that we're ashamed of and hope nobody ever discovers about us. But when Jesus comes into your heart, things change.

He cleans out the skeletons in your closet. He replaces fear with confidence. He throws out despair and replaces it with hope.

Jesus is the Good Shepherd. He'll fill your life with love, joy, peace, power, prosperity, and victory! You see, once you confess your sins to Jesus and ask Him to wash them away, He does, and you're free. You no longer care who finds out about your past because you've rolled all of your cares over on Jesus. They're His cares now—not yours!

If it's been a while since you had a heart-to-heart talk with Jesus, do it today. Tell Him all your troubles. He hears the voice of His children. He will clean up everything in your life and make you brand new again.

Remember, you are strong in the Lord and in the power of His might!

Thank You, Father, for blessing me with Your presence and loving conviction. I know that when I repented of my sin, You made me a new creation in Christ. Today I ask You to search my heart and show me if there is any sin I am overlooking in my life. Convict me of any hidden faults and cleanse me through the power of Your blood.

Peace Will Guard Your Mind

*...His [God's] peace will keep your thoughts and your hearts
quiet and at rest as you trust in Christ Jesus.*

—Philippians 4:7

The mind is the devil's battleground. His only entrance into your personality, your body, your thinking, and your emotions is through your mind. So understand that you must guard your mind. You don't have to accept every thought that pops into your head.

Whatever you gaze at, meditate on, or gravitate toward in your mind will draw you. Allowing wrong thoughts into your mind causes so many problems—jealousy, suspicion, envy, hatred, lust—even divorce and murder begin with a thought.

We watch terrible things on television and get a visual thought started. But television and Hollywood don't reflect real life. Television has changed America's thinking—depreciating our moral standards. You have to fight against the things that defile your mind.

Recognize that those disturbing thoughts are not your own, and say, "Devil, get out of here. I refuse to think those thoughts!" Recognize the enemy for who he is. Say, "Greater is He that is in me than he that is in the world. I am more than a conqueror through Christ who loves me and lives in me. He is able to do exceedingly, abundantly above all that I can ask or think. Glory be to God!"

❧

*Father, I refuse to allow the devil's lies and thoughts to dominate my mind.
Your peace will keep my thoughts, and my heart will be quiet and at rest because
my trust is in You. I choose to think Your thoughts today.*

Jesus: Preparing Your Place

In my Father's house are many mansions: if it were not so,
I would have told you... I go [to] prepare a place for you....
—John 14:2 KJV

Several years ago, a little preacher came through Houston from Florida. He was up in his eighties, and John invited him to testify at our morning services. This precious man just got up and said, "I'm on my way to heaven, and I just came through Houston to ask you to go with me!"

Our congregation—always open to a move of the Holy Spirit—went wild with applause. We started singing, "Come and go with me to my Father's house."

Have you thought much about our Father's house? We have some exclusive areas in Houston, with what we call "mansions." But compared to the mansions our Father is preparing for us we haven't seen anything yet! He didn't say there are many little condos, apartments, and houses. He said, "In my Father's house are many mansions! If it weren't so, I'd have told you!"

What a shame it would be for anyone to miss all that God has prepared for us. This is why evangelizing the world is so important to our family and church. We don't want anybody to miss out! We want everyone to shout for joy on the hillsides of glory.

God is there now—preparing our mansions. And I think everybody ought to know...and go!

❦

Father, thank You for sending Jesus to shed His blood for my sins, giving me eternal life, and for resurrecting Him to prepare my place of glory with You in heaven. I look forward to living with You there, Father, and I'll be bold in asking others to go with me!

A Prayer for Marriages

*There are three things that remain—faith, hope, and love—
and the greatest of these is love.*

—1 Corinthians 13:13

Faith, hope, and love are so important in the marriage relationship. God can restore love, trust and security in your marriage. It is never beyond repair—if you both work at it.

I know Jesus is interested in your marriage.

❦

Father, in the name of the Lord Jesus Christ, I pray that You will touch this husband and this wife. Mend any hurts in their hearts and restore the love they had for one another at the beginning, making it stronger than ever before.

Help them be merciful and forgiving toward one another, preferring their mates' desires above their own. I rebuke you, Satan, and I command you in the name of Jesus Christ to take your hands off this couple and this family. I believe that any healing that needs to take place in their home begins now, in Jesus' name. Amen.

The Devil Is a Liar

"...[The devil] was a murderer from the beginning and a hater of truth—there is not an iota of truth in him. When he lies, he is perfectly normal; for he is the father of liars."

—John 8:44

*M*arriage was meant to have life, and life more abundantly. Now, the devil may tell you that your marriage is dead, but God can give it life. The devil doesn't even know how to tell the truth, so it's important for you to know that you cannot believe his lies—ever!

If God can take two million Israelites through the wilderness for forty years, providing them clothes and shoes that didn't wear out and food that rained down from heaven, He knows how to work a miracle in your marriage.

The devil often tells couples that their marriage is over. We need to know that Jesus comes through for us in every crisis if we'll let Him. He never takes His eyes off of us, and He'll come through for you!

In Jesus there is love, joy, peace, and happiness. When it seems that all hope is gone, and no one has a positive word for your situation, stand your ground! Call the devil the liar that he is and claim your victory in Christ Jesus! Jesus is truly a Healer, and He can restore your marriage.

❧

Father, thank You for reminding me in Your Word that it is the devil who has told me lies that my marriage won't work. I rebuke you, Satan, in the name of Jesus and bind your lies in my life and marriage. You are a liar, and the father of lies, but Jesus is the Healer and Restorer of my marriage. I reject your lies and command you to flee NOW! Thank You, Jesus, that Your Word is truth!

There Is Hope for Your Marriage!

"Listen to me! You can pray for anything, and if you believe, you have it; it's yours!"

—Mark 11:24

There is hope for Christian marriages even when the devil is coming in like a flood to destroy them. God is raising up people in the body of Christ who are taking a stand, saying, "No, devil, you can't have my mate! You can't have my children! As for me and my house, we will serve the Lord!"

We know God can restore and bring marriages back to life. We know that nothing is too difficult for God. No situation is hopeless. We have seen marriages restored when only one of the partners faithfully stood on God's Word, trusting Him to deliver their mate.

God loves you. He doesn't want you to live in brokenness and rejection, and divorce is not God's best. He wants everyone to have a beautiful marriage—especially Christians. He has a wonderful plan for your life, and it includes happiness with your spouse!

God's plan involves changing each one of us into a totally new person. That means your husband or your wife can be made brand new by the miracle-working power of the living God! He changes people's lives every day—and He can turn your relationship into something straight from heaven!

❧

God, I know that nothing is too difficult for You. Our situation is not hopeless. Our hearts are in Your hands. Show us how to have a happy and fulfilled marriage. I believe that we are receiving Your miracle-working power now in Jesus' name.

Wisdom for Your Marriage

If you want to know what God wants you to do, ask him, and he will gladly tell you, for he is always ready to give a bountiful supply of wisdom to all who ask him....

—James 1:5

*P*eople who face a marriage crisis need wisdom for their particular situation. This scripture in James 1 says to ask God who gives you a bountiful supply of wisdom. He will show you why there is turmoil in the marriage, as well as how to change the situation.

God knows all about you. Psalm 139:1-4 says, *O Lord, you...know everything about me. You know when I sit or stand. When far away you know my every thought. You chart the path ahead of me, and tell me where to stop and rest. Every moment, you know where I am. You know what I am going to say before I even say it.*

God knows what it will take to bring His very best to your marriage. He knows how to turn your situation around—whatever it is. You and your mate may or may not be ready to split, but God will always bring something good into your marriage when you put Him in the center of it.

He created marriage, and He knows how to make it work. He can restore the love you had for one another at the beginning and make it stronger than ever. Listen and learn divine wisdom from the Healer of marriages!

My Father, thank You for the bountiful supply of wisdom that You freely give all those who ask. I ask You today to reveal Your wisdom for my marriage and to show me and my spouse what we need to do to change our relationship and make it better. Open Your Word to us and speak to our hearts. In Jesus' name I pray.

Do What You Can Do

Stop being mean, bad-tempered and angry. Quarreling, harsh words, and dislike of others should have no place in your lives. Instead, be kind to each other, tenderhearted, forgiving one another, just as God has forgiven you because you belong to Christ.

—Ephesians 4:31,32

The Lord expects us to do what we can do. He expects us to do the possible, and He'll take care of what looks impossible in our marriages.

You may ask, "But what can I do?" You can forgive. You can go the extra mile. You can get up and write a letter, make a phone call, admit that you were wrong, confess your sins, and release anger and bitterness from your heart.

You can overcome evil with good as Romans 12:21 instructs you to do. You can ask God to show you how to be a better husband or wife. You can pray and intercede for your mate until you see him or her delivered.

If you'll do what you can do, Jesus will do what you can't do. If you'll do the natural, Jesus will do the supernatural!

God wants to restore marriages and return what the devil has stolen and destroyed. Remember, God forgave you, so you can forgive others—your mate, your child, or whoever has hurt you. Now is the time for healing to come to your home and family!

❧

Father, I commit myself today to always forgive my mate and to admit when I am wrong. I am willing to walk any extra mile my marriage may require to stay strong and healthy. I will not quarrel or be bad tempered, but will be tender-hearted and kind. I will not let the sun go down on my wrath and will not let a root of bitterness or resentment take hold of my heart, because Jesus lives in me.

Love Never Fails

Let the husband render to his wife the affection due her, and likewise also the wife to her husband.

—1 Corinthians 7:3

*W*hen we got married, I couldn't cook at all. John used to say, "Dodie couldn't boil water!" He would go to a restaurant and eat before he came home to eat my food! But he loved me—and it's the love that counts.

As husbands and wives, we need to always demonstrate our love for each other—even in our sexual relationship. Sexual intimacy should never be used as a tool to punish our mates for supposed wrongs. God commands us to be happily joined together, and He wants us to be lovers because love never fails.

You and I have the potential and ability to love like God loves. Romans 5:5 says that God has poured out His love in our hearts by the Holy Spirit.

Nobody has to lose their mate or their home if they will take the time to seek God's face. Put God first even though the devil will do everything in his power to keep you from seeking God. God can do the impossible, and the devil is no match for Him. If you need a healing touch in your marriage, read God's Word, fellowship daily with Him in prayer, and allow His love to flow through you to your spouse. Love never fails!

❦

Father, Your love has been shed abroad in my heart by the Holy Spirit. I do love my mate, and I will show it by giving of myself in the marriage relationship. Your love never fails, and I'm glad You teach me to love as You love!

Enjoy Your Marriage

You wives, submit yourselves to your husbands, for that is what the Lord has planned for you. And you husbands must be loving and kind to your wives and not bitter against them, nor harsh.
—Colossians 3:18,19

These verses in Paul's letter to the Colossians are similar to his message on marriage to the Ephesian church where he addresses the subject more fully (see Ephesians 5,6). He instructs us to honor Christ by submitting to one another. He exhorts husbands to love and be in charge of their wives in the same way Christ is in charge of the church, remembering that Christ sacrificed His very life for us!

He admonishes wives to submit to their husbands' leadership in the same way we submit to the Lord. He says a wife must deeply respect her husband—obeying, praising, and honoring him.

I feel sorry for people who aren't happily married. If you're reading this exhortation today and you're not happy with your marriage, you can change the atmosphere if both of you are willing to work on it and follow Paul's instructions.

If you think you're the only one who's working at your marriage, pray and ask God to cause your spouse to be willing to work on it too.

When you both put God first in everything you do and spend time trying to make each other happy, you will have a blessed life.

❦

Jesus, I honor my spouse today as a gift straight from Your throne. You have commanded us to love one another and submit to one another. Therefore, I repent today for any unkind words or ungrateful actions I have shown toward my spouse lately and for taking my spouse for granted. I will put You in the center of our marriage relationship and spend time making my spouse happy.

God's Word Works

He replied, "Yes, but even more blessed are all who hear the Word of God and put it into practice."

—Luke 11:28

It is important for you to ~~know~~ understand that the Word of God works. If you have a need in your life, just remember that God's Word is forever settled in heaven and He is as close as the very breath you breathe.

When you hide the Word of God in your heart and put it into practice every day, you will see such a difference in your life. God's Word is alive—it is the sword of the Spirit. Spoken out of our mouths, it will defeat the devil!

In the Old Testament, the Lord commanded Joshua to be strong and courageous! Reading and putting into practice the Word of God will make you strong and courageous. It will pierce the darkness around you with the light and life of almighty God. By speaking the Word of God, you will defeat the devil for yourself!

Practice God's Word in your life, and see what the Lord will do!

❦

I know Your Word works, Father. I will not only be a hearer of the Word, but I will put it into practice by speaking it out of my mouth. Your Word is alive and forever settled in heaven and will defeat the devil every time.

Be Instructed in the Word of God

> *Philip ran over and heard what he was reading and asked, "Do you understand it?" "Of course not!" the man replied. "How can I when there is no one to instruct me?" And he begged Philip to come up into the chariot and sit with him.*
>
> —Acts 8:30,31

*T*his story of the Ethiopian eunuch reading the book of Isaiah touches my heart. *The Holy Spirit said to Philip, "Go over and walk along beside the chariot"* (v. 29). This man was in need of a teacher or preacher to guide him into understanding what he was reading. He was putting forth the effort to read Isaiah, but he couldn't understand it without a teacher to explain.

Do you see what these verses are saying? We can read and try to understand God's Word, but we're all in need of good teachers and preachers.

If you're not already, I encourage you to become involved in a local, Bible-believing and Bible-teaching church where you can be instructed in the Word of God. Watch Christian television and expose yourself to the leadership of a good teacher and preacher.

Understanding will come as you submit yourself to biblical, godly instruction. God's Word is packed with life-changing wisdom that you can apply to every situation!

❧

Lord God, I want to understand the Bible as I read it. Thank You for sending teachers and preachers to instruct me and help me understand Your Word. I know I will receive life-changing wisdom as I receive their instruction.

Let God's Word Sink into Your Heart

*So also is my Word. I send it out and it always produces fruit. It
shall accomplish all I want it to, and prosper everywhere I send it.*
—Isaiah 55:11

The Word of God has given me great delight over the years. I read the
Word, meditate on it, confess it before the Lord, and really let it sink down into
my spirit. Then I lift up my voice and make my confessions several times each day.
It has been helpful to me to confess the Word out loud so I could speak it out
with assurance.

Such strength comes from saying, "Father, I come before You today with Your
Word in my heart and upon my lips. I refuse to say that I am weak and defeated
or that I have trouble and sorrow. I will not say that I cannot do the things I have
to do. I will say what the Word of God says. It says I can do all things through
Christ who gives me strength and power (see Philippians 4:13)."

You can create an atmosphere in which you live by the thoughts you
entertain for constant meditation. Begin to fill your mind, mouth, heart, home,
and surroundings with marvelous, loving thoughts of God about health, victory,
peace, prosperity, and all the other things you desire in life. Base these thoughts
on definite promises of God. Think them...talk them...act on them!

❧

*Father, I believe Your Word accomplishes all that You want it to—Your Word
always produces fruit. I confess the things that Your Word says about me. Speaking
Your Word brings good health, victory, peace, and prosperity in my life. Thank You,
Father, for Your Word.*

He Sent His Word to Heal

He sent His word and healed them, and delivered them from their destructions.

—Psalm 107:20 NKJV

*Ps 138:2
7, 8*

When I was fighting cancer, I knew how important it was to know the Word and to act on it for health and healing. If it had not been for the Word of God—knowing that God's Word works, that God would never lie, and that He keeps His promises—I would not be alive today. God sent His Word, and I was healed.

But when our daughter Lisa was born with brain damage similar to cerebral palsy, my husband and I knew very little about healing. John was the pastor of a traditional church that didn't teach about healing. Lack of knowledge could have destroyed us (see Hosea 4:6), but somehow we knew that God's Word was true.

We started by reading the four Gospels—Matthew, Mark, Luke, and John—where it tells about the miraculous healings Jesus performed. Then we read Hebrews 13:8, where it says Jesus is the same yesterday, today and forever. We prayed and asked God to touch and heal our baby girl.

Jesus did just that. He sent His Word and healed Lisa. She is a perfectly normal adult now—strong in the Lord and in the power of His might.

My family has reaped the benefits of learning that God desires for everybody to be well. And He sent His Word to make sure we would know it.

He is no respecter of persons—He'll do the same for you just because He wants to.

Thank You, Lord, for sending Your Word to heal us. You never change—Your Word always brings us healing. I'm glad my family and I are delivered from the destructions the enemy has planned for us. I believe that You heal and deliver us daily.

All of God's Promises Come True

Every good thing the Lord had promised them came true.
—Joshua 21:45

*N*early every Sunday morning just before the message is given, Joel leads our church in this confession: "This is my Bible. I am what it says I am. I have what it says I have. I can do what it says I can do. Today I will be taught the Word of God. I boldly confess my mind is alert. My heart is receptive. I will never be the same. I am about to receive the incorruptible, indestructible, ever-living seed of the Word of God. I will never be the same. Never, Never, Never I'll never be the same. In Jesus' name."

Just as they did for Joshua and the children of Israel, all of God's promises come true when we confess His Word and stand on its promises. Every time our congregation makes that confession together, they're affirming to themselves and to those around them that they are becoming the powerhouse Christians God wants all of us to be.

The devil can't stand it when you know who you are in Christ Jesus! When you refuse to lie down and just absorb every fiery dart the devil sends your way, he gets upset and discouraged. Hallelujah!

If you struggle with believing that God's promises are true and apply to you, try a little experiment for just a week. Act as though they were written just for you. You'll be blessed by the results!

Lord God, every good thing in my life has come from You. I'm glad Your Word tells me who I am, what I have, and what I can do as Your child. Your promises always come true.

Test God's Promises

I have thoroughly tested your promises, and that is why I love them so much.

—Psalm 119:140

The 119th Psalm is wonderful. It is especially good in the Living Bible. It is so easy to understand. It talks about God's laws and how they're all right. If we obey them, then we won't get ourselves in a mess.

I have thoroughly tested God's promises, and most of our congregation at Lakewood Church has thoroughly tested God's promises also. That's why we love them so much. I'll just tell you that God's promises will work in your life.

Look up and meditate on the promises in God's Word—hold on to them, and they will come to pass, in Jesus' name.

Father, I have not tested all of Your promises, but if they work for others, they will work for me too. I thank You for all the promises set forth in Your Word, and I'll start claiming them daily for my life.

Let the Word Penetrate Your Heart

God's Word [handwritten]

> *Listen, son of mine, to what I say. Listen carefully. Keep these thoughts ever in mind; let them penetrate deep within your heart, for they will mean real life for you, and radiant health.*
>
> —Proverbs 4:20-22

Do you see that part in these verses about storing away the Word of God in your thoughts and deep in your heart? It will mean real life and radiant health for you! Hallelujah!

When you're sick, you don't have a real life—you don't feel like doing anything. You're certainly not walking in radiant health. When I was fighting cancer many years ago, I let God's Word penetrate my heart. I "took" forty healing scriptures every day like medicine. I let absolutely nothing keep me from confessing those scriptures over my body. *& mine & into* [handwritten] *heal* [handwritten]

I do it to this very day! And I can truly say that I enjoy radiant health—not just health, but radiant health! I have a real life again. God gave me back my life when Jesus touched my cancer-stricken body. *Jesus is - Word* [handwritten]

Now I pray for the sick and love doing it. I believe they will recover. I'm so happy and fulfilled in my calling. You will be too as you let the Word of God actually penetrate your heart. *, minds, bodies, our beings Amen!* [handwritten]

❀

Father, thank You for giving me life and radiant health as I allow Your thoughts *words,* [handwritten] *to penetrate my heart.* *our bodies* [handwritten] *How I praise You for the truth of Your Word. I will continue to store Your words in my heart and mind and take them as preventive medicine daily.*

Take Delight in God

Praise the Lord! For all who fear God and trust in him are blessed beyond expression. Yes, happy is the man who delights in doing his commands.

—Psalm 112:1

*D*o you realize that you can take delight in God even when you get tired and weary? Even when I'm feeling worn out, I have often walked around my house saying, "I take delight in You, Lord. It is delightful to do what You command."

Every time I do that, it's just like He takes hold of my hand. As I reach up to God and praise Him, it is just as though He reaches down, takes hold of my hand, and says, "Look, Dodie, I am always here for you. I love your expressions of praise and thanksgiving. Don't be afraid of anything. I'm here to help you. I know you get tired, but I'll see you through."

I say that to you today—God will see you through whatever is troubling you today. Just lift up your hands and say, "Jesus, I take delight in You."

❧

Lord Jesus, I praise You. I take delight in You. I delight in doing Your commands. I am happy to revere and trust You because in You I am blessed beyond expression!

He's a Great God!

Great is the LORD, and greatly to be praised....
—Psalm 48:1 KJV

*G*od's greatness is unsearchable. Who can fathom the greatness of God? His name is to be continually praised. He's a great God. He's a mighty God. He's a loving God—filled with kindness and tender mercy.

Sometimes we just need to stop and tell Him how much we love and adore Him and thank Him for who He is and all that He's done for us.

Praise is an important part of a successful Christian life. If you're not accustomed to praising God, you may find it easier to do if you get into the Psalms of David. David is known as a psalmist.

For example, in Psalm 33:1-3, David praises: *Let all the joys of the godly well up in praise to the Lord, for it is right to praise him. Play joyous melodies of praise upon the lyre and on the harp. Compose new songs of praise to him, accompanied skillfully on the harp; sing joyfully.*

God's Word, which is always right, says it is an appropriate thing to do. If you are musically inclined, you may want to sing some of the psalms aloud or play an instrument in praise of the goodness of God. You may just want to play music on the radio or CD.

No matter how many troubles you've had or how serious they've been, you have to admit that God has done something good in your life. Let Him know how much you appreciate Him.

God, You are great and I praise You greatly. I praise You for who You are and for all You've done for me. Every good thing in my life has come from You. I just want to tell You how much I love and adore You. You are filled with kindness and tender mercy. Your greatness is truly unsearchable!

Thank God for Answered Prayer

Don't be weary in prayer; keep at it; watch for God's answers and remember to be thankful when they come.

—Colossians 4:2

*M*any times when we receive the answer to prayers we've prayed for a period of time, we forget to give God praise and thank Him for it. I've done that on so many occasions. I think back on it sometimes, and I'm reminded that He really came through for me in a certain situation and I failed to thank Him for His answer.

Do you remember the story of the ten lepers who were healed? Only one cleansed leper came back to express his gratitude to Jesus. How sad!

I believe Jesus delights in answering the prayers of His children, but He also likes for us to thank Him when He does something for us.

Let your heart soar today with thanksgiving to God for all He has done for you. And develop a habit of thanksgiving unto God for all the good things that He's done and will do in the future. Let your thanksgiving be a sweet, sweet sound in God's ear...beginning now!

❧

Help me, Lord, not to become weary in prayer. Help me to pray until I see Your answer come. You have already answered many of my prayers, and I stop to give You thanks right now for Your goodness and Your faithfulness.

As Long as You Have Breath, Praise the Lord

Let every thing that hath breath praise the Lord. Praise ye the Lord.

—Psalm 150:6 KJV

If you're breathing, you ought to be praising the Lord. It's that simple. God has given us so much to be thankful for. Every day He loads us with His benefits. They are listed specifically in Psalm 103:1-17:

1. He forgives all your sins.
2. He heals you.
3. He ransoms you from hell.
4. He surrounds you with lovingkindness and tender mercies.
5. He fills your life with good things, so your youth is renewed like the eagle's.
6. He gives justice to all who are treated unfairly.
7. He reveals His will and nature to you.
8. He is merciful and tender toward you.
9. He is slow to get angry and full of kindness and love.
10. He has removed your sins as far away as the east is from the west.
11. He is a like a tender and sympathetic father to those who reverence Him.
12. His lovingkindness is from everlasting to everlasting.

If you're not used to praising God, just try it this week. I believe you'll have a better week than you've had for a long time.

❀

O God, I praise You! I will remember all the benefits that You daily unload in my life. Thank You for being a tender and sympathetic Father.

Grateful for God's Mercies

Yet there is one ray of hope: his compassion never ends. It is only the Lord's mercies that have kept us from complete destruction. Great is his faithfulness; his lovingkindness begins afresh each day.

—Lamentations 3:21-23

*J*ohn and I walked together with the Lord for most of our lives, and I can tell you that God blessed us richly every day we enjoyed together! When we fell, He lifted us up. When we sinned, He had mercy on us. When we were wrong, He forgave us. When we were weak, He strengthened us. When we lacked faith, He restored our hope.

He walked beside me when John went home to be with Jesus for eternity, and He has never left me. He has never forsaken me. Glory be to God!

I often think of the Good Shepherd's mercies toward His flock. Yes, we fail God from time to time, but God never fails to welcome us back into His fold. I am so grateful for God's mercy—thankful that He rescues us out of the hands of the enemy every time we ask Him to.

What a joy to be given the responsibility of sharing the message that Jesus loves everyone and that our calling on His name will bring eternal life! Oh, how I praise the name of Jesus!

I exhort you to take a moment to ponder God's mercies toward you and your family. I believe you'll find that He has been faithful to you, as He has been to us. Then express your gratitude to God for His mercies that are new this morning. You'll feel good, and God will be happy to hear from you.

Thank You, Lord, that Your compassion never ends. It is Your mercy and lovingkindness that sustain us. Thank You for the family You have given me in this life. Great is Your faithfulness. Your mercies are new every morning.

Give Thanks and Bless His Name

Go through his open gates with great thanksgiving; enter his courts with praise. Give thanks to him and bless his name.
—Psalm 100:4

I believe it makes a difference when we pray with grateful hearts. The Bible tells us to come into God's house with thanksgiving on our lips—in an attitude of praise. We have much to be thankful for! First Timothy 2:1-6 tells us to pray for others, pleading for God's mercy upon them, and *giving thanks* for all He is going to do for them.

I bless the name of the Lord Jesus Christ with every fiber of my being. I rejoice in my salvation and my healing, and I am thankful for my family, our staff, and our church family at Lakewood—truly an Oasis of Love in a troubled world.

What are you thankful for? Do you demonstrate your gratitude to God on a daily basis? Think about what you would do if God decided to remove from your life all the things for which you haven't been thankful? Would you be in trouble? Most of us would be, because we often take our many blessings for granted.

During this season when our country sets aside time to reflect on our many blessings, remember some of the things the Lord has done for you. Look around and give honor and glory to Jesus. He's worthy of your praise.

❧

I give You thanks today, Lord, with a grateful heart for all Your lovingkindness and generosity to my family and our nation. Thank You for the salvation, healing, redemption, and abundance we enjoy. I praise You for all those today who are in authority in this land of freedom. Bless our nation with peace...and we bless You for it, Father, in Jesus' name.

Reverence the Lord

But the lovingkindness of the Lord is from everlasting to everlasting to those who reverence him....

—Psalm 103:17

*R*épeat after me. Say this aloud: Everlasting to everlasting. That's a pretty long time. The verse goes on to say, *...to those who reverence him.* Does that make you wonder? If things are not going well in your life, you might just ask yourself: *Am I reverencing God?* Check yourself out. Do you spend time worshipping the Lord? Do you devote your life to serving Him as best you can?

Reverential fear doesn't mean God is someone to be afraid of, but that He's a God that is worthy of great respect and devotion. You might discover if you start reverencing God—having a reverential fear of Him in your heart—that you will begin to be blessed with His lovingkindness from everlasting to everlasting, as promised in this psalm of David!

Spend time worshipping the Lord. Set aside time for just you and God to be together. Play some praise music in the background, and just begin to tell Him how important He really is to you. Revere who God is—not just what He can do for you. Your efforts to praise Him will be a sweet sound in His ear. And He'll reward your reverence of Him in ways you couldn't begin to imagine!

❧

Lord God, I worship You today. I reverence You and Your holy name. Thank You that Your lovingkindness is from everlasting to everlasting. You are great and greatly to be praised!

God Is Faithful

What is faith? It is the confident assurance that something we want is going to happen. It is the certainty that what we hope for is waiting for us, even though we cannot see it up ahead.

—Hebrews 11:1

*H*ebrews 11 is an especially good faith-building chapter in the Bible. Imagine God telling one-hundred-year-old Abraham and his wife Sarah that they would have a son at their age. You probably know the story—Sarah laughed. But Abraham believed that if God said it, He was well able to do anything He promised. Sarah later realized that God, who gave her His promise, would certainly do what He'd said.

Now all we have to do is take the promises of God and believe them. It's so simple. If God said it, you can believe it because He sure wouldn't lie to you. So let's judge Him faithful as Abraham and Sarah did.

He'll do great things for you when you judge Him faithful and believe that He won't go back on His Word.

❦

My Father, I judge You faithful. Thank You for Your faithfulness to me even when I have not been as faithful to You. I stand on Your promises for my life. I believe that Your Word is true, and I have confident assurance that all of Your precious promises belong to me and my family.

God Will Never Leave You in the Dark

...I will never leave thee, nor forsake thee.
—Hebrews 13:5 KJV

We were enjoying an evening with all of the family, and our little granddaughter, Christiana, had joined her Aunt Lisa and me for a walk outdoors after dark. We had walked along with Christiana for a while, and had somehow gotten ahead of her.

Suddenly she said, so profoundly with her little voice, "Lisa, you wouldn't leave me, would you?" That touched me so much. I almost cried because I thought of how it relates to Jesus.

Sometimes it seems like God is so far away from us. Maybe we're a few steps behind, and it feels as though we've been left behind. If that ever happens to you, you need to do what Christiana did. Say, "Jesus, You wouldn't leave me, would You?"

The truth is, He never will. The Word of God says so. We can be certain God is always with us no matter how we feel.

❦

Thank You, Lord, for never leaving me behind. You always wait for me to catch up to where You are leading me so we can walk together through life.

Jesus Can Stop Your Storm

...So he spoke to the storm: "Quiet down," he said, and the wind and waves subsided and all was calm!

—Luke 8:24

*T*his story of the disciples who were in the boat with Jesus when the storm came up never fails to remind me of God's ability to settle all the storms of our lives. Jesus was in the back of the boat, sleeping peacefully when the wind began to rise. The Bible says that a fierce storm developed — not unlike the fierce storms that arise in our lives today.

The disciples grew very upset, thinking that Jesus didn't seem to be demonstrating any concern for them. So they awakened Him and screamed, *Master, Master, we are sinking!* Don't we do the same thing when we're faced with a crisis? We cry, "Where are You, God? Why aren't You doing something?"

Jesus asked the disciples, *"Where is your faith?"* (v. 25) And that's the same question He asks us today. Where is our faith when we get bent out of shape over issues we could easily transfer to Him if only we were willing?

I encourage you today that this same Jesus who calmed the stormy sea is still in charge of the rough waters you're facing. All you have to do is call upon Him, for He is a God of mercy, and He won't let you down.

❦

Jesus, I face stormy seas of problems from time to time, and I grow desperate for Your help. Climb into my boat during those times, Lord, and calm the storm raging around me that I might have Your peace.

God Gives You the Strength You Need

When I pray, you answer me, and encourage me by giving me the strength I need.

—Psalm 138:3

In today's fast-paced world, it is easy to feel overworked, tired, and even discouraged. Sometimes it seems that we can't keep up the pace. But when we feel weak, we need to go to God and draw from His supernatural strength. Second Corinthians 12:9 tells us that His strength is made perfect in weakness.

God likes to answer the prayers of His children, and His Word says that He will encourage you and give you the strength you need. So when you're tired, just pray. God will answer you and give you strength.

❦

Father, I am so glad that I can come to You when I am tired and weak, knowing that You are waiting to encourage me and give me Your strength. Thank You for loving me and providing just what I need...whenever I need it.

Jesus Is Willing

And behold, a leper came and worshiped Him, saying, "Lord,
if You are willing, You can make me clean." Then Jesus put out His
hand and touched him, saying, "I am willing; be cleansed." And
immediately his leprosy was cleansed.

—Matthew 8:2,3 NKJV

*J*esus had just finished teaching and preaching to a large gathering of people on a mountainside. A crowd had followed Him down the mountain because they were so amazed at His teaching—He spoke with such authority.

Along came a leper. Although he had been shunned and considered untouchable by the crowd, Jesus had amazed him. Something in Jesus' teaching had given this man hope. I think he saw the compassion of Jesus. He could tell that Jesus wasn't like other teachers. He took a chance that Jesus might notice Him in the crowd. He was sick and tired of being sick and tired. Have you ever felt like that? I have.

Jesus touched the leper, and immediately he was healed. His leprosy disappeared!

He is willing to touch you too. He is willing to do whatever it takes to restore you to health when you come to Him as this leper did. Jesus did not love this man any more than He loves you.

Whatever you need, Jesus is willing. Press through the "crowd" of problems and circumstances, reach out to Jesus, and receive His touch. Someone is going to be blessed today—it might as well be you.

❀

Thank You, Lord, that Matthew 8 settles the fact that You are willing to make me clean and whole in every area of my life. I ask You to reach out and touch me today. I praise You, Jesus, and thank You for doing it just because I ask.

God Is Faithful

Let Jesus Reveal Himself to You

"The one who obeys me is the one who loves me; and because he loves me, my Father will love him; and I will too, and I will reveal myself to him."

—John 14:21

This was Jesus talking. He said that He and the Father will love us when we are obedient. And Jesus will reveal himself to us!

Do you want Jesus to reveal himself to you? I do. I say, "Here I am, Jesus. Right here. Reveal yourself to me because I love You, and I love the Father." When we do this, then He will reveal himself to us.

Reveal means "to make known." God reveals or shows himself to us in a variety of ways. James 1:17 says, *But whatever is good and perfect comes to us from God, the Creator of all light, and he shines forever without change or shadow.*

God reveals himself every time something good happens to us. Isn't that good news? Every good thing that comes our way is something God uses to reveal how important we are to Him.

Be quick in obeying God. When He says to do something, don't ponder it for days or weeks or months or even years—just do it. When you do, He will reveal himself to you!

❈

Reveal Yourself to me, O God. I will not put off obeying Your commands because I want You to show yourself to me. I want to know You well because I desire to be like You. I love You, and I know You love me too.

The Seed Is the Word

"A farmer went out to his field to sow grain... The seed is God's message to men."

—Luke 8:5,11

𝒢od uses many illustrations to describe the importance of His Word. This parable from Luke 8 demonstrates how to get the Word to produce results.

Just as you can release the power of seeds by obeying the laws of God in the natural world, you can release the power of the Word of God by obeying the same laws in the spiritual realm.

Seeds carry life to reproduce themselves in miraculous ways. That's also true of the words in the Bible. Each promise has the life that God breathed into it! Jesus said, *...the words that I speak...are spirit...and life* (John 6:63 KJV).

God uses His Word as seed to produce a harvest. What do you want from God? If you want healing, look up healing seeds (scriptures that apply to healing)! If you want a miracle, sow some miracle seeds (scriptures that describe miracles)! If you need deliverance from fear, habits, or Satan's power, then get the appropriate seeds (find where it is written in the Word) and sow them in your heart.

Make a list of the verses that apply to your situation. Keep them in the midst of your heart.

These are the promises of God to you! My husband always said they are living seeds with divine potential. Put God's Word in your heart and nourish it daily with prayer and thanksgiving. God is faithful to make it grow, and your harvest will surely come.

❧

Father, I love Your Word. I can see its divine potential to change situations and circumstances in my life. Thank You for the seeds of Your Word. I will plant them in my heart and expect a glorious harvest!

We Have Received the Spirit of God

And God has actually given us his Spirit (not the world's spirit)
to tell us about the wonderful free gifts of grace and blessing that
God has given us.

—1 Corinthians 2:12

Although the Bible clearly states that we have not received the spirit of the world but the Spirit of God, many wonderful Christians still deny the work of the Holy Spirit. They demonstrate a lack of faith for healing and deliverance from demonic forces. They don't know how to use the wonderful name of Jesus, the power of His blood, and the truth of His Word.

God has freely given us the Holy Spirit so that we might know more about Him and His unending desire to bless us. I'll use my late husband as an example. He was a born-again Christian and Baptist minister for nineteen years before he was baptized in the Holy Ghost. And that was when John really began to understand who he was in Christ. John always said the revelation knowledge he received after his baptism in the Holy Ghost was a continual unfolding in the Lord Jesus.

The apostle Paul wrote to the Christians in Colosse that *in him* [Jesus] *lie hidden all the mighty, untapped treasures of wisdom and knowledge* (Colossians 2:3). You and I have many blessings in Christ Jesus! He has all the wisdom and knowledge we'll ever need, and He wants us to tap into it—so jump in today!

❧

Father, Your free gifts of grace and blessing are mine in Christ Jesus. I want to partake of the blessings of Your Holy Spirit. I desire for revelation knowledge to be poured out on me, so teach me from the treasures of wisdom and knowledge hidden in You.

Good Enough for God

So give yourselves humbly to God. Resist the devil and he will
flee from you. And when you draw close to God, God will draw
close to you. Wash your hands, you sinners, and let your hearts be
filled with God alone to make them pure and true to him.

—James 4:7,8

*A*s pastors, we often are asked questions relating to faith, healing, salvation, and many other subjects. I'll always remember a woman who asked, "How do I know that I'm good enough to use Jesus' name to make the devil flee? I love to hear you tell Satan to leave when you rebuke him and yell at him in Jesus' name. But, you see, sometimes I don't know that I'm a good person. I don't really think I am. So I'd like for you to tell me how to get the same boldness in my life that you have in yours."

That boldness comes from the assurance you receive once you've accepted Jesus as your Savior and realize that the devil no longer has a right to control any part of your life.

You can enjoy boldness like you've never known before when you are assured of who you are in Christ. You have power because Jesus lives in you!

❀

Father, I humbly give myself to You. I resist the devil, and he has no choice but
to flee from me. I draw close to You, Lord, so that You will draw close to me. Cause
my heart to always be pure and true to You.

Treat the Devil Like a Snake

> *The serpent was the craftiest of all the creatures the Lord God had made....*
>
> —Genesis 3:1

I lived in a townhouse that had a little courtyard area where I enjoyed gardening. One evening when I was watering my plants, I noticed that a snake had invaded my garden. I thought, *I have such a little place to begin with, and now a snake has come in here.* My husband got a shovel out of the garage and started poking around the bushes, but that snake would not come back out—it had simply disappeared.

I was instantly reminded of the devil because the Bible refers to him as a snake. I thought, *We've got authority in the name of Jesus, and I'm going to use it!* I said, "Snake, in the name of Jesus, come out!" And all of a sudden, that snake came out, and my husband killed it with the shovel.

So many times we let the devil just run over us. I could have let that snake stay in my garden, but then I wouldn't have enjoyed working there. I would have been uncomfortable knowing that a snake was there. So, in the name of Jesus, that snake came out.

I encourage you to use the authority that Jesus has given to us in His powerful name, and treat the devil like the snake he is.

Father, I thank You for Your power and the authority You have given to all believers. I will exercise my authority over the devil in the name of Jesus. I won't have him staying at my house!

You Don't Have to Wander in Darkness

"I have come as a Light to shine in this dark world, so that all who put their trust in me will no longer wander in darkness."

—John 12:46

*H*ave you ever seen someone wandering around the streets at night? They don't seem to have anything to do or know where to go. Praise God, we don't have to live like that. When we put our trust in Jesus, the Light of the world, then we no longer wander in darkness—naturally or spiritually.

The King James Version of the Bible says you won't "abide" in darkness. *Abide* means "to remain; to go on being; to stay; to dwell." No one wants to dwell in darkness, and you don't have to. When Jesus is Lord of your life, you'll no longer wander aimlessly through life, but you'll have purpose. You will know where you are going.

If you find yourself wandering through life without direction, try taking Jesus' pathway. Try reading His Word. Jesus and His Word will only do you good and never harm you. He'll set you on the path that leads to light and life everlasting!

❈

Jesus, You are the Light of the world, and I refuse to walk in darkness. I have no desire to wander through life purposeless and without direction. I choose to walk in Your path that gives me light and life.

Rebuke Sin Fearlessly and Be Blessed

...blessings shall be showered on those who rebuke sin fearlessly.
—Proverbs 24:25

This wonderful scripture promises that the blessings of the Lord will be showered on us—but there is an important condition or requirement. We must be determined to take a fearless stand against sin. The word *rebuke* means to "criticize or reprove sharply; to reprimand, to check, or repress."

Has the devil ever come against you and tempted you to sin? Or has a family member or friend ever suggested that you do something you knew was wrong? You are to fearlessly stand up to the devil or that person who is trying to get you to sin and say, "I rebuke that in Jesus' name. I will have nothing to do with that, and you shouldn't either."

After you refuse to sin, then do what God has told you to do. When you are obedient to Him, you'll be showered with blessings!

❧

O Lord, I take a fearless stand against sin because I want to be blessed. I turn my back on sin and rejoice in following You. Thank You for showering me with Your blessings.

Deliverance and Salvation Are Right Now!

For I am offering you my deliverance; not in the distant future, but right now! I am ready to save you....

—Isaiah 46:13

What kind of a God do you serve? Is He a good God? Is He a bad God? Let's talk about the true and living God!

The true and living God is a good God. Wherever you are today, God's not a God who wants to save or deliver you somewhere down the road…in the distant future. He wants you to begin enjoying the abundant life He died to provide for you—starting today!

Won't you open your heart and the eyes of your understanding and give heed to what God says? He gives You power to be saved and delivered.

❧

What a blessing to know, Lord, that You are a God of the now. I don't have to wait for You to deliver and save me somewhere down the road. You are a good God, and I thank You for giving me power to receive Your salvation and deliverance right now!

The Benefits of the Holy Spirit's Baptism

*And God has actually given us his Spirit (not the world's spirit)
to tell us about the wonderful free gifts of grace and blessing that God
has given us. ...The spiritual man has insight into everything....*
—1 Corinthians 2:12,15

Until we received the Holy Spirit, John and I weren't completely aware of the wonderful things God had given to us. We didn't know we had access to the spiritual gifts of wisdom, knowledge, faith, healing, miracles, prophecy, discerning of spirits, tongues, and interpretation of tongues (see 1 Corinthians 12:1-11).

Without the fullness of the Spirit, we would have continued to deny that these gifts are for us today. Jesus said when the fullness of the Spirit comes to us, He shows us His power to save, heal, perform miracles, and drive out devils.

Spirit-filled people talk, act, and preach differently about Jesus. The Holy Spirit has shown us the real Jesus as described in the Bible. We no longer see a traditional Jesus who has lost His power to save and deliver people. We see the One who is ...*the same yesterday, today, and forever* (Hebrews 13:8).

When we learned that Jesus had not lost His power or compassion, John couldn't keep from preaching about Jesus' healing and delivering power!

You too can experience God's endowment of power in your life.

❧

Lord Jesus, I want everything You have for me. Teach me to flow in the supernatural gifts of Your Spirit to reach hurting, suffering people with Your love and healing power. Thank You for giving me spiritual insight into everything You have planned for my life.

Thank God for Our Heritage

Thank God for his Son—his Gift too wonderful for words.
                                                                    —2 Corinthians 9:15

There really aren't adequate words to describe how wonderful Jesus is. God gave His Son so that we might have this wonderful gift—actually I believe the gift of Jesus is a heritage to us. The dictionary says one of the meanings of the word *heritage* is "the status gained by a person through birth."

Your heavenly Father loved you so much that He gave His only Son to be your brother—a brother too wonderful to describe, too wonderful for words. With Jesus as your brother, your station in life has been raised to the highest possible level.

He has left you a heritage for all eternity. I trust that you are claiming that heritage today.

❦

God, I thank You for the wonderful gift of Your Son Jesus. I claim my heritage today, and I am grateful to be part of Your family.

Have a Heart for Lost Souls

*Jesus told him, "This shows that salvation has come to this
home today. This man was one of the lost sons of Abraham, and I,
the Messiah, have come to search for and to save such souls as his."*
—Luke 19:9,10

A lonely businessman was sitting in a California hotel when he turned on the TV and watched our program. The message was about the need to find the roots of our Christian faith and the power the early Christians had, which seems to be missing from our lives today. Searching for the roots of our Christianity, the message said, would show us who we really are in Christ Jesus.

As the man thought about it, he realized this was true. And he was impressed that all we cared about was seeing people come to a relationship with the Lord. Before he went to bed, he thought about all the other businessmen sitting in hotel rooms, single parents, the lost, desperate, and lonely people of the world who were probably watching TV about the same time he was.

He thought about us preaching to an audience we would never meet and reaching souls we would never know about until we get to heaven. It blessed him to know that we weren't doing it for money, fame, or to be on the evening news.

He wrote to us and said, "I hope the next time you wonder about the impact and effectiveness of your ministry, you know that the lives of thousands of people are being changed for the better every week!"

Never forget that you can impact the life of another by caring and showing them the God you serve with your life. Develop a heart for lost souls and use your relationship with God to encourage someone today.

❧

My Father, use me today to lift up another. Help me to be a friend to someone who is lonely, a hand of hope to those whose hope is gone. Thank You for giving me opportunities to bless someone else today as You have blessed me.

Restoring the Fallen

I am amazed that you are turning away so soon from God who, in his love and mercy, invited you to share the eternal life he gives through Christ; you are already following a different "way to heaven," which really doesn't go to heaven at all.

—Galatians 1:6

*A*ll Christians make mistakes once in a while—we occasionally do things that displease the Lord. I believe most Christians are truly miserable and experience sadness in their hearts when they've failed God in some area, and they can't wait to confess it and repent. I know that is true for me.

Others are deceived into thinking they have no need to repent. Both scenarios result in separation from God until the sin is confessed and repented of.

God always forgives us when we ask Him to—that's His part. What, then, is our part when one of our Christian brothers or sisters is overtaken in a fault? The Bible clearly says that we who are spiritual are to restore our brothers and sisters with a spirit of meekness.

Not many people deliberately plan to just go out and sin. But the devil blinds people's minds sometimes, and suddenly they're presented with a temptation. If they fall into it, they soon find themselves out of fellowship with God.

It is not our part to point fingers and make judgments against others. We must restore the fallen with a kind and tender heart that forgives and forgets by following the example of Jesus, who forgives us when we repent of sin.

❦

Father, help me to forgive others today who are overtaken by temptation. Help me to gently encourage them to get back into fellowship with You by turning away from sin and embracing Your life again. You are a good God who forgives and restores all things.

Go and Tell

And the disciples went everywhere preaching, and the Lord
was with them and confirmed what they said by the miracles that
followed their messages.

—Mark 16:20

*I*f we Christians don't go out into the world and tell people about the love
and saving grace of Jesus, who will? Few Christians, however, seem to realize that
they need to participate in evangelizing the world. Why? Satan's primary attack is
in the mind. We think, *Oh, that's the preacher's job. I'm not a preacher!* Or we say
things like, "I'm just not called to be a witness. I'm a background person."

If Christians wait for others to do their job, Jesus' return will be delayed,
because He won't come back until everyone has heard the salvation message.

Second Corinthians 10:5 speaks about casting down strongholds and
imaginations. If we imagine that we can't do something, we won't do it. But
we have the mind of Christ! When we win the battle over our "I can't" thoughts,
we'll go out and tell the whole wide world that Jesus Christ is Lord!

There's a world out there just waiting to hear the Good News. Yes, they have
fallen short of the glory of God—there's no one on earth who hasn't! But it's up to
you and me to let them know that Jesus loves them and can wash away their sins.

Jesus will go with you and confirm what you tell others about Him with His
miracle-working power!

Jesus, I commit myself today to be Your witness and to share Your Good News
of salvation to this lost and dying world. I will be sensitive to any opportunity that
may present itself today on the job, while out shopping, or in my home to let others
know that You love them and will help them start a new life in You. Use me, and
stand with me to touch others with Your saving power.

Lowly Shepherds Heard the Good News

...shepherds were in the fields...guarding their flocks of sheep. Suddenly an angel appeared among them.... They were badly frightened, but the angel reassured them. "Don't be afraid!" he said. "I bring you the most joyful news ever announced, and it is for everyone! The Savior—yes, the Messiah, the Lord—has been born tonight in Bethlehem!"

—Luke 2:8-11

*W*hy do you suppose Jesus' birth announcement came to shepherds in a pasture? Perhaps they were more open to God's plan than the religious leaders of their day. History records that shepherds were not highly thought of by society's standards. Yet they were the first witnesses to Jesus' birth.

I read somewhere that shepherds might have been chosen because they represented all who needed cleansing. How fortunate those shepherds were to be included. They were a little frightened by the angel, but their fear soon turned into wonder.

"Come on! Let's go to Bethlehem! Let's see this wonderful thing that has happened, which the Lord has told us about" (v. 15).

Just as God brought the shepherds good news of the Savior's birth, so He reminds us of that same joyful announcement every year.

❧

Thank You, Father, for revealing Your joyful news to the humble hearts of lowly men. Your announcement to the shepherds and Your plan to bring Christ forth in a stable show me that You reach down to every person to lift them and bring them into Your presence. Help me reach out in love this Christmas to those who may need to be lifted and encouraged.

Joy to the World!

... "*I bring you the most joyful news ever announced, and it is for everyone! The Savior—yes, the Messiah, the Lord—has been born tonight in Bethlehem!*"

—Luke 2:10,11

*T*his is a special time of year. If you look at the lights and decorations on display throughout cities, towns, and villages, you'll recognize that this is no ordinary season—but the birthday celebration of the Savior of the world! Even the air itself is electric with expectancy!

I love the old Christmas carols. They represent a perfect application of the truth of our Savior's birth in poetic verse. George Handel wrote, "Joy to the world! The Lord is come: Let earth receive her King; let every heart prepare Him room, and heaven and nature sing...".

In other words, the heavens and the earth were urged to rejoice with singing at the announcement of Jesus' birth. It brought joy then, and His birth continues to bring joy now as our hearts make preparation to receive Him again.

Don't let this busy season get you so bogged down with hurry, worry, shopping, baking—and the exhaustion that comes with all of these things—that you fail to remember why we celebrate Christmas. Prepare room in your heart for Jesus.

Another verse of "Joy to the World!" says, "He came to make His blessings flow...". Take time this Christmas to enjoy the blessings Jesus came to give you and the entire world. And, as for you, bring joy to your world!

❧

Jesus, just as You brought joy into the world long ago, help me to bring joy to others in this generation. Your joy is for everyone!

Jesus Makes Room for You

*And she gave birth to her first child, a son. She wrapped him in
a blanket and laid him in a manger, because there was no room for
them in the village inn.*

—Luke 2:7

When Joseph and Mary arrived in Bethlehem to pay their taxes to Caesar,
there was no room open to them, but the birth of the newborn King soon drew
attention. Angels came to see Him. Shepherds came. And wise men came from
the East bearing gifts (see Matthew 2:1,2). Jesus had drawing power!

People from all around the little town of Bethlehem gathered at the stable to
see for themselves what the prophets of old had long foretold.

The world had no room for Jesus, but Jesus always makes room for everyone
in the world—rich or poor...red, yellow, black, brown, or white...saint or sinner.

Maybe you feel that no one has room for you this Christmas, or maybe you
know people who don't have a home and may feel left out at Christmastime. Why
don't you open your heart to someone less fortunate than you by helping them
find God's love during this special season? Jesus makes room for everyone.

*Thank Him, Jesus, for making room in Your heart and in heaven for me. I want
others to know that You love and care about them, too, this Christmas. Show me
someone who needs encouragement, and use me to help them find joy and peace
through Your love.*

God So Loved That He Gave

For God so loved the world, that he gave his only begotten Son, that whosoever believeth in him should not perish, but have everlasting life.

—John 3:16 KJV

This message that God loved the world so much that He gave us Jesus is really the Bible's message from Genesis to Revelation. It isn't easy for some people to believe that God loves them, but He does.

When God looked down from heaven on the human race, He didn't say, "They're rubbish!" He said, "They are a treasure! I'm going to give heaven's best for them. I am going to come in the person of My Son who shall be called Immanuel."

Immanuel means "God with us." God looked down on us and said, "They're wonderful. They are my potential sons and daughters. I'm going to go down and live with them. I'll feel what they feel, and do for them what they could never do for themselves. I'll provide the way out of their sin, sickness, heartache, and pain."

God thought you were valuable enough to send Jesus so that you might be saved. He loves you with an everlasting love. Give thanks to the Father for His unspeakable gift. You have been delivered from the power of darkness, and the same bright star that guided the wise men to Bethlehem now shines on you to show you the way, the truth, and the life.

Thank You, Father, for sending Your Son Jesus into the world to give us eternal life. Lord Jesus, thank You for leaving Your glorious place in heaven to take on human flesh to redeem my life from sin. Thank You that You delivered me from the power of darkness and gave me Your light so I would not walk in darkness. Use me this Christmas season to show others how You can give them eternal life too.

Let Us Adore Jesus

For unto us a Child is born; unto us a Son is given; and the government shall be upon his shoulder. These will be his royal titles: "Wonderful," "Counselor," "The Mighty God," "The Everlasting Father," "The Prince of Peace."

—Isaiah 9:6

Isaiah 9:6 is one of my favorite scriptures. Many Bible scholars call Isaiah the greatest of the Old Testament prophets. Isaiah predicted that a remnant would be spared even after Israel fell to their enemies because of disobedience.

Isaiah knew in his heart that God had a plan and that His work would continue. The confident prophet fearlessly charged that the political system of those times displayed a total lack of trust in God, but his advice was ignored. A study of the Old Testament reveals that Isaiah's prophecies were exactly right.

He said, *The people who walk in darkness shall see a great Light—a Light that will shine on all those who live in the land of the shadow of death. For Israel will again be great...for God will break the chains that bind his people...* (Isaiah 9:2-4).

We now know that Jesus was the "Light" Isaiah spoke of. He knew that, ultimately, the Savior would usher in a peaceful government that would never end. Jesus is the light of the world. We must not limit ourselves to celebrations of His birth at this season only. We should thank God every day for Jesus, our Savior.

In the words of the great Christmas hymn written by Frederick Oakeley, "O come, let us adore Him, Christ, the Lord."

❦

Thank You, Father, for giving Your Son as my Royal Lord. Jesus, today You are my Wonderful Counselor, Mighty God, Everlasting Father, and Prince of Peace. I adore You and worship You, and ask that You use me today as an ambassador of Your Kingdom to help set other captives free.

The Stairway of Heaven

"Glory to God in the highest...."
—Luke 2:14

*T*here is a story that says on the first Christmas, God came down the stairway of heaven with a baby in His arms. I sometimes wonder if it was God's plan to send His Son in the form of an infant because babies are just so irresistible.

I love being a mother and a grandmother. There is something so special about bringing life into the world. When our first daughter was born, the doctors said she had something similar to cerebral palsy.

This is when we discovered that sickness was of the devil. I loved the Bible, but suddenly I was disinterested in what Jesus did for babies in the Bible—I wanted to know what He would do for *my* baby!

John and I learned that God had not afflicted our baby. We met Jesus, the Healer. Jesus said, *For I came down from heaven, not to do mine own will, but the will of him that sent me* (John 6:38 KJV). We learned to confess health and healing over our baby daughter. We saw no immediate changes, but we told everyone that God had healed her. The Word declares that we are healed and we are. She was completely healed and is a vital part of the ministry of Lakewood Church.

I believe God descended the stairway of heaven to bring me that beautiful baby girl, and, along with her, He brought her healing and wholeness.

Begin to act on your faith. God wants you well. He will come down heaven's stairway to meet you right where you are today because He has a miracle for you!

❧

Father, Your Word declares that I am healed, and I confess and receive Your healing touch today. Thank You that You brought Jesus down heaven's stairway to bring healing to my house. You said in Exodus 23:25 that because we serve You, You bless our food and water and take sickness from the midst of us. Glory to God!

Happy Birthday, Jesus!

Through the tender mercy of our God...the dayspring from on high hath visited us.

—Luke 1:78 KJV

The Bible gives no indication of the date of Jesus' birth. Some say He might have been born in summer or early fall. December is traditionally cold and rainy in Judea, and in those circumstances, the shepherds probably would have found shelter for the sheep as night approached.

Scholars disagree as to when and where festivals originated that celebrate the Christ-child's birth. But it really doesn't matter. Most important is the fact that the child who was born is Jesus, God's Son, the Messiah, and our Savior.

Gloria Gaither wrote some wonderful lyrics for a musical program that is often presented during this time of year called "His Love...Reaching." In it, she says, "His love still is longing, His love still is reaching, right past the shackles of my mind. And the Word of the Father became Mary's little Son. And His love reached all the way to where I was."

Jesus is reaching out to you right now—whether you've just paused in all the Christmas turmoil to get quiet and honor Him with a moment of your time or you're feeling lonely and forgotten. Reach out to Jesus today and, in your own quiet way, wish Him a happy birthday. And thank God for His unspeakable gift—the King of Kings and Lord of Lords!

Happy Birthday today, Jesus, my Savior and Lord. Thank You for taking on flesh and for walking this earth as a human being. Use me as Your vessel this next year—as You used Joseph and Mary to bring us the dayspring from on high. Fill me to overflowing with Your love so it will flow out to refresh others.

Love People

Let love be your greatest aim....
—1 Corinthians 14:1

*M*y family and I love God's people and desire to help everyone we meet find the best for their lives. We believe God wants to use us to reach others, and He wants the same thing for you. You can win souls! You can bring people back to God! You can see the sick healed, broken hearts and homes mended by His power, and you can see miracles performed.

You are probably asking, "Me? How can God use me?" Through love. If you read much about Jesus in the Bible, you'll soon find out that He was moved with divine compassion rising up in His heart. He felt love flowing out of His Spirit. The end result was that the healing love of God brought deliverance to the suffering people of that day.

The divine flow of God's love can move you toward the people God wants to reach. We need to watch for the rising of this supernatural love and be ready to follow wherever it flows.

When you accepted Jesus Christ as your personal Savior, the Holy Spirit shed the love of God abroad in your heart. After Jesus baptizes you in the Holy Spirit, that love flows out far more freely.

Follow the divine flow of love, and be guided by it today and every day!

❧

Father, thank You for the powerful gifts of Your Spirit that all operate through Your love. The flow of Your love as You minister through me is what Your gifts are all about. Your Word says, ...now abide faith, hope, love, these three; but the greatest of these is love. So I will make love my greatest aim. Teach me to love others as You love them, and use me as Your vessel of love today.

A Happy Christian Wins the Lost

And then he told them, "You are to go into all the world and preach the Good News to everyone, everywhere."

—Mark 16:15

After Jesus rose from the dead, He gathered His disciples around Him and told them to go into the world and preach the Good News to everybody. Everybody has the right to hear the good news about Jesus. There's enough bad news in this world—that's for sure.

This is very meaningful to me because we got a letter from someone who said they had once been very hardened because they'd made a lot of mistakes. This person had no joy, no peace, and no happiness, and all of this because of his own bad behavior in the past. He wrote, "I've always denied the existence of God. But I turned on your program one time, and I was taken by your positive, joyous message, and by your demeanor, suggesting that you were quite happy.

"Twice since then, I have tuned in to your program, and now I've given my heart to Jesus and I trust God to forgive me."

It just thrills me that our happiness and joy were contagious enough to cause someone to want what we have—and that's Jesus! I'm so happy to know that this man has received Jesus' forgiveness, and now joy and peace and happiness are also his!

Share your joy with others and tell them about Jesus. Let your happiness be contagious...starting today!

❧

Lord Jesus, I truly desire to share the good news joyfully so others may be attracted to You because of Your joy in me. Everyone everywhere has a right to know they can have the same joy, peace, and happiness I found in You. Help me to be a happy Christian so others will want to know You too.

Good News Is Spreading Everywhere

...The Good News that Jesus died for you...is now spreading all over the world. And I, Paul, have the joy of telling it to others.

—Colossians 1:23

*I*f what is being preached in your church isn't changing your life, there's something wrong with what's being preached. There is power in the Gospel to change your life and to break the power of the devil.

First, you must *hear* the gospel. Romans 10:17 tells us that faith comes by hearing and hearing by the Word of God. Some preachers preach such deep theological messages that you don't even know what they've talked about when they're finished. I'd rather just hear a practical message that's at my level—where the rubber meets the road.

Second, we have to *understand* the Good News! I like the Living Bible because it makes God's Word easy to understand. In Joel 2:13, the Good News to sinners is: *...Return to the Lord your God, for he is gracious and merciful. He is not easily angered; he is full of kindness and anxious not to punish you.* All kinds of sinners come to our church and watch our television program. But ours is not a message of condemnation.

We share the Good News. I don't think a message that says God just wants to throw you into hell is good news. In fact, it's bad news, and it isn't true at all!

Rejoice that Jesus became what you were that you might become what He is— free from sin and sickness, the curse of the law, and death. Spread this great Good News to everyone around you. Once everybody knows, Jesus will come back to earth to pick us up and take us home to be with Him. Glory!

❦

Thank You, Father, for the Good News that Jesus died for me. Now I have the joy of telling the Good News to others that Jesus died for them too.

Evangelizing the World for Jesus

...And all who love the Father love his children too. So you can find out how much you love God's children—your brothers and sisters in the Lord—by how much you love and obey God.
—1 John 5:1,2

I love all of God's people, and I love to give to His people. I like investing money in spreading the Gospel. I enjoy it so much when our church evangelizes the world through TV, home missions and other things.

Some of those precious saints will be in heaven when I get there, and they're going to say, "It was your money that brought the Gospel to me. Thank you." What a joy to have a part in evangelizing the whole wide world!

The nations of the world are going to hear about Jesus. They are going to get saved and delivered whether you give toward missions and evangelizing or you don't. But won't it be fulfilling to know that you had a part in bringing them the Good News?

Proverbs 11:25 says, *The generous soul will be made rich, and he who waters will also be watered himself* (NKJV). I like that! Do what God asks you to do with your money, and help evangelize the world for Him!

❦

I thank You and praise You, Father, for using my substance to win the lost and for Your promise to refresh me for blessing the earth with the money you bless me with. I love You, Lord, and I love to obey You in my giving.

"Tell Them I Need Them"

And I sought for a man among them, that should make up the hedge, and stand in the gap before me for the land, that I should not destroy it: but I found none.

—Ezekiel 22:30 KJV

*O*ne Saturday morning several years ago, my husband had gone out to run some errands, stopping at the cleaners and the alterations shop to pick up some of his clothes. Suddenly, as John was driving along, the Lord spoke to him saying, "Tell My people I need them."

John was eager to get home and tell me about it. He told me He'd said to God, "You're almighty God. You have all power in heaven and earth. Why do You need me to tell them You need them?"

The Lord began to pour out scripture after scripture to prove to John that God clearly states in His Word that He needs us.

God is searching for people He can trust. He needs people like you and me. He needs our eyes, arms, hands, hearts, and feet to evangelize the world. He's looking for somebody to help Him reach out to the lost with the Gospel of the Lord Jesus Christ.

As you reflect on the past year and plan for the new one, think about what you can do in response to God's need. He said He would do what you cannot do. If you'll do the possible, He'll do the impossible. If you will work in the natural, He'll work in the supernatural. Do your part. Cooperate with God. He needs you.

Lord God, use me this next year as Your mouth, hands, and feet to bring the good news of salvation to this lost and dying world. Use my hands to heal and my life as a witness of Your goodness toward all men. Show me where You want me to stand in the gap this year to bless the world in Jesus' name.

Go Win Souls

"Therefore go and make disciples in all the nations, baptizing them into the name of the Father and of the Son and of the Holy Spirit, and then teach these new disciples to obey all the commands I have given you; and be sure of this—that I am with you always, even to the end of the world."

—Matthew 28:19,20

I believe most Christians want to be used by God, but they do not know exactly how to go about it. We often fail to realize that God's love flowing through us can move us toward the very people God wants us to reach.

Throughout my husband's many years as a pastor, he always felt that demonstrating genuine love toward others was God's greatest witnessing tool. No amount of words could compare to a simple demonstration of heartfelt love. He said, "Love goes to the door, opens it, and commands fear to go out!"

God is love, and His love brings life, health, and peace. It never brings fear and torment. God wants all of His children to be fruitful. He never wants us to feel inadequate and afraid of witnessing about His goodness and mercy. Being timid about sharing Christ will not bear fruit.

All things are possible to those who believe. Believe that you can make a difference in the life of another as you share the love of Jesus, and you will be a soul winner!

Open a door of opportunity for me today, Father, to show Your lovingkindness to someone I may not even know. Because You are love and Your love is in me, I can love others with Your love. Help me to comfort those I encounter today who may be seeking You, as I will obey Your commandments, in Jesus' name.

About the Author

Dodie Osteen has seen the miracle-working power of God not only in her life but in the lives of over 40,000 people who attend Lakewood Church in Houston, Texas. Dodie and her late husband, Pastor John Osteen, co-founded Lakewood Church in 1959, where they were pastors together for 40 years. They ministered in many nations and co-hosted a national television program that has reached millions of people worldwide.

Dramatically healed of metastatic cancer of the liver in 1981, Dodie continues to minister in the weekly services at Lakewood where she lovingly prays for the sick and ministers compassionately to hurting people. Working alongside her family members and together with the leadership of her youngest son, Pastor Joel Osteen, Dodie is a vital part of making Lakewood Church a place of new beginnings for thousands.

A registered nurse, Dodie is the author of *Healed of Cancer*, a frank and candid story of her supernatural healing. Dodie received an honorary Doctorate of Humane Letters degree from Oral Roberts University in Tulsa, Oklahoma, and was named Christian Woman of the Year in a nationwide, live television broadcast in 1991.

A great tribute to Dodie's personal ministry is the fact that her five children are all active in full-time ministry today. Through the years, Dodie's ability to balance multiple callings as a minister of the Gospel, as well as that of a successful wife and mother, have made her a role model for an entire generation.

Topical Index

The Ten Club
Bible Reading Plan

❧

$\mathcal{T}$he Ten Club Bible Reading Plan was one that my late husband John Osteen recommended we use at Lakewood Church for years. It is about thirty minutes of Bible reading a day where you read **two chapters out of the Old Testament, two chapters out of the New Testament, five Psalms, and one Proverb a day** (10 chapters). This will cause you to read through the Old Testament in one year, the New Testament four times yearly, and the books of praise and wisdom every month.

You can even alter this reading plan and just read one chapter out of the Old Testament, one chapter out of the New Testament, one Psalm and one Proverb (five chapters a day). The main thing is to get the Word of God in your spirit daily.

The Apostle Paul wrote, *All scripture is given by inspiration of God, and is profitable for doctrine, for reproof, for correction, for instruction in righteousness: that the man of God may be perfect, thoroughly furnished unto all good works* (2 Timothy 3:16,17). Doctrine is something God wants you to believe. Reproof means something God wants you to stop doing. Correction means something God wants you to do better. Instruction in righteousness is something God wants you to start doing.

Romans 12:2 says, *And be not conformed to this world: but be ye transformed by the renewing of your mind, that ye may prove what is that good, and acceptable, and perfect, will of God.* God bless you now as you let the Holy Spirit teach you God's Word.

Daily Bible Reading Plan

❧❧

Month 1

DAY	OLD TESTAMENT	NEW TESTAMENT	PSALMS	PROVERBS
_____ 1	Gen. 1-2	Matt. 1-2	Ps. 1-5	Prov. 1
_____ 2	3-4	3-4	6-10	2
_____ 3	5-6	5-6	11-15	3
_____ 4	7-8	7-8	16-20	4
_____ 5	9-10	9-10	21-25	5
_____ 6	11-12	11-12	26-30	6
_____ 7	13-14	13-14	31-35	7
_____ 8	15-16	15-16	36-40	8
_____ 9	17-18	17-18	41-45	9
_____ 10	19-20	19-20	46-50	10
_____ 11	21-22	21-22	51-55	11
_____ 12	23-24	23-24	56-60	12-13
_____ 13	25-26	25-26	61-65	14
_____ 14	27-28	27-28	66-70	15
_____ 15	29-30	Acts 1-2	71-75	16
_____ 16	31-32	3-4	76-80	17
_____ 17	33-34	5-6	81-85	18
_____ 18	35-36	7-8	86-90	19
_____ 19	37-38	9-10	91-95	20
_____ 20	39-40	11-12	96-100	21
_____ 21	41-42	13-14	101-105	22
_____ 22	43-44	15-16	106-110	23
_____ 23	45-46	17-18	111-115	24
_____ 24	47-48	19-20	116-119, v32	25
_____ 25	49-50	21-22	119, v33-120	26
_____ 26	Ex. 1-2	23-24	121-130	27
_____ 27	3-4	25-26	131-135	28
_____ 28	5-6	27-28	136-140	29
_____ 29	7-8	Mark 1-2	141-145	30
_____ 30	9-10	3-4	146-150	31
_____ 31				

Choosing Life—One Day At A Time

Month 2

DAY	OLD TESTAMENT	NEW TESTAMENT	PSALMS	PROVERBS
_____ 1	Ex. 11-12	Mark 5-6	Ps. 1-5	Prov. 1
_____ 2	13-14	7-8	6-10	2
_____ 3	15-16	9-10	11-15	3
_____ 4	17-18	11-12	16-20	4
_____ 5	19-20	13-14	21-25	5
_____ 6	21-22	15-16	26-30	6
_____ 7	23-24	Rom. 1-2	31-35	7
_____ 8	25-26	3-4	36-40	8
_____ 9	27-28	5-6	41-45	9-10
_____ 10	29-30	7-8	46-50	11
_____ 11	31-32	9-10	51-55	12
_____ 12	33-34	11-12	56-60	13
_____ 13	35-36	13-14	61-65	14
_____ 14	37-38	15-16	66-70	15
_____ 15	39-40	Luke 1-2	71-75	16
_____ 16	Lev. 1-2	3-4	76-80	17
_____ 17	3-4	5-6	81-85	18
_____ 18	5-6	7-8	86-90	19
_____ 19	7-8	9-10	91-95	20
_____ 20	9-10	11-12	96-100	21
_____ 21	11-12	13-14	101-105	22
_____ 22	13-14	15-16	106-110	23
_____ 23	15-16	17-18	111-115	24
_____ 24	17-18	19-20	116-119, v32	25
_____ 25	19-20	21-22	119, v33-120	26
_____ 26	21-22	23-24	121-130	27
_____ 27	23-24	1 Cor. 1-2	131-135	28
_____ 28	25-26	3-4	136-140	29
_____ 29	27; Num. 1	5-6	141-145	30
_____ 30	2-3	7-8	146-150	31
_____ 31				

Month 3

Day	Old Testament	New Testament	Psalms	Proverbs
___ 1	Num. 4-5	1 Cor. 9-10	Ps. 1-5	Prov. 1
___ 2	6-7	11-12	6-10	2
___ 3	8-9	13-14	11-15	3
___ 4	10-11	15-16	16-20	4
___ 5	12-13	John 1-2	21-25	5
___ 6	14-15	3-4	26-30	6
___ 7	16-17	5-6	31-35	7
___ 8	18-19	7-8	36-40	8
___ 9	20-21	9-10	41-45	9-10
___ 10	22-23	11-12	46-50	11
___ 11	24-25	13-14	51-55	12
___ 12	26-27	15-16	56-60	13
___ 13	28-29	17-18	61-65	14
___ 14	30-31	19-20	66-70	15
___ 15	32-33	21; 2 Cor. 1	71-75	16
___ 16	34-35	2-3	76-80	17
___ 17	36; Deut. 1	4-5	81-85	18
___ 18	2-3	6-7	86-90	19
___ 19	4-5	8-9	91-95	20
___ 20	6-7	10-11	96-100	21
___ 21	8-9	12-13	101-105	22
___ 22	10-11	Gal. 1-2	106-110	23
___ 23	12-13	3-4	111-115	24
___ 24	14-15	5-6	116-119, v32	25
___ 25	16-17	Eph. 1-2	119, v33-120	26
___ 26	18-19	3-4	121-130	27
___ 27	20-21	5-6	131-135	28
___ 28	22-23	Phil. 1-2	136-140	29
___ 29	24-25	3-4	141-145	30
___ 30	26-27	Col. 1-2	146-150	31
___ 31				

Month 4

Day	Old Testament	New Testament	Psalms	Proverbs
1	Deut. 28-29	Col. 3-4	Ps. 1-5	Prov. 1
2	30-31	Matt. 1-2	6-10	2
3	32-33	3-4	11-15	3
4	34; Josh. 1	5-6	16-20	4
5	2-3	7-8	21-25	5
6	4-5	9-10	26-30	6
7	6-7	11-12	31-35	7
8	8-9	13-14	36-40	8
9	10-11	15-16	41-45	9
10	12-13	17-18	46-50	10
11	14-15	19-20	51-55	11
12	16-17	21-22	56-60	12-13
13	18-19	23-24	61-65	14
14	20-21	25-26	66-70	15
15	22-23	27-28	71-75	16
16	24; Judg. 1	1 Thess. 1-2	76-80	17
17	2-3	3-4	81-85	18
18	4-5	5; 2 Thess. 1	86-90	19
19	6-7	2-3	91-95	20
20	8-9	1 Tim. 1-2	96-100	21
21	10-11	3-4	101-105	22
22	12-13	5-6	106-110	23
23	14-15	2 Tim. 1-2	111-115	24
24	16-17	3-4	116-119, v32	25
25	18-19	Titus 1-2	119, v33-120	26
26	20-21	3; Philem.	121-130	27
27	Ruth 1-2	Heb. 1-2	131-135	28
28	3-4	3-4	136-140	29
29	1 Sam. 1-2	5-6	141-145	30
30	3-4	7-8	146-150	31
31				

Month 5

DAY	OLD TESTAMENT	NEW TESTAMENT	PSALMS	PROVERBS
_____ 1	1 Sam. 5-6	Heb. 9-10	Ps. 1-5	Prov. 1
_____ 2	7-8	11-12	6-10	2
_____ 3	9-10	13; James 1	11-15	3
_____ 4	11-12	2-3	16-20	4
_____ 5	13-14	4-5	21-25	5
_____ 6	15-16	1 Peter 1-2	26-30	6
_____ 7	17-18	3-5	31-35	7
_____ 8	19-20	2 Peter 1-3	36-40	8
_____ 9	21-22	1 John 1-5	41-45	9
_____ 10	23-24	2&3 John; Jude	46-50	10
_____ 11	25-26	Mark 1-2	51-55	11
_____ 12	27-28	3-4	56-60	12-13
_____ 13	29-30	5-6	61-65	14
_____ 14	31; 2 Sam. 1	7-8	66-70	15
_____ 15	2-3	9-10	71-75	16
_____ 16	4-5	11-12	76-80	17
_____ 17	6-7	13-14	81-85	18
_____ 18	8-9	15-16	86-90	19
_____ 19	10-11	Rev. 1-2	91-95	20
_____ 20	12-13	3-4	96-100	21
_____ 21	14-15	5-6	101-105	22
_____ 22	16-17	7-8	106-110	23
_____ 23	18-19	9-10	111-115	24
_____ 24	20-21	11-12	116-119, v32	25
_____ 25	22-23	13-14	119, v33-120	26
_____ 26	24; 1 Kings 1	15-16	121-130	27
_____ 27	2-3	17-18	131-135	28
_____ 28	4-5	19-20	136-140	29
_____ 29	6-7	21-22	141-145	30
_____ 30	8-9	Luke 1-2	146-150	31
_____ 31				

Month 6

DAY	OLD TESTAMENT	NEW TESTAMENT	PSALMS	PROVERBS
_____ 1	1 Kings 10-11	Luke 3-4	Ps. 1-5	Prov. 1
_____ 2	12-13	5-6	6-10	2
_____ 3	14-15	7-8	11-15	3
_____ 4	16-17	9-10	16-20	4
_____ 5	18-19	11-12	21-25	5
_____ 6	20-21	13-14	26-30	6
_____ 7	22; 2 Kings 1	15-16	31-35	7
_____ 8	2-3	17-18	36-40	8
_____ 9	4-5	19-20	41-45	9
_____ 10	6-7	21-22	46-50	10
_____ 11	8-9	23-24	51-55	11
_____ 12	10-11	Acts 1-2	56-60	12-13
_____ 13	12-13	3-4	61-65	14
_____ 14	14-15	5-6	66-70	15
_____ 15	16-17	7-8	71-75	16
_____ 16	18-19	9-10	76-80	17
_____ 17	20-21	11-12	81-85	18
_____ 18	22-23	13-14	86-90	19
_____ 19	24-25	15-16	91-95	20
_____ 20	1 Chron. 1-2	17-18	96-100	21
_____ 21	3-4	19-20	101-105	22
_____ 22	5-6	21-22	106-110	23
_____ 23	7-8	23-24	111-115	24
_____ 24	9-10	25-26	116-119, v32	25
_____ 25	11-12	27-28	119, v33-120	26
_____ 26	13-14	John 1-2	121-130	27
_____ 27	15-16	3-4	131-135	28
_____ 28	17-18	5-6	136-140	29
_____ 29	19-20	7-8	141-145	30
_____ 30	21-22	9-10	146-150	31
_____ 31				

Daily Bible Reading Plan

Month 7

DAY	OLD TESTAMENT	NEW TESTAMENT	PSALMS	PROVERBS
_____ 1	1 Chron. 23-24	John 11-12	Ps. 1-5	Prov. 1
_____ 2	25-26	13-14	6-10	2
_____ 3	27-28	15-16	11-15	3-4
_____ 4	29; 2 Chron. 1	17-18	16-20	5
_____ 5	2-3	19-20	21-25	6
_____ 6	4-5	21; Rom. 1	26-30	7
_____ 7	6-7	2-3	31-35	8
_____ 8	8-9	4-5	36-40	9
_____ 9	10-11	6-7	41-45	10
_____ 10	12-13	8-9	46-50	11
_____ 11	14-15	10-11	51-55	12
_____ 12	16-17	12-13	56-60	13
_____ 13	18-19	14-15	61-65	14
_____ 14	20-21	16; Heb. 1	66-70	15
_____ 15	22-23	2-3	71-75	16
_____ 16	24-25	4-5	76-80	17
_____ 17	26-27	6-7	81-85	18
_____ 18	28-29	8-9	86-90	19
_____ 19	30-31	10-11	91-95	20
_____ 20	32-33	12-13	96-100	21
_____ 21	34-35	Matt. 1-2	101-105	22
_____ 22	36; Ezra 1	3-4	106-110	23
_____ 23	2-3	5-6	111-115	24
_____ 24	4-5	7-8	116-119, v32	25
_____ 25	6-7	9-10	119, v33-120	26
_____ 26	8-9	11-12	121-130	27
_____ 27	10; Neh. 1	13-14	131-135	28
_____ 28	2-3	15-16	136-140	29
_____ 29	4-5	17-18	141-145	30
_____ 30	6-7	19-20	146-150	31
_____ 31				

Choosing Life—One Day At A Time

Month 8

DAY	OLD TESTAMENT	NEW TESTAMENT	PSALMS	PROVERBS
1	Neh. 8-9	Matt. 21-22	Ps. 1-5	Prov. 1
2	10-11	23-24	6-10	2
3	12-13	25-26	11-15	3
4	Est. 1-2	27-28	16-20	4
5	3-4	1 Cor. 1-2	21-25	5
6	5-6	3-4	26-30	6
7	7-8	5-6	31-35	7
8	9-10	7-8	36-40	8
9	Job 1-2	9-10	41-45	9
10	3-4	11-12	46-50	10
11	5-6	13-14	51-55	11
12	7-8	15-16	56-60	12
13	9-10	Mark 1-2	61-65	13
14	11-12	3-4	66-70	14
15	13-14	5-6	71-75	15-16
16	15-16	7-8	76-80	17
17	17-18	9-10	81-85	18
18	19-20	11-12	86-90	19
19	21-22	13-14	91-95	20
20	23-24	15-16	96-100	21
21	25-26	2 Cor. 1-2	101-105	22
22	27-28	3-4	106-110	23
23	29-30	5-6	111-115	24
24	31-32	7-8	116-119, v32	25
25	33-34	9-10	119, v33-120	26
26	35-36	11-12	121-130	27
27	37-38	13; Gal. 1	131-135	28
28	39-40	2-3	136-140	29
29	41-42	4-5	141-145	30
30	Eccl. 1-2	6; Eph. 1	146-150	31
31				

Month 9

Day	Old Testament	New Testament	Psalms	Proverbs
_____ 1	Eccl. 3-4	Eph. 2-3	Ps. 1-5	Prov. 1
_____ 2	5-6	4-5	6-10	2
_____ 3	7-8	6; Phil.1	11-15	3
_____ 4	9-10	2-3	16-20	4
_____ 5	11-12	4; Col.1	21-25	5
_____ 6	Song 1-2	2-3	26-30	6
_____ 7	3-4	4; 1 Thess.1	31-35	7
_____ 8	5-6	2-3	36-40	8
_____ 9	7-8	4-5	41-45	9
_____ 10	Isa. 1-2	2 Thess.1-3	46-50	10
_____ 11	3-4	1 Tim. 1-2	51-55	11
_____ 12	5-6	3-4	56-60	12-13
_____ 13	7-8	5-6	61-65	14
_____ 14	9-10	2 Tim. 1-2	66-70	15
_____ 15	11-12	3-4	71-75	16
_____ 16	13-14	Titus 1-3	76-80	17
_____ 17	15-16	Philem. 1	81-85	18
_____ 18	17-18	Luke 1-2	86-90	19
_____ 19	19-20	3-4	91-95	20
_____ 20	21-22	5-6	96-100	21
_____ 21	23-24	7-8	101-105	22
_____ 22	25-26	9-10	106-110	23
_____ 23	27-28	11-12	111-115	24
_____ 24	29-30	13-14	116-119; v32	25
_____ 25	31-32	15-16	119; v33-120	26
_____ 26	33-34	17-18	121-130	27
_____ 27	35-36	19-20	131-135	28
_____ 28	37-38	21-22	136-140	29
_____ 29	39-40	23-24	141-145	30
_____ 30	41-42	Heb. 1-2	146-150	31
_____ 31				

Choosing Life—One Day At A Time

Month 10

Day	Old Testament	New Testament	Psalms	Proverbs
_____ 1	Isa. 43-44	Heb. 3-4	Ps. 1-5	Prov. 1
_____ 2	45-46	5-6	6-10	2
_____ 3	47-48	7-8	11-15	3
_____ 4	49-50	9-10	16-20	4
_____ 5	51-52	11-12	21-25	5
_____ 6	53-54	13; James 1	26-30	6
_____ 7	55-56	2-3	31-35	7
_____ 8	57-58	4-5	36-40	8
_____ 9	59-60	1 Peter 1-2	41-45	9
_____ 10	61-62	3-4	46-50	10
_____ 11	63-64	5; 2 Peter 1	51-55	11
_____ 12	65-66	2-3	56-60	12
_____ 13	Jer. 1-2	1 John 1-2	61-65	13
_____ 14	3-4	3-4	66-70	14
_____ 15	5-6	5; 2 John	71-75	15-16
_____ 16	7-8	3 John; Jude	76-80	17
_____ 17	9-10	Rev. 1-2	81-85	18
_____ 18	11-12	3-4	86-90	19
_____ 19	13-14	5-6	91-95	20
_____ 20	15-16	7-8	96-100	21
_____ 21	17-18	9-10	101-105	22
_____ 22	19-20	11-12	106-110	23
_____ 23	21-22	13-14	111-115	24
_____ 24	23-24	15-16	116-119; v32	25
_____ 25	25-26	17-18	119;v 33-120	26
_____ 26	27-28	19-20	121-130	27
_____ 27	29-30	21-22	131-135	28
_____ 28	31-32	John 1-2	136-140	29
_____ 29	33-34	3-4	141-145	30
_____ 30	35-36	5-6	146-150	31
_____ 31				

Month 11

Day	Old Testament	New Testament	Psalms	Proverbs
_____ 1	Jer. 37-38	John 7-8	Ps. 1-5	Prov. 1
_____ 2	39-40	9-10	6-10	2
_____ 3	41-42	11-12	11-15	3
_____ 4	43-44	13-14	16-20	4
_____ 5	45-46	15-16	21-25	5
_____ 6	47-48	17-18	26-30	6
_____ 7	49-50	19-20	31-35	7
_____ 8	51-52	21; Acts 1	36-40	8
_____ 9	Lam. 1-2	2-3	41-45	9
_____ 10	3-4	4-5	46-50	10
_____ 11	5; Ezek. 1	6-7	51-55	11
_____ 12	2-3	8-9	56-60	12-13
_____ 13	4-5	10-11	61-65	14
_____ 14	6-7	12-13	66-70	15
_____ 15	8-9	14-15	71-75	16
_____ 16	10-11	16-17	76-80	17
_____ 17	12-13	18-19	81-85	18
_____ 18	14-15	20-21	86-90	19
_____ 19	16-17	22-23	91-95	20
_____ 20	18-19	24-25	96-100	21
_____ 21	20-21	26-27	101-105	22
_____ 22	22-23	28; Rom. 1	106-110	23
_____ 23	24-25	1-3	111-115	24
_____ 24	26-27	4-5	116-119; v32	25
_____ 25	28-29	6-7	119; v33-120	26
_____ 26	30-31	8-9	121-130	27
_____ 27	32-33	10-11	131-135	28
_____ 28	34-35	12-13	136-140	29
_____ 29	36-37	14-15	141-145	30
_____ 30	38-39	16; Matt. 1	146-150	31
_____ 31				

Choosing Life—One Day At A Time

Month 12

Day	Old Testament	New Testament	Psalms	Proverbs
1	Ezek. 40-41	Matt. 2-3	Ps. 1-5	Prov. 1
2	42-43	4-5	6-10	2
3	44-45	6-7	11-15	3
4	46-47	8-9	16-20	4
5	48; Dan. 1	10-11	21-25	5
6	2-3	12-13	26-30	6
7	4-5	14-15	31-35	7
8	6-7	16-17	36-40	8
9	8-9	18-19	41-45	9
10	10-11	20-21	46-50	10
11	12; Hos. 1	22-23	51-55	11
12	2-3	24-25	56-60	12
13	4-5	26-28	61-65	13
14	6-7	2 John	66-70	14
15	8-9	3 John	71-75	15-16
16	10-11	Nah. 1	76-80	17
17	12-13	2-3	81-85	18
18	14; Joel 1	Hab. 1-3	86-90	19
19	2-3	Zeph. 1-3	91-95	20
20	Amos 1-2	Hag. 1-2	96-100	21
21	3-4	Zech. 1-2	101-105	22
22	5-6	3-4	106-110	23
23	7 8	5 6	111-115	24
24	9; Obad.	7-8	116-119; v32	25
25	Jonah 1-2	9-10	119; v33-120	26
26	3-4	11-12	121-130	27
27	Mic. 1-2	13-14	131-135	28
28	3-4	Mal. 1-2	136-140	29
29	5-6	3-4	141-145	30
30	7	Isa. 58	146-150	31
31				

Notes

Notes

Notes